realistic assessments of possibilities in comparison with other requirements for economic growth, and to demands for expenditures in such areas as the military. He discusses discrepancies between economic demands and educational input and output both in the industrialized and the developing countries, and the mounting problem of the educated unemployed throughout the world.

He considers formative influences on student attitudes, educational aims and cross-tensions between modernists and traditionalists, institutional inertia, and administrative and managerial arrangements at various levels in the educational process; and he makes a strong plea for a massive strengthening of non-formal education. He weighs the effects of educational gaps between urban and rural areas of developing nations, between elites and masses, and between the world's industrialized and underdeveloped sectors; and he urges that universities take the initiative in innovation, and in the formulation of strategies to match the components of the crisis. Finally, he suggests the elements of a positive approach to the crisis, taking into account the possibilities of educational interchange among nations, and untapped potential contributions from the developing countries.

Philip H. Coombs has been an international leader in educational development as Director of the International Institute for Educational Planning, a division of Unesco. He served as Assistant Secretary of State for Education and Cultural Affairs during the Kennedy Administration, and before that as Research Director of the Ford Foundation's Fund for the Advancement of Education. Mr. Coombs was formerly a Professor of Economics at Amherst College, and taught also at Williams College.

THE WORLD EDUCATIONAL CRISIS: *A Systems Analysis*

# THE WORLD EDUCATIONAL CRISIS

## *A Systems Analysis*

*By Philip H. Coombs*

NEW YORK
OXFORD UNIVERSITY PRESS 1968
LONDON    TORONTO

*Preface*

This book has two main aims. The first is to assemble in one place the root facts about an unfolding world crisis in education, to make explicit the tendencies inherent in these facts, and to suggest the elements of a strategy for dealing with them. The second aim is related to the first but goes beyond it. It is to present a method for looking at an educational system not piecemeal, where every facet stands alone, but *as* a system, whose interacting parts produce their own 'indicators' as to whether the interaction is going well or badly.

Both aims call for the use of a lens with a wider angle of vision than is ordinarily trained on educational topics. They also call for the use of analytical terms and concepts drawn from other fields, such as economics, engineering, and sociology. These alien terms may at first confound and even exasperate some of our colleagues in the educational world—but hopefully they will reserve judgment long enough to hear us out. The world of education, as we see it, has become so complex and is in so serious a state that no one vocabulary—including that of pedagogy—can describe the whole of it. Hence we need languages and ideas from many intellectual disciplines and spheres of action to widen our view of the educational process, to see the whole ever more clearly, and thus accomplish more and benefit more.

Our use of the word 'crisis' to describe education's state of affairs may also evoke initial dissent, even by some who accept the general thrust of the analysis presented here. This was the case with European educational leaders who reviewed an earlier draft of this book in late 1967. They readily agreed that *other* nations, especially the developing ones, no doubt faced a crisis, but not *their* nation—it simply faced educational 'problems.' The violent events since then in leading universities of Czechoslovakia, France, the Federal Republic of Germany, Italy, Poland, Spain, the United States, and Yugoslavia have put the matter abruptly into sharper focus. Having examined the facts of the situation at large, we are more inclined than ever to call it by its right name—and 'crisis' seems entirely fitting.

A brief genealogical note should be added here. This book had its start as the basic working paper for the International Conference on the World Crisis in Education, held at Williamsburg, Virginia, in October 1967. The initiative for this conference came from an erstwhile elementary teacher, President Lyndon B. Johnson, but its actual planning and management were in private hands, led by Cornell University's president James A. Perkins. As chairman, he requested the International Institute for Educational Planning (established by Unesco in 1963 in Paris) to prepare a paper which would set the intellectual framework of the conference; his request was accepted, and as the institute's director I personally undertook to be its author, aided by my colleagues.

The participants in the conference—some 150 leaders from fifty 'developing' and 'developed' nations—included ministers of education, university heads, professors, researchers, adult educators, and social scientists. They, too, were there in a private capacity, without 'official' constraints, free to speak their minds. In this setting, the working paper was put to the test of critical scrutiny and debate, from which the present book—a greatly revised version of the original paper—profited greatly. It profited also from the suggestions of numerous other informed critics who kindly consented to review it later, and from exposure to a series of follow-up meetings to the Williamsburg Conference, held in various parts of the world in late 1967.

It would stretch the truth to say that all the Williamsburg conferees endorsed every element of the working paper—much less the whole of what is stated in this book. Yet it seems fair to say that its method of approach and the main burden of its argument and conclusions were generally accepted by the conference participants. In all events, having examined the paper, the conference spoke its own mind, through the voice of its chairman, whose admirable Summary Report is reproduced here as the Epilogue.

No man, and certainly no author, is an island unto himself. Accordingly, I wish to acknowledge my great indebtedness and gratitude to the many individuals and organizations who contributed in a host of ways to the preparation of this book. In particular I owe an immeasurable debt to the International Institute for Educational Planning—to which, in appreciation, any earnings of this book will flow—and to its parent organization, Unesco. My immediate colleagues at the IIEP who lent a helping hand are too numerous to name—but four in particular who played major roles from the outset must be mentioned: Sidney Hyman, Jacques Hallak, John Chesswas, and Ta Ngoc Chau.

This said, I also wish to acknowledge full personal responsibility for all the views, interpretations, and conclusions set forth in the pages that follow. What is said should in no way be construed as the official position of Unesco, the International Institute for Educational Planning, or any other organization. Still, in line with the broad purposes of such organizations, it is hoped that these pages will contribute to a wider dialogue about the grave problems and challenges facing educational systems all over the world today, to the better orientation of young people who are preparing themselves to be tomorrow's custodians of education, and to the unleashing of greater energies to advance the progress of this most important of social enterprises.

Paris                                                                          P. H. C.
June 1968

# Contents

THE WORLD EDUCATIONAL CRISIS: *A Systems Analysis*

# I

## Angle of Vision

NATURE OF THE WORLD-WIDE EDUCATIONAL CRISIS · ITS BASIC
CAUSES · REQUIREMENTS FOR OVERCOMING IT · CONCEPTUAL VIEW OF
EDUCATION AS A 'SYSTEM,' SUBJECT TO 'SYSTEMS ANALYSIS' · CAVEATS
BEARING ON THE ANALYSIS.

In the early 1950's, educational systems the world over began a process of expansion without precedent in human history. Student enrollments more than doubled in many places, expenditures on education rose at an even faster rate, and education emerged as the largest local industry. This graphic process held out the promise of continued educational progress.

How does the matter stand at present?

A partial answer lies in a dry fact—dry as gunpowder. Despite this great educational expansion, a parallel population growth has led to an increase in the aggregate number of adult illiterates in the world. The figure for Unesco's member states currently exceeds 460 million illiterate adults, or almost 60 per cent of their active population.[1] But a larger answer to the question sounds in the warning note now being struck with increased frequency by worried leaders in many lands. They caution that crisis conditions are encroaching on educational systems everywhere and already hold many countries in their grip. This book joins in that warning.

It is true that national educational systems have always seemed tied to a life of crisis. Each has periodically known a shortage of funds, teachers, classrooms, teaching materials—a shortage of everything except students. It is also true that these systems have usually managed somehow to overcome their chronic ills or else have learned to live with them. The

1. Unesco, 'Unesco's Contribution to the Promotion of the Aims and Objectives of the United Nations Development Decade: Report by the Director-General,' General Conference, Fourteenth Session, 25 October–30 November 1966, Paris, September 1966, 14 C/10.

present case, however, differs profoundly from what has been common-place in the past. This is a *world* educational crisis—more subtle and less graphic than a 'food crisis' or a 'military crisis,' but no less weighted with dangerous potentialities.

Because of special local conditions, the crisis varies in form and severity from one country to the next. But its inner lines of force appear in all nations alike, whether they are old or new, rich or poor, whether they have stable institutions or are struggling to build them in defiance of heavy odds.

The nature of this crisis is suggested by the words 'change,' 'adaptation,' and 'disparity.' Since 1945, all countries have undergone fantastically swift environmental changes, brought about by a number of concurrent world-wide revolutions—in science and technology, in economic and po-litical affairs, in demographic and social structures. Educational systems have also grown and changed more rapidly than ever before. But they have adapted all too slowly to the faster pace of events on the move all around them. The consequent disparity—taking many forms—between educational systems and their environments is the essence of the world-wide crisis in education.

There are assorted specific causes of this disparity, but four in particu-lar stand out. First is the *sharp increase in popular aspirations for educa-tion,* which has laid siege to existing schools and universities. Second is *the acute scarcity of resources,* which has constrained educational systems from responding more fully to new demands. Third is *the inherent inertia of educational systems,* which has caused them to respond too sluggishly in adapting their internal affairs to new external necessities, even when resources have not been the main obstacle to adaptation. Fourth is *the inertia of societies themselves*—the heavy weight of traditional attitudes, religious customs, prestige and incentive patterns, and institutional struc-tures—which has blocked them from making the optimum use of educa-tion and of educated manpower to foster national development.

If the crisis is to be overcome there must obviously be substantial mu-tual adjustment and adaptation by *both* education and society. If these are not forthcoming, the growing disparity between education and society will inevitably crack the frame of educational systems—and, in some cases, the frame of their respective societies. This is inevitable, because as the educational needs of national development continue to grow and change, and as pressures on the demand side of the educational systems continue to build, it will not be possible to meet the situation by increasing at will the resources made available to the systems.

To do their part in meeting the crisis, educational systems will need help from every sector of domestic life, and in many cases, much more help also from sources beyond their national boundaries. They will need more money. But money will be harder to get since education's share of national incomes and budgets has already reached a point that restricts the possibilities for adding on further increments. They will need the real resources that money buys. They will especially need a fuller share of the nation's best manpower, not merely to carry on the present work of education, but to raise its quality, efficiency, and productivity. They will need buildings, equipment, and more and better learning materials. In many places, they will need food for hungry pupils, so that they will be in a condition to learn. Above all, they will need what money alone cannot buy—ideas and courage, determination, and a new will for self-appraisal, reinforced by a will for adventure and change. This in turn means that educational managers in particular must face up to the way the relevance of their systems is being challenged. No more than a grown man can suitably wear the clothes that fitted him as a child, can an educational system successfully resist the need to change itself when everything around it is changing.

Education, of course, is not a cure for all the ills of the world, any more than it is responsible for causing them. Education at best has at its disposal only limited time and means for satisfying all the expectations that individuals and society bring to the educational process. It is a hopeful act of faith—faith that education is doing what is best for the individual and his society, and that it is not wasting too much of its scarce resources and everyone's time (the scarcest of all resources) in doing things that are wrong or irrelevant. The question to be asked in this connection is whether a blind, dogmatic faith guides any particular system, or whether it is a faith enlightened by rational analysis, reflection, and imagination.

An educational system can lose the power to see itself clearly. If it clings to conventional practices merely because they are traditional, if it lashes itself to inherited dogmas in order to stay afloat in a sea of uncertainty, if it invests folklore with the dignity of science and exalts inertia to the plane of first principles—that system is a satire on education itself. Individuals showing authentic gifts may still emerge from such a system. But they will not have been produced by it; they will merely have sur-

vived it. Moreover, from the standpoint of society, the resources invested
in perpetuating such a system are misused resources—misused because a
high proportion of its students will emerge ill-fitted to serve well either
themselves or their society.

On the other hand, any society, however limited its means, makes a
wise investment in an educational system that has the courage to heed
the Socratic injunction: 'Know thyself.' It invests wisely if that system is
objective in judging its own performance, if it ceaselessly examines the
living testimony offered by its own former students in order to determine
what it has done reasonably well, poorly, or not at all—and if it then cor-
rects itself in the light of that testimony. The managers of such a self-
aware system will be able to catch and deal with errors before the errors
harden into habits able to resist even the stoutest hammers later used
against them.

As things stand, the educational profession itself, viewed in the mass,
shows no great propensity for searching self-criticism. Nor is it quick to
seize opportunities for innovations that will help teachers achieve more in
classrooms, where they are now subject to so many distractions that they
have little time to think. Indeed, the world-wide educational crisis is shot
through with irony. While the crisis has occurred amid a virtual explosion
of knowledge, education, as the prime creator and conveyor of knowledge, has generally failed to apply to its own inner life the research function it performs for society at large. It has failed to infuse the teaching
profession, for transmittal into the classroom, with the new knowledge
and methods that are required in order to correct the present disparity
between educational performance and needs. Education thus places itself
in an ambiguous position. It exhorts everyone else to change his ways, yet
seems stubbornly resistant to innovation in its own affairs.

Why should there be this resistance to change?

It is not that teachers are more conservative than anyone else. There
was a time when farmers, even in the more advanced countries, resisted
innovation in agriculture, and the way their outlook was changed points
to an analogy and a moral for education. Agriculture, like education, is a
vast 'industry' of many small and widely scattered 'firms,' each with its
own decision-makers and implementers. Like education, it lacked scientific methods to analyze its affairs, and scientific research to improve its
practices, efficiency, and output. Scattered small farms, like schools, simply did not have the means to conduct their own scientific investigations,
to challenge their traditional practices and develop new and better ones.

Traditional practices thus tended to perpetuate themselves as sacred doctrine, and from one generation to the next they were clung to for security.

Eventually, however, governments and universities organized agricultural research and development on a large and economical scale on behalf of scattered farmers, supplemented by efficient informational and advisory services which transmitted to individual practitioners the tested and useful results of research. Only then did the farmers break out of the grip of traditional methods.

While this development (with some exceptions) has unfolded only in the agricultural context of today's more advanced countries, there has been nothing like it as yet in education, even in the richer countries. Education's technology, by and large, has made surprisingly little progress beyond the handicraft stage, whereas remarkable strides have been made in the technology and productivity of many other sectors of human activity, such as medicine, transportation, mining, communications, and manufacturing. Yet perhaps this should not be so astonishing, for education is surely among the most complex of all human endeavors. Educating a nation, and keeping that nation's educational system in step with the times, seems to be many times harder than putting a man on the moon.

We noted earlier that in addition to resource scarcities and the inertia of educational systems, society itself is a cause for the present disparity between its own needs and the state of education. The point here needs amplifying.

When a society decides—as many have lately done—to transform its 'elitist' educational system into one that will serve the mass of people, and when it further decides to use that system as an instrument for national development, it is beset by many novel problems. One is that while many more people want more education, they do not necessarily want the *kind* of education that under new circumstances is most likely to serve both their own future best interests and the best interests of national development. Most students naturally hope that education will help them get a good job in their developing society. But their job preferences are often dictated by a prestige-carrying hierarchy of jobs, set in the past, which does not fit the new hierarchy of manpower requirements bearing on economic growth. When the incentive structure and the employment demands of the market place also reflect the old hierarchy of prestige, there is a serious disjunction between the nation's manpower needs and its actual manpower demands. Such a disjunction is usually a signal that the nation is not deploying its available educated manpower in ways most conducive to development. Thus the student in choosing an academic field, and the educational system in trying to change its student flows to match the requirements of national development, are both caught in the cross-tensions between the stated development goals of society and society's antidevelopment patterns of prestige and incentives. In a larger sense, therefore, the crisis in the foreground is not simply a crisis of education, but one that embraces the whole of society and the economy.

Against this background, at this point we can usefully restate the main aims of this book as set out in the Preface. The first is to assemble in one place the root facts about the world crisis in education, to make explicit their inherent tendencies, and to suggest some of the possible elements for a strategy to deal with the crisis. The second aim is to present a method for examining an educational system, not piecemeal where every facet stands alone, but *as* a system—a system with interacting parts that produce their own 'indicators' as to whether the interaction is going well or badly.

Charts I and II, below, form a conceptual model for a 'systems analysis' of an educational system. In contrast to the meaning which the phrase 'systems analysis' has in some other contexts, it should at once be stressed that its use here does not entail the mathematical expression and measurement of all that is involved. Rather, it functions as a wide-angled lens trained on an organism so that it can be seen in its entirety, including the relationships among its parts and between the organism and its environment.

A 'systems analysis' of education resembles, in some respects, what a doctor does when he examines the most complicated and awe-inspiring 'system' of all—a human being. It is never possible, nor is it necessary, for the doctor to have complete knowledge of every detail of a human being's system and its functional processes. The strategy of the diagnosis is to concentrate upon selected critical indicators and relationships within the system and between the system and its environment. The doctor, for example, is concerned especially with correlations between such critical indicators as heartbeat, blood pressure, weight, height, age, diet, sleeping habits, urinary sugar content, white and red corpuscles. From these he appraises the way the total system is functioning, and prescribes what may be needed to make it function better.

What the doctor does in his analysis of the human body, modern management does in its 'systems analysis' approach to the operations and plans of everything from department stores to military establishments. The 'indicators' differ from context to context, but the strategy remains much the same. By extension, this is also true of a systems analysis applied to an educational system.

There is no incompatibility between looking at an educational system in this way and the time-honored view that education, though a means to many ends, is first and foremost an end in itself. This is not at issue here. What is at issue is the organized *process* by which a society pursues education, and whether that process and its results can be made more relevant, efficient, and effective within the context of the particular society.

In our use of the phrase 'educational system' we mean not merely the several levels and types of formal education (primary, secondary, postsecondary, general, and specialized) but also all those systematic programs and processes of education and training that lie outside 'formal' education. These, called nonformal education, include, for example, worker and farmer training, functional literacy training, on-the-job and in-service training, university extension (extramural), professional refresher courses, and special youth programs. The formal and nonformal educational activities collectively comprise the nation's total organized educational efforts, irrespective of how such activities may be financed or administered.

Even beyond these wide limits, of course, there are a myriad of other matters which, in any broad view of learning, are educative in nature, often profoundly so. They include things that are often taken as much for granted as the air we breathe—books, newspapers, and magazines; movies, radio, and television broadcasts; and above all the learning that goes on daily in every home. For the present, however, we must confine our view to those activities which are consciously organized for the express purpose of achieving certain prescribed educational and training objectives.

An educational system, *as* a system, obviously differs greatly from the human body—or from a department store—in what it does, how it does it, and the reasons why. Yet in common with all other productive undertakings, it has a set of *inputs,* which are subject to a *process,* designed to attain certain *outputs,* which are intended to satisfy the system's *objectives.* These form a dynamic, organic whole. And if one is to assess the health of an educational system in order to improve its performance and to plan its future intelligently, the relationship between its critical components must be examined in a unified vision.

This, however, is not the way we customarily view an educational system. We call it a system but we do not treat it as one. The school board meets to deal item by item with a laundry list of things. Each item is taken up and examined seriatim on its own terms. The daily calendar of the overworked school administrator is typically a similar mélange of 'items to handle.' He moves as expeditiously as he can from one to the next, having little time to reflect on how they impinge on each other, or on yesterday's and tomorrow's calendar of things.

Chart I—to deal with it briefly—presents a simplified diagram showing some of the more important internal components of an educational system. How they interact on each other can be illustrated by the following two examples:

Let us assume that a decision is made to alter the system's aims or priorities in some fashion—for example, a decision to diversify secondary education, to include a new 'technical' track to higher education and new 'terminal' programs with a vocational bias. To implement this decision may require far-reaching changes in the system's academic structure, in the curriculum and teaching methods, in facilities and equipment, and in the distribution of teachers and the flow of students within the structure. In short, virtually every component is substantially affected by such a change.

Similarly, without any change of basic aims or priorities, a significant innovation in the curriculum, such as the adoption of 'new mathematics' in place of traditional mathematics, may entail substantial alterations in teaching and learning methods, which in turn may require changes in the deployment of time, in physical facilities and equipment, and in the number and kind of teachers required. This chain reaction may thus have considerable consequences for the system's input requirements and for the quantity and quality of its final outputs.

Chart I, however, does not show the whole of what must be looked at in a systems analysis. The chart is confined to the internal components of the system, detached from the environment. Yet since it is society which supplies the educational system with the means of functioning—just as the educational system in turn is expected to make vital contributions to society—something more must be added to the picture of systems analysis. Education's inputs and outputs must be examined in their external relationships with society, for these reveal both the resource constraints that limit the system and the factors that ultimately determine its productivity to society. Hence Chart II shows the multiple components of the inputs

Chart I.    The major components of an educational system

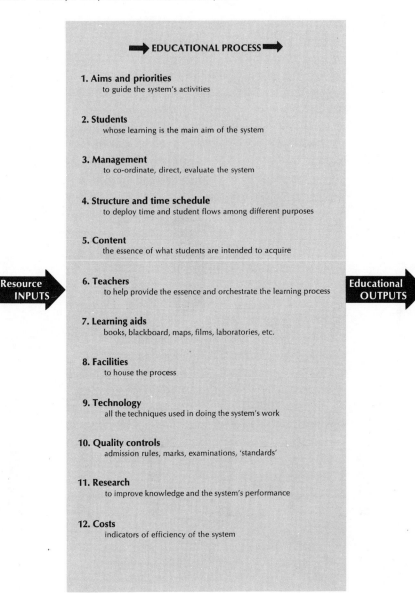

**EDUCATIONAL PROCESS**

**1. Aims and priorities**
    to guide the system's activities

**2. Students**
    whose learning is the main aim of the system

**3. Management**
    to co-ordinate, direct, evaluate the system

**4. Structure and time schedule**
    to deploy time and student flows among different purposes

**5. Content**
    the essence of what students are intended to acquire

Resource **INPUTS**

**6. Teachers**
    to help provide the essence and orchestrate the learning process

Educational **OUTPUTS**

**7. Learning aids**
    books, blackboard, maps, films, laboratories, etc.

**8. Facilities**
    to house the process

**9. Technology**
    all the techniques used in doing the system's work

**10. Quality controls**
    admission rules, marks, examinations, 'standards'

**11. Research**
    to improve knowledge and the system's performance

**12. Costs**
    indicators of efficiency of the system

from society into the educational system, followed by the multiple outputs from that system which flow back into society, upon which they
ultimately have many diverse impacts.

Chart II.  Interactions between an educational system and its environment

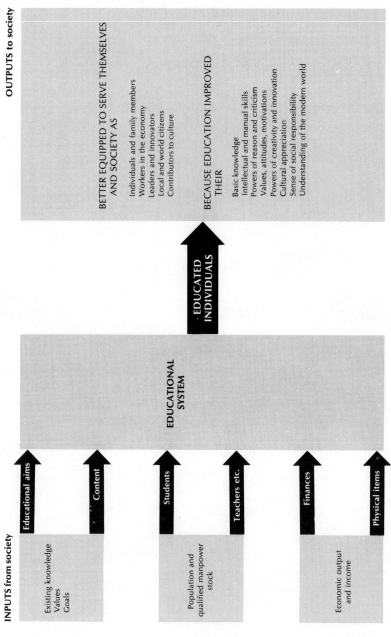

**INPUTS from society**

Educational aims

Content

Students

Teachers etc.

Finances

Physical items

Existing knowledge
Values
Goals

Population and
qualified manpower
stock

Economic output
and income

EDUCATIONAL
SYSTEM

EDUCATED
INDIVIDUALS

**OUTPUTS to society**

BETTER EQUIPPED TO SERVE THEMSELVES
AND SOCIETY AS

Individuals and family members
Workers in the economy
Leaders and innovators
Local and world citizens
Contributors to culture

BECAUSE EDUCATION IMPROVED
THEIR

Basic knowledge
Intellectual and manual skills
Powers of reason and criticism
Values, attitudes, motivations
Powers of creativity and innovation
Cultural appreciation
Sense of social responsibility
Understanding of the modern world

To illustrate how things interact, suppose that an educational system is called upon to produce more scientists and technologists. For this it needs more specialized teachers, but they are in scarce supply because they are being underproduced by the system, relative to market demand. To raise its production, education must get back from its own limited output of such people enough of them to serve as inputs. But to this end its offers to such qualified personnel must be able to meet the market competition from other users. This may require a considerable change in its teacher-salary policies and structure.

Charts I and II raise many questions but these will be dealt with later. They include such matters as the meaning of 'management,' the nature of educational 'technology,' the meaning of 'efficiency' and 'quality,' and doubts about the reliability of resource inputs as indicators of the quality of educational outputs. They include the need to define the difference between the internal and external ways of judging the quality and productivity of an educational system's performance, and to suggest how these different angles of vision can lead to different judgments. They also include the need to identify key and reliable indicators of an educational system's performance on both the input and output side.

Though all these matters will be discussed later, it is in point here to establish a clearer relationship between the two charts—the first dealing with the internal aspects of an educational system, and the second with its external linkages. The relationship can be put in a capsule by postulating the following: First, if external conditions lead to changes in the inputs available to the system—as when a national manpower shortage and an unfavorable salary structure result in a shortage of teachers—the effect within the system may be a decline in the size and quality of its outputs. On the other hand, the input stringency may conceivably provoke a change in 'technology' and in the use of resources calculated to avert a decline in the size and quality of the outputs. The systems analysis thus shows that *there need be no rigid pattern of internal responses* to which an educational system must adhere in meeting external stringencies. Aided by such an analysis, the system is in a position to choose its own response, and the choice it actually makes can have a considerable influence on the quantity and quality of its output, and on its internal efficiency and external productivity.

Chart III adds an international dimension to the systems analysis. It assumes that country X has been analyzed in the combined lights of Charts I and II. But it adds to the analysis the inputs into its educational

Chart III.  The interdependence of educational systems of the world

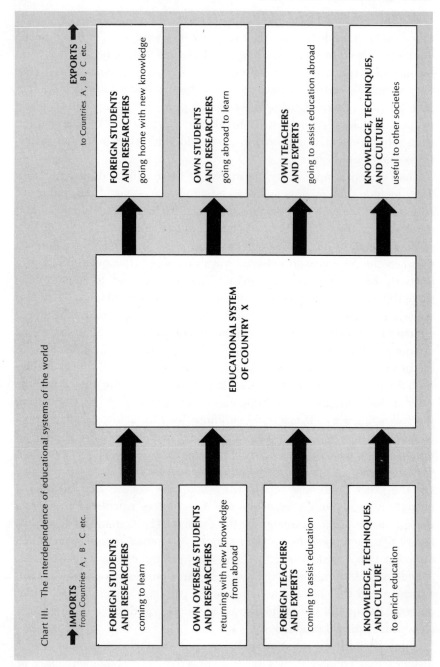

**IMPORTS** from Countries A , B , C etc.

**EXPORTS** to Countries A , B , C etc.

EDUCATIONAL SYSTEM OF COUNTRY X

FOREIGN STUDENTS AND RESEARCHERS coming to learn

OWN OVERSEAS STUDENTS AND RESEARCHERS returning with new knowledge from abroad

FOREIGN TEACHERS AND EXPERTS coming to assist education

KNOWLEDGE, TECHNIQUES, AND CULTURE to enrich education

FOREIGN STUDENTS AND RESEARCHERS going home with new knowledge

OWN STUDENTS AND RESEARCHERS going abroad to learn

OWN TEACHERS AND EXPERTS going to assist education abroad

KNOWLEDGE, TECHNIQUES, AND CULTURE useful to other societies system of components imported in different forms from a number of foreign countries which enter into the process of country X's educational system (such as foreign teachers or students, foreign-made equipment or teaching materials, new teaching methods developed abroad). Similarly, it adds outputs from country X's educational system (teachers, students, new curriculum ideas, etc.) which are exported to become input components of a foreign educational system, completing the circuit of international educational trade.

So much for the moment about a systems analysis. The schematic models sketched above will provide the analytical framework for the balance of this book. Within this framework, the various elements and relationships thus far mentioned only briefly will be examined in greater detail.

What remains to be added are some caveats about the material to be presented in these pages. No spread-eagle claims are being made—or can be made—for the material. We are keenly aware of the sparse facts and tools available for examining and comparing educational systems. For all sorts of reasons well known to experienced educational statisticians, official figures on matters such as enrollments, dropout and repeater rates, expenditure patterns, and unit costs must be taken (particularly in developing countries) with a grain of salt. This is nobody's fault in particular; it is simply the 'state of the art.' Indeed, while working on this study, it occurred to us many times that if the world's financial systems were forced to guide their decisions on the basis of facts no better than those by which educational systems live, a financial panic would swiftly seize all world capitals. The raw material we have drawn on has consisted of bits and pieces of recent and current data, some informal experiences by practitioners in the field of education, along with their personal observations. Many other sources have also been tapped. But we have, in particular, drawn heavily on Unesco's mine of data, and on the field research conducted by the International Institute for Educational Planning.

A mosaic of generalizations formed of so many different sources is vulnerable from two sides. First, as the passing years reveal what the days now hide, the generalizations may prove to be wide of the truth. Second, no generalization can cover all the exceptional aspects of individual cases. Still, as between choices, would it be better to abandon all attempts at rational analysis in planning and entrust the future to the play of accident? Or would it be better to move into the future with some sort of rationally conceived road map? We make the latter choice.

We make another choice as well.

Since much of the material to be presented here does not convey a rosy picture of things to come, this book could be wrongly understood as a cry of hopelessness and a call to stoic resignation in the face of impending doom. The risk of being so misunderstood is nonetheless accepted, for the alternative is worse still. The alternative is to corrupt the integrity of words by affirming, contrary to realities, that all is well with educational systems around the world. As a matter of fact, in the very act of presenting the kind of bleak material that will appear in these pages, we place ourselves among the optimists, not through a prejudice of the heart, but through a conviction of the mind. We firmly believe that the world crisis in education can be overcome—if: If the people concerned candidly and systematically diagnose their educational problems and plan their educational future in the light of what they uncover in their self-diagnosis. If they do that, and especially if nations will do it together, the action will generate the national energies and the will power required to deal with the findings of fact that appear in the pages that now follow.

# II

# The Inputs of Educational Systems

*Students Viewed as Inputs*
SWIFT RISE IN SOCIAL DEMAND FOR EDUCATION · RISE IN
ENROLLMENTS AND PARTICIPATION RATES · GAP BETWEEN SOCIAL
DEMAND AND EDUCATIONAL CAPACITY · IMBALANCED GROWTH RATES
DETER NATIONAL DEVELOPMENT · IMPACT OF POPULATION 'EXPLOSION'
IN DEVELOPING COUNTRIES · ALTERNATIVE STRATEGIES FOR DEALING
WITH EDUCATIONAL GAP.

We begin with students because they are the prime inputs of any educational system. Their development is its prime object, their attitudes greatly affect its process, and in the end they are its prime outputs.

When we send children to school, we expect that the experience will make a desirable difference in their lives. They are also moulded, of course, by their families, friends, church, and other environmental forces, each in its own distinctive way. But we expect the school to give them things they cannot get elsewhere. Among others, we expect the school to endow children with the means to lead fuller, more satisfying lives and to enjoy the 'humanistic' aspect of education as an end in itself. All this comprises what may be called the 'consumption' dimension of education. We also expect the school to endow children with the means to be better citizens, to get a better job, and to contribute more to society's welfare— this comprises what may be called the 'investment' dimension of education. The two dimensions are not mutually exclusive.

The number of students trying to enter school, or trying to stay in and go further, reflects society's *social demand* for education. This is not the same as society's *manpower requirements* for economic and social development. The two may interact, yet behave quite independently. Social demand for education, for reasons to be stated presently, has a way of grow-

17

ing faster than manpower requirements, leading on some occasions to 'unemployment of the educated.'

Here, first, we shall view students as 'inputs,' while holding in reserve a view of them as the 'outputs' of the educational system. We will ask: What forces account for the recent explosive growth in the social demand for education? Have school systems been able to meet that demand? If not, how have they coped with the consequent demand-supply gap? Looking ahead, what can we reasonably expect will happen to the trend of social demand, and for what reasons?

There are three main reasons why the social demand for education has been rising rapidly since the end of World War II. The first is the mounting educational aspirations of parents and their children. The second is the new stress of public policy almost everywhere on educational development as a precondition for over-all national development, and the parallel stress on the democratic imperative of increased 'educational participation rates'—which means sending a higher proportion of each age group to school, and for more years. The third reason is the population explosion, which has acted as a quantitative multiplier of the social demand.

The interaction among these forces since 1950 accounts for the phenomenon that is depicted in Chart IV. World-wide primary school enrollments have increased by more than 50 per cent, and secondary and higher education enrollments by more than 100 per cent. Since the developing countries started from a smaller base, their *percentage* increase, especially at the primary level, has been much greater than is the case in the developed countries. In absolute numbers, however, the developed countries have had a much greater increase in secondary and higher education.[1]

The whole of these enrollment figures, showing that compared with a generation ago, twice the proportion and number of the world's children are today being exposed to formal schooling, forms the bright side of the case. The figures, however, are silent about the dark side. They do not reveal the vast social waste and the human tragedy in the high rate of dropouts and failures. They hide the large number of costly 'repeaters.' And, most important, they say nothing about the nature, quality, and usefulness of the education received.

More will be said later about all these matters. What must be noted here is a dual aspect of the increased demand for education. The rising enrollment curves reflect the compounded effect of an over-all expansion

1. See Appendix 1.

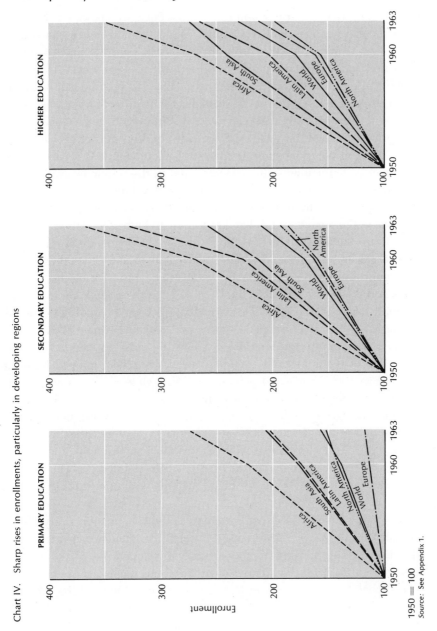

Chart IV.  Sharp rises in enrollments, particularly in developing regions

HIGHER EDUCATION

SECONDARY EDUCATION

PRIMARY EDUCATION

Enrollment

1950 = 100

*Source:* See Appendix 1.

in the *absolute size* of each age group, and a rise in the *percentage* of each age group participating at each educational level.

It is true that viewed retrospectively, most countries show a slow rise in their educational participation rates. In recent years, however, the rate of the rise has been sharply accelerated. Why? One crucial reason is that educational demand, feeding on itself, creates its own dynamic. A population that suddenly starts getting more education soon wants still more. An African child of illiterate parents who learns to read and do sums in primary school wants to go on to secondary school; from there, he wants to go on to the university if he can make it. But even if he gets no further than primary school, he will insist that *his* children do better. Thus the social demand for education is inexorably compounded, regardless of what may be happening to the economy and to the resources available to education. This phenomenon is not unique to developing countries. It has shown itself markedly in the postwar years in western Europe and North America, at the secondary level and especially in higher education.

What are the implications for the future, of this tendency of education to generate its own demand? A hint of what is in store for other industrial countries can be found in the educational histories of the United States and the Soviet Union. In the United States the population increased 2½ times from 1900 to date. This alone would have boosted educational enrollments, even if participation rates had stayed constant. But public demand, if nothing else, would not allow the rates to stand still. The proportion of the age group attending secondary school jumped from 12 per cent in 1900 to over 90 percent in 1967, while in the same period, higher educational enrollments rose from 4 to 44 per cent of the corresponding age group. What this, in addition to the postwar baby boom, has meant for enrollments in United States higher education is shown in Chart V. Total enrollments in all educational institutions now exceed 57 million—well over one-quarter of the whole population. The United States has thus become an 'educational society,' with education its largest industry.[2]

In 1967 the Soviet Union, commemorating the fiftieth anniversary of the October Revolution, had good reason to celebrate its achievements on the educational front. Starting from a vertically developed but narrow educational system in 1914, the number of primary and secondary students per 10,000 inhabitants in the Soviet Union more than trebled in 1966, while in higher education, this same ratio multiplied more than twenty-one times, all concurrently with a substantial population rise.[3]

2. See Appendix 2.
3. K. Nozhko, *et al.*, *Educational Planning in the USSR*, including a report by an IIEP mission to the USSR, headed by R. Poignant (Paris: Unesco/IIEP, 1968); see also Appendix 3.

Chart V. Effect of postwar baby boom and rising participation rates on U.S. college and university enrollments, 1939-1965

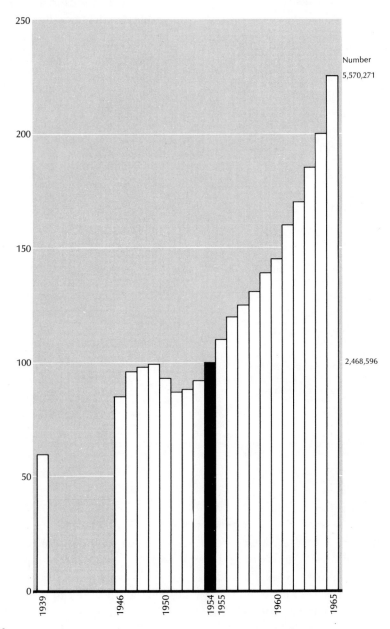

1954 = 100
*Source:* U.S. Department of Health, Education and Welfare, *Digest of Educational Statistics,* Washington, D.C., Office of Education, 1965 and 1966.

Western European countries have belatedly been moving in the same direction since World War II. While the figures for different countries in Table 1 below are not entirely comparable, in each case they show a substantial rise in participation rates.

TABLE 1.

*Growth in educational participation rates in Western Europe*

| | ENROLLMENT RATIO IN PER CENT | |
|---|---|---|
| LEVEL OF EDUCATION | 1950 | 1963 |
| *Secondary* | | |
| Greece | 35 | 47 |
| Ireland | 34 | 50 |
| Italy | 29 | 63 |
| Netherlands | 62 | 111[a] |
| Portugal | 11 | 39 |
| Spain | 17 | 31 |
| Austria (15-19 years) | 22 | 36.7[b] |
| Sweden (16-18 years) | 25 | 44[b] |
| *Higher* | | |
| Austria (20-24 years) | 1.9 | 5.6[b] |
| (25 and 26 years) | 0.8 | 1.7[b] |
| France (1st year of higher education) | 5.0 | 13.8[c] |
| Germany (Fed. Rep.) | | |
| (1st year of higher education) | 4.2[d] | 5.8 |
| Sweden (19-24 years) | 10 | 21[b] |

Sources: Unesco, *Statistical Yearbook, 1965* (Paris, 1966); R. Poignant, *L'Enseignement dans les pays du Marché commun* (Paris: Institut pédagogique national, 1965); OECD, *Educational Planning and Economic Growth in Austria, 1965-1975* (Paris: Directorate for Scientific Affairs, 1968); OECD, *Educational Policy and Planning. Sweden* (Paris: Directorate for Scientific Affairs, 1967).

a Includes students younger and/or older than the population 'age group' on which the enrollment ratio is based.

b Figure for 1965.

c Figure for 1964.

d Figure for 1957.

Because of the vital relationship between education and economic growth, a two-sided point is worth inserting here. On the one side, the industrialized countries of Europe achieved much of their present economic growth with quite low educational participation rates above the primary level. However, it did take them a long time to get where they now are economically. On the other side, there is reason to believe that the higher participation rates of the United States, the Soviet Union, and Japan, at relatively earlier stages of their development, paid substantial dividends in promoting their present high level of economic and technological advancement.[4] Recent participants in the debate over the 'technological gap' and the 'management gap' between western Europe and the United States have criticized lags in European education as one of root causes.[5]

TABLE 2

*Rising enrollment ratios in a sample of developing countries*

| COUNTRIES | PRIMARY LEVEL (percentage of 5-14-year-olds) | | | | SECONDARY LEVEL (percentage of 15-19-year-olds) | | | |
|---|---|---|---|---|---|---|---|---|
| | 1950 | 1955 | 1960 | 1963 | 1950 | 1955 | 1960 | 1963 |
| Africa | | | | | | | | |
| Cameroon | 25 | 37 | 57 | 79 | 0.7 | 2 | 5 | 8 |
| Niger | 1 | 2 | 4 | 7 | 0.1 | 0.2 | 0.5 | 0.8 |
| Nigeria | 16 | 27 | 35 | 31 | 1 | 2 | 5 | 6 |
| Tunisia | 18 | 26 | 44 | 57 | 9 | 11 | 15 | 20 |
| Asia | | | | | | | | |
| Afghanistan[a] | 3 | 4 | 5 | 9 | 0.5 | 0.7 | 1 | 3 |
| Indonesia[b] | 29 | 39 | 42 | 45 | 3 | 7 | 9 | 10 |
| Korea, Republic of | 53 | 54 | 60 | 69 | 20 | 36 | 32 | 38 |
| Pakistan | 16 | 19 | 22 | 25 | 15 | 15 | 16 | 22 |
| Latin America | | | | | | | | |
| Argentina | 66 | 71 | 69 | 68 | 21 | 28 | 32 | 37 |
| Bolivia | 24 | 34 | 38 | 49 | 9 | 12 | 15 | 19 |
| Brazil | 28 | 33 | 45 | 50 | 10 | 12 | 18 | 25 |
| Venezuela | 40 | 44 | 70 | 72 | 6 | 11 | 27 | 34 |

Source: Unesco, *Statistical Yearbook, 1965* (Paris, 1966), pp. 117-137.
a Public education only.
b Not including West Irian.

As for the developing countries of Asia, Latin America, and Africa, they have lately been driven by motives of economic growth and social equity to follow hard on the educational tracks of the advanced countries. For them, increased participation rates have been a matter of high priority, and the results of their efforts since 1950 are reflected in Table 2. (The figures shown should be taken as indicative only, since there is a tendency

4. See, for example, E. F. Denison, 'Measuring the Contribution of Education (and the Residual) to Economic Growth' in *The Residual Factor and Economic Growth* (Paris: OECD, 1964); T. H. Schultz, *Education and Economic Growth* (Chicago: University of Chicago Press, 1961); Th. W. Schultz, *The Economic Value of Education* (New York and London: Columbia University Press, 1964); S. Strumilin, 'The Economics of Education in the USSR' in *International Social Science Journal,* Paris, Unesco, XIV, no. 4 (1962).

5. See, for example, J.-J. Servan-Schreiber, *Le Défi américain* (Paris: Denoël, 1967); and OECD, *The Over-all Level and Structure of Research and Development Efforts in OECD Member Countries* (Paris: OECD, 1967).

for official enrollment figures in developing countries to overstate the reality.)

What up to this point has been implied can now be stated explicitly. The crucial relationship between social demand and an educational system's capacity to satisfy it is a key indicator in diagnosing any educational system. Political leaders, for their part, need no statistics to measure a widening gap in this relationship; they sense it intuitively from the mounting protests they face each day.

By the test of the key indicator just set forth, the world-wide educational picture looks like this. Despite the remarkable rise in school enrollments after 1950, the rise did not keep pace with an even faster growing social demand for education. The gap between the desire for education and school admission is greatest in developing countries where, even now, elementary school participation rates are often below 50 per cent. But in these countries the gap is frequently even greater, proportionately, at the secondary and higher levels, due partly to an earlier priority given to primary education. The latter priority has already set in motion the powerful dynamic whereby educational demand is rapidly feeding on itself.

All the developing countries thus face a severe problem, which lies at the heart of their educational crisis. The encouraging fact that their people are enthusiastically demanding education is offset by the nerve-racking fact that grave political and social consequences can ensue if that demand is not satisfied. How can they bridge the great and growing gap between the burgeoning aspirations of their people for more education and the limited ability of their educational systems to fulfill those aspirations?

In a less acute but still marked degree, many of the advanced countries face the same problem. The point was explicitly voiced by the French minister of education, M. Christian Fouchet, at a meeting in Caen late in 1966, where leading science professors were unsparing in their criticism of French educational conditions:

> No French Minister of Education, no French university has ever had to face so many problems as you and I. It was not until 1940 that there was a rise in population; until then, no real social demand for education, no scientific revolution. During the past twenty years, on the contrary, there have been explosions in all sectors.[6]

The reality of the same dilemma has been expressed in different ways by other industrially advanced countries. British universities, for example,

6. *Bulletin quotidien du Colloque de Caen* (November 1966).

have been forced by a shortage of places in recent years to turn away more than one-quarter of the qualified candidates applying to them. Austrian secondary and technical trade schools between 1955 and 1965 refused admission to as many as 2.7 to 22.2 per cent of qualified applicants.[7] In the winter term of 1966-67, 6500 qualified candidates applied for entry into Federal Republic of Germany medical faculties; only 2800 places were available. In 1966 about one-quarter of the applicants to universities of Victoria State in Australia was rejected.[8] Examples could be multiplied from other advanced countries.

Is there any reason to believe that this boom in education's market will subside in coming years? On the contrary, the signs indicate that the forces of the recent past which account for the increased social demand for education will not only continue but may even accelerate. Further, the signs say that the intensity of the human pressures embraced by these forces will undergo a kind of 'quantum jump' in the case of the developing countries—this, because of the extraordinarily high rate of increase in their youth population.

The latter point warrants calm and objective examination. Many developing countries show a marked but readily understandable sensitivity to any comments about their extraordinary population growth. Any such comments ring in their ears as unwelcome toplofty outside interference in the most private aspects of their own family life. It is important, therefore, to define precisely what is really at issue. The issue is not whether these countries can ultimately have a much larger, better-educated, and better-fed population than they now have. Many have the basic natural resources to support larger populations, given ample time to develop these resources. The issue, rather, involves the question of timing and relative rates of growth. It is part of a broader problem of *unbalanced growth* affecting the whole national development process, as suggested by the following propositions:

If population grows faster than food production, each year there will be less available on the average for each person to eat.

If the educational system grows faster than the Gross National Product,

7. See Appendix 4.
8. Committee on Higher Education, *Higher Education: The Demand for Places in Higher Education. Appendix One to the Report of the Committee Appointed by the Prime Minister under the Chairmanship of Lord Robbins, 1961-63* (London: HMSO, 1964), Pt. IV, p. 120; Commonwealth of Australia, *Third Report of the Australian Universities Commission, Australian Universities 1964-69* (Canberra: Commonwealth Government Printer, 1966).

and it has been doing so for some time, it will sooner or later have to slow its growth until the economy catches up.

If the educational system turns out graduates faster than the economy can give them jobs, unemployment among the educated will increase.

If the child population expands faster than the educational system can absorb them and give them a decent education, there will be either a lower participation rate than desired or overcrowded schools of poor quality.

If *all* these critical rates of growth—economic, agricultural, demographic, and educational—get seriously out of balance, the nation's whole development process will be in trouble, not merely economically, but socially and politically.

We will return to the issue of imbalance when we consider the financial inputs into an educational system, and after that, the fitness of education's outputs to manpower needs. Here, the main proposition to be advanced about population growth subdivides into a present and future tense. As to the present, the rise thus far in school-age population in most developing countries plainly exceeds what their educational systems can digest while still doing an acceptable education job. As to the future, certain crucial facts, which are concealed in the gross statistics of population growth, point to an even more severe state of imbalance between the prospective demands on school systems and the capacity of the systems to cope with them.

One set of facts shows that in many developing countries, the youth population has been growing more rapidly than the population as a whole because improved health measures have led to a sharper decrease in infant mortality rates than in adult mortality rates. Thus in Central America, for example, *total* population is estimated to have been growing at a rate of 3.25 per cent in recent years, whereas *school-age* population has been growing at a rate of 3.75 per cent. A broader world picture is given in Chart VI.[9] Wherever such a disparity exists, the over-all figures of population growth may seriously understate the growth in the educational system's potential clientele.

A second set of facts tells us that the already rapid growth of the school-age population in developing countries is likely to grow even more rapidly in the future. For despite the dramatic decline in infant mortality rates in recent years, there still exists a large potential for further decline. To illustrate: the infant mortality rate averages 20 per 1000 in western Europe,

9. See also Appendix 5.

Chart VI.   The school-age population in developing countries is growing very rapidly . . .

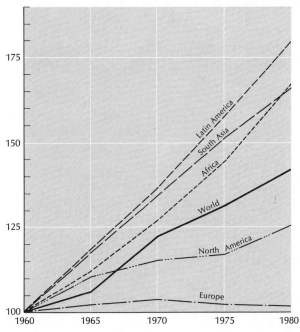

1960 = 100
*Source:* See Appendix 5.

. . . and more rapidly than the total population

| Region | Population | 1960 | 1970 | Annual growth rate |
|---|---|---|---|---|
| **Africa** | | | | |
| Northern[a] | School-age (5-14 years) | 17 174 | 22 656 | 2.75 |
| | Total | 65 955 | 86 712 | 2.75 |
| Western | School-age (5-14 years) | 23 478 | 31 117 | 2.85 |
| | Total | 85 973 | 112 862 | 2.75 |
| Eastern[a] | School-age (5-14 years) | 18 927 | 22 420 | 1.75 |
| | Total | 75 032 | 90 397 | 1.90 |
| **South Asia** | | | | |
| South East | School-age (5-14 years) | 52 024 | 74 218 | 3.70 |
| | Total | 218 866 | 282 032 | 2.60 |
| Middle South | School-age (5-14 years) | 138 938 | 184 097 | 2.85 |
| | Total | 579 906 | 730 334 | 2.30 |
| **Latin America** | | | | |
| Middle America | School-age (5-14 years) | 12 523 | 18 011 | 3.75 |
| | Total | 46 811 | 64 595 | 3.25 |
| Tropical South | School-age (5-14 years) | 29 068 | 40 546 | 3.40 |
| | Total | 112 479 | 152 896 | 3.15 |

*Source:* Unesco, *Statistical Yearbook, 1965* (Paris, 1966).
[a] These seem to be the 'exceptions that prove the rule,' but may instead simply result from dubious population data.

Chart VII.   Schools must expand fast to stay even with population growth— the example of Uganda's primary schools

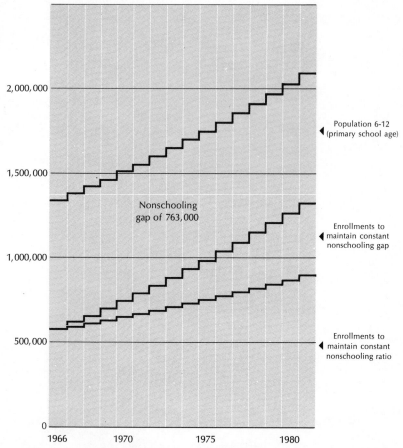

Note: Nonschooling gap equals total school-age group in the population minus those enrolled in school.

*Source:* IIEP estimations, prepared from data of the Uganda Government, in *Educational Statistics, 1965* (Kampala: Ministry of Education) and *Work for Progress. The Second Five-year Plan, 1966-71* (Entebbe: Government Printer).

whereas Latin American countries have lately been in the range of 80 per 1000. Recent averages in African countries have been in the neighborhood of 100 per 1000.[10] There is a revealing contrast between Burma's infant mortality rate of 128 per 1000, and a rate of less than 30 per 1000 in Hong Kong and Singapore.[11]

We can get an idea of what these population forces do to school enroll-

10. United Nations, *Demographic Yearbook* (New York, 1961 and 1964).
11. See Appendix 6.

ments by glancing at several illustrative cases. One is provided by Uganda (Chart VII). Uganda and many other countries similarly situated will have to expand their primary school enrollments very considerably in the next fifteen years just to keep their participation rates from falling. That is, they will have to expand even faster in order to prevent a rise in the absolute number of youngsters who are not getting any primary schooling at all, and are thus condemned to permanent illiteracy.

Another view of how rising population *plus* rising participation rates will affect future school enrollments is provided by Chart VIII. It shows the projections contained in the 1966 report of the Indian Education Commission.[12]

Yet another view of the same phenomenon appears in Table 3, below,

TABLE 3

*Recent and projected trends in enrollment in industrial countries*
*( in thousands )*

| COUNTRY | YEAR | PRIMARY | SECONDARY | HIGHER |
|---|---|---|---|---|
| France | 1951 | 5,358 | 1,181 | 162 |
| | 1961 | 7,301 | 2,509 | 283 |
| | 1964 | 7,406 | 3,112 | 412 |
| | 1972 | 7,280 | 4,980 | 792 |
| Netherlands | 1950 | 1,615 | 325 | 30 |
| | 1960 | 1,915 | 655 | 40 |
| | 1965 | 1,965 | 725 | 65 |
| | 1970 | 2,105 | 760 | 80 |
| | 1975 | 2,375 | 805 | 110 |
| Austria | 1955 | — | 127 | 17 |
| | 1963 | 905 | 135 | 40 |
| | 1970 | 1,116[a] | 159 | 44 |
| | 1975 | 1,184[a] | 217 | 50 |
| Ireland | 1963-64 | 496 | 132 | 16 |
| | 1970-71 | 515 | 173 | 24 |
| U.S.A. | 1949 | 22,207 | 6,453 | 2,659 |
| | 1959 | 32,412 | 9,600 | 3,216 |
| | 1965 | 35,900 | 12,900 | 5,400 |
| | 1970 | 37,300 | 15,000 | 6,959 |
| | 1973 | 38,000 | 16,000 | 7,951 |

*Sources:* (France): R. Poignant, *Education and Economic and Social Planning in France* (Paris: to be published); (Netherlands): OECD, *Educational Policy and Planning. Netherlands* (Paris: Directorate for Scientific Affairs, 1967); (Austria): OECD, *Educational Planning and Economic Growth in Austria, 1965-1975, op. cit.;* (Ireland): OECD, *Investment in Education. Ireland* (Paris: Directorate for Scientific Affairs, 1966); (United States): U.S. Department of Health, Education and Welfare: (past), *Digest of Educational Statistics* (Washington, D.C., 1965), pp. 114-116; (projection), *Projection of Educational Statistics, 1973-74* (Washington, D.C., 1964), p. 3.
  a Compulsory education.

12. See Appendix 7.

Chart VIII.   The projected impact of rising youth population and rising participation rates on
enrollments in India (1950 = 100)

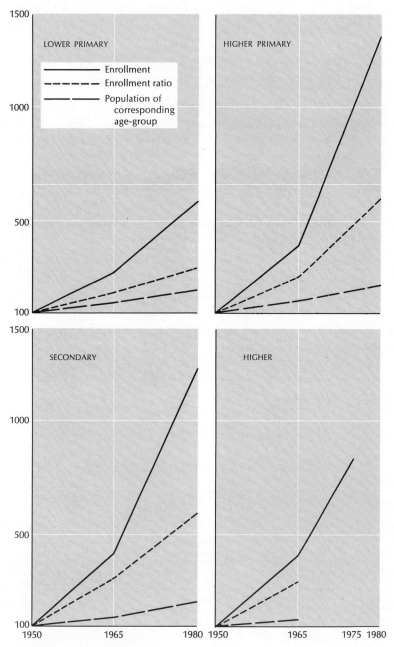

*Source:* Prepared from data given in: Government of India. *Report of the Education Commission (1964-66). Education and National Development* (New Delhi; Ministry of Education, 1966)

applying to certain industrially developed and educationally advanced countries. Their postwar 'baby boom' has now subsided somewhat. It put great pressures on their elementary schools in the 1950's, but it is still putting great pressures on the higher echelons of their educational systems. This, however, is not the end of the matter. When these postwar babies start having babies of their own—as they are even now doing—this will create yet another population bulge for the educational systems to cope with. This, together with rising educational participation rates, explains the rising trends projected in Table 3 (which may well prove to be on the low side).

There are different strategies an educational system can use to deal with the demand-supply gap. It can, at one extreme, throw open its doors, let everyone in who wishes, allow them to stay in for as long as they like, and go as far as they please. If this is done within a compressed period, it leads directly to bulging enrollments, crowded classrooms, and probably a sharp dip in quality. This strategy may satisfy social demand, or at least appear to do so, but at the price of a storm of protests about high dropout rates, poor quality, and the waste of public resources. India and Latin American countries have had this experience.

At the opposite extreme from this 'wide-open' system, there is the policy whereby everyone (if it can be afforded) is given a chance for a primary education, but a severely selective process governs who goes on from there. In this way, elementary education serves to screen the academically bright, the students in secondary and higher education can be held down to a manageable number, and quality can more readily be maintained. This policy of competitive selectivity and promotion, based on individual academic performance, seems at first glance to be fair and democratic. It makes the examination the impartial arbiter of who will continue into secondary and higher education; it accepts the 'ablest' and ruthlessly rejects the rest, thereby, incidentally, stamping more young people with the identifying mark of 'failure' than 'success.' The strategy is designed to produce an 'educated elite,' which will provide society with its essential leadership. It is in fact admirably efficient for this purpose—up to a point—and for a long while worked well for many of today's advanced nations.

The same strategy, however, is now in deep trouble almost everywhere, and the reasons for this bring us back full circle to the matter of increased social demand for education. For one thing, families will not take no for an answer when they are convinced that children need at least a secondary education to rise in the present world. And in industrialized countries more people are becoming convinced that even a secondary education is not enough. Second, a highly selective system, entailing open competitive examinations, only *seems* to be democratic. In practice it is not—because of the inherent social bias of the academic system, whatever the political doctrines of the nation. Its 'standards' and examination systems inevitably tilt the scales on the side of children whose parents are educated and who thus provide their children with a good vocabulary and a culturally rich environment. Schools judge students especially by their verbal dexterity, and this is largely acquired *outside* the school. The youngster who brings a good vocabulary to school, and all else that this implies, has a strong head start, and for the same reasons is likely to keep his lead all through the system, over an equally bright youngster with a culturally impoverished background.

The social bias of educational systems which are seemingly democratic has been repeatedly shown in studies made of the socio-economic origins of European students who have managed to get through secondary school and into the university.[13] In France, for instance, the chances of receiving a university education are 58.5 per cent for children of professionals, against less than 2 per cent for children of agricultural and other workers.[14] The bias is particularly marked, in fact, in older nations, such as in Europe and Latin America, that have long had a substantial educated elite and a highly structured social system. It is much less of a problem in Africa today, for its educated elite has been so small that any substantial expansion in education is bound to reach extensively into the educationally handicapped families. In later generations, however, when Africa has formed a broader educated elite, the problem of bias is bound to crop up there too, as it has even in the socialist countries of eastern Europe.

There is yet another reason why a highly selective, elitist educational system, unless drastically modified, is bound to be in deep trouble these days in industrial countries. It is that the same elitist system which does well by the young people it favors, wastes the human resources represented by those of its rejects who, if given an authentically fair chance for advanced education, would profit considerably and pass the benefits on to society. No modern economy, if it is to prosper, can afford such waste of human talent.[15] Nor will any democratic people, if they can find a way out, tolerate forever an educational system which denies equality of op-

13. See Appendix 8.
14. P. Bourdieu and J. Passeron, in *Les Héritiers. Les étudiants et la culture* (Paris: Editions de Minuit, 1964).
15. See Appendix 9.

portunity to youngsters of inherently equal intellectual ability but unequal social background. To state the problem, however, is far easier than to solve it; and certain types of efforts to solve it can readily damage the whole educational effort.

What has just been said shows a different face in the case of a country that is at an early stage of its educational and economic development. A selective system for such a country is no easier to manage from a political standpoint, but its adoption can be justified on practical grounds: first, the country is not in an economic position to afford a more open system; second, by trying to adopt one, it may slow its economic growth and thus postpone the day when it can in fact afford one.

The case of Tanzania is illustrative. Tanzania has been trying to hold primary schooling to the quantitative level of 50 per cent of the age group; the object is to conserve scarce resources for use in expanding secondary and higher education, both being vital preconditions for economic growth.[16] As things stand in that country—and elsewhere in East Africa— only about one out of ten primary school graduates can find a place in secondary schools. Prospects are no greater for secondary school graduates getting into the university. Curbing primary school expansion and applying highly selective admission to secondary and higher education are not, in Tanzania's case, a permanent policy. They are viewed as being only a transitional necessity for building a balanced educational system, for safeguarding its higher levels from being crushed by a landslide of students, and for accelerating economic growth. The ultimate aim is universal primary education, and higher participation rates beyond there. Such a strategy, however, aimed at reaching long-term goals more quickly, is bound to encounter extreme pressures in the shorter run from those whose educational opportunities have been abruptly cut short.

We can put very simply in capsule form the world-wide outlook for 'student inputs.' Virtually everywhere, more and more students will be knocking on education's door each year. In the industrialized countries the pressures will be greatest beyond the secondary level; in the developing countries they will be great at all levels. Even in the extremely unlikely event that birth rates suddenly dropped sharply all over the world, this would provide little relief to education's 'numbers problem' for many years to come. In all countries the die is already cast. The primary school pupils of the next 6 to 12 years, the secondary school pupils of the next 12 to 18

16. See, for example, G. Skorov, *Integration of Educational and Economic Planning in Tanzania,* African research monographs, No. 6 (Paris: Unesco/IIEP, 1966).

years, and the college students of the next 18 to 24 years, are already with us. We can count their little noses.

## Teachers—An Issue of Quality and Cost

EDUCATION'S COMPETITIVE DISADVANTAGE · REASONS FOR TEACHER SHORTAGES · IMPROVED SUPPLY PROSPECTS · AMBIGUOUS SALARY PROSPECTS · EFFECTS OF TEACHER SALARY STRUCTURES · TEACHER TRAINING CAPACITY · HIGH LOSS RATES · RURAL TEACHER PROBLEM.

Teachers, next to students, are the largest, most crucial inputs of an educational system. They are also, by all odds, the most expensive inputs, even when they are underpaid. Teachers, in fact, lie at the heart of the educational crisis, and for many reasons. Here we look at factors pertaining to teacher supply and specifically at such matters as the salaries, status, and costs of teachers. Later we will examine other factors having to do with the job of teaching itself—how teachers spend their time.

What needs to be said in prologue is that the problem of teacher supply is not one of simple numbers. It is first and foremost a problem of quality —of getting a large enough quantity of the right quality. One schoolman put the case tersely. 'We can,' he said, 'usually find enough willing warm bodies to keep order in the classrooms. Our problem is to find enough *who can also teach.*' Looked at in this light—and in the full context of a nation's over-all manpower position—the teacher supply problem is seen to have its origins in three hard facts.

The first fact is that education is a mass production, *labor-intensive* industry, still tied to a handicraft technology.

The second fact is that education, in contrast to other industries, is both a producer and a consumer of high-level manpower; if it is to serve all other consumers of manpower well—and each generation better—it must constantly recoup enough of its own best output to reproduce a good further crop.

The third fact, tied to the other two, is that in the competition to win back enough of its own best quality products, education is usually at a disadvantage. It often ends up with a high proportion of 'second choice' candidates. Education is at a disadvantage because other competitors with larger purses set the standards for attractive salaries. This applies especially to capital-intensive modern industries, whose new technologies and rising labor productivity permit steady increases in wages and salaries without corresponding increases in the real costs of production. A 10 per cent salary increase for education, on the other hand, usually translates into a 7 to 8 per cent increase in its total 'costs of production.'

These hard economic facts have far-reaching repercussions on the social status and general attractiveness of teaching. They have the power to set in motion an educational variant of Gresham's Law—meaning, that too many poor teachers will drive good ones out of the market. There are, of course, many happy exceptions to the generalization just made. But the larger generalization stands firm. As the educational enterprise grows increasingly larger relative to the whole economy, and as it retains its labor-intensive character while competing enterprises become more capital-intensive, it is progressively more difficult for education to match competitive salaries attractive to topflight personnel. In the degree to which it fails, it contributes to a downward spiral of teacher status, and thus further compounds the difficulty it has in attracting precisely the kind of people it needs to improve education's quality and productivity.

A set of specific questions intrude themselves at this point. What has been happening to teacher supply in the past ten years, and what are the future prospects? Is the potential supply of teachers likely to improve, and if so, will enough of the best people comprising that potential be willing to teach? Can the present stock of poorly qualified teachers be upgraded? What will this cost, and can it be afforded?

It is an open secret that in the last decade most countries have been plagued by teacher shortages. This condition has generally reflected both an over-all shortage of well-qualified manpower and the competitive disadvantage of education. In many places it has also reflected a lag in the expansion of teacher-training capacity. The most acute shortages of well-qualified teachers have cropped up in the sciences, mathematics, and various technical fields, where over-all manpower shortages have also been greatest. The net result of these various factors has been a widespread decline in teacher qualifications.

Fortunately, modest improvements can be reported. In a good number of countries the combined effects of an improving high-level manpower supply, of teacher 'upgrading,' and of earlier initiatives to expand teacher training have begun to increase the quantity and proportion of qualified teachers.[17] But there is a 'relativistic' air to this picture of improvement,

17. See Appendix 10.

since the take-off point for the expansion and upgrading was a poor situation. And there is something more. What may seem in statistical terms to be an upgrading of teacher stock, may in reality be only an upgrading of labels. This is by no means always the case. But it does happen, for example, when in-service training programs endow teachers with higher grade certificates without a commensurate improvement in their professional competence.

There is good reason to hope that in the coming years the teacher supply will improve. Yet the hope rests on an ambiguous center premise: that as education's own output in many countries closes the supply-demand gap for higher level manpower, education will be able to claim a larger share of this output for its own needs.

The strong side of this premise can be seen in evidence drawn from the developing world. In India, for example, the supply of secondary and university graduates has caught up with (and indeed has exceeded) the effective market demand for their services, except for certain specialized fields. This happened in parts of Latin America as well. Then again, an African country like Nigeria, which once seemed to face unsolvable manpower shortages, has recently begun to wonder how it will place its greatly enlarged supply of university graduates.[18] In many industrialized countries, the over-all manpower supply-demand balance, and hence the teacher supply, also seem to be improving steadily. France is an example. It is past the time of greatest strain when its 'thin' population born in prewar years had to provide teachers for the postwar bumper crop of babies. By now these babies are almost old enough to be teachers themselves, and the marginal birth rate has receded somewhat.[19] Add to this another example, though it is in the form of an opinion rather than a concrete fact. Specifically, a prominent United States educator has recently forecast that the 'seller's market' for Ph.D.'s for college teaching is due to

18. L. Cerych, *The Integration of External Assistance with Educational Planning in Nigeria*, African research monographs, No. 14 (Paris: Unesco/IIEP, 1967).

19. Broadly speaking, we may say that students who are in school now (1968), in primary, secondary, or higher education, were born after 1945, while teachers in all levels of education were recruited among generations born before 1945. This fact may be important for some countries. In France, for instance, in addition to the deficit of births during the two world wars, there was a sharp decline in the birth rate from 1922 to 1940. Since World War II, on the contrary, there has been a marked increase in the birth rate, which recently began subsiding.

This important change in the birth rate can by itself account for the relative shortage of teachers. Of course, this situation is only temporary and will certainly improve in the future when it will be possible to recruit teaching staff from the more numerous generations born after 1945.

be reversed. He sets the time at around 1968 to 1970, when supply will mount rapidly against a possible leveling in the demand, as shown in Chart IX.

So far, so good. However, there is a weak side to the premise being considered here. There is no guarantee that education will, in fact, attract a growing share of the best quality part of an expanding high-level man-

Chart IX.  Ph.D.'s available versus number required to maintain faculty quality at 1963-64 level in the United States

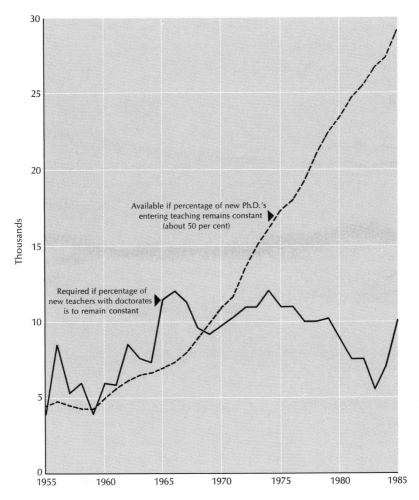

Available if percentage of new Ph.D.'s entering teaching remains constant (about 50 per cent)

Required if percentage of new teachers with doctorates is to remain constant

*Source:* Allan M. Cartter, *The Journal of Human Resources,* Madison, University of Wisconsin (Summer, 1966), I, no. 1.

power supply. The doubt arises in connection with teacher salaries, the character of teacher salary structures, and their relationship to each nation's ability to pay for mounting teacher costs per pupil. Beyond this, there are other complicating factors, such as teacher-training capacity, teacher loss rates, the pull of the cities and the push of rural areas, special shortages in special fields, and the heavy dependence of some countries on expatriate teachers.

The future quality of the teacher corps in every country will be decisively influenced by what happens to teacher salaries *relative to other salaries*. We must therefore here ask a crucial question. What can happen, and what is likely to happen, to those salaries? The answer will vary enormously from country to country depending on an assortment of factors —the level and speed of economic development, the behavior of competing salaries, the priority given to expanding and improving education, and the rate of inflation. Above all, it will vary depending on the supply-demand balance for high-level manpower generally.

We noted a moment ago that the supply-demand balance promises to improve in many countries—owing to education's increased output, but owing also in some unfortunate cases to a slow rate of economic growth, along with a bad structuring of the employment market and incentives. But leaving the fine points out of account, the case of India provides an example of what happens to teachers' salaries once the scarcity value of education diminishes. In India the rather early emergence of a so-called 'educated manpower surplus,' combined with price inflation, has plainly had a depressing effect on teacher salaries, though the impact has been unevenly distributed. After adjustment for a 65 per cent rise in the cost of living between 1950 and 1966, primary school teachers gained only 9 to 16 per cent in real income during this whole sixteen-year period, secondary teachers lost 6 per cent, while professors in higher education either gained or lost 5 to 10 per cent according to where they were teaching.[20]

The race against inflation and the effects of a 'softening' manpower position are by no means confined to India. In most of Latin America, though there are exceptions, the typical pattern has been for the real income of teachers to fall behind the onrush of inflationary prices, then to catch up briefly through a grant of salary increases to teachers, only to fall behind again. To make ends meet, many teachers have been forced to combine teaching with other jobs (something which also happens in many countries of Asia and the Middle East). It is safe to say generally that if infla-

20. See Appendix 11.

tion does not subside—especially in Latin America—education will be the loser.

The blunt reality that confronts a good many developing countries is that the prospect for substantial increases in the real incomes of teachers in the next several years is not good. A 'softening' manpower market and budget stringencies will deter such increases. Inflation, wherever it occurs, will make the matter worse. For reasons to be considered later, the brakes on teacher salary rises will be strongest where such salaries are already a high multiple of average per capita income, as they are throughout most of Africa.

There are brighter prospects for such increases in the industrialized nations, though even here a word of caution is in order. The study of supply-demand prospects for Ph.D's in the United States, just cited, concluded that 'academicians may experience again [as in the 1940's] a decline in their relative income position.' How the matter actually works out in the case of individual nations will depend on whether the improvement in manpower supply will be more than offset by the upward pressure exerted by competition from rising productivity industries. In the long view, teacher salaries in developed countries undoubtedly will rise, as they have before, as part of the progressive rise of real incomes generally throughout the economy. But, if the rise in teacher salaries continues to lag behind other salaries, education will continue to get the poorest pickings of the available manpower supply. Timing is of great importance. It is not enough for teachers' salaries to rise; they must also rise soon enough.

So far we have considered only the general level of teacher salaries. But the structures of these salaries also have a strong bearing upon teacher recruitment and turnover, and upon teacher costs to the educational system. For one thing, the typical teacher salary structure in most countries has built-in automatic increases and retirement provisions, based on years of service. So long as the average age of the teaching force remains constant or is falling, this does not produce significant annual cost increases. But a young teaching force starts to grow older as soon as educational expansion starts to slow down. At that point, which has already been reached in many countries, 'automatic increments' and retirement payments take a larger bite out of each year's over-all budget.

Even more important, however, for many developing countries especially, is the extreme spread in salary structures between the starting level for poorly qualified teachers and the pay of fully qualified teachers. In such situations, the upgrading of a poorly qualified teacher through in-service training, or his replacement by a qualified one, raises the cost to the system considerably. Again, Africa is the extreme case but an instructive one, as exemplified in the salary structures of Northern Nigeria and Uganda.[21] In both these places, for example, a 'standard *trained* primary teacher' who reaches the maximum salary, earns four times as much as an entering 'standard *untrained* primary teacher.' In Uganda, a university graduate teaching in secondary school can reach a maximum of nearly three times the salary of an entering secondary teacher who is trained but lacks a full university degree. It requires no imagination to see what happens when an African educational system makes rapid progress in 'upgrading' its teaching staff. This is true, on a lesser scale, of virtually all educational systems. These teacher salary structures are protracted devourers of an educational budget. The full implications are only beginning to be realized.

The hope is sometimes expressed that in the long run African countries can counteract rising teacher costs by replacing expatriate teachers with local ones. To a degree perhaps they can, but the possibility should not be overestimated; and for some it could conceivably work in reverse. In the former British colonies in Africa, for example, a hired expatriate teacher often costs about 40 per cent more than a local one; his replacement should save money. But a volunteer expatriate teacher—from the Peace Corps, for instance—typically costs the host country less than a local teacher. Many French-speaking African countries are now liberally supplied with regular French teachers. Their cost to the host country is about the same as for a local teacher; the French government typically provides most or all of any necessary supplement. They, too, have less expensive volunteer teachers, whose eventual replacement may raise costs. All things considered, the ultimate replacement of both hired and volunteer expatriate teachers may make relatively little difference in the educational costs of many African countries.

In any event, this process is likely to take a good while. African countries, conscious of their heavy dependence on expatriate teachers, mainly in secondary and higher education, have tried hard to produce more of their own. Some have already succeeded in increasing the percentage of local teachers in the system, but even so the total number of expatriate teachers has continued to grow, owing to the rapid expansion of education. In Northern Nigeria, for example, in the period 1961-1964, expatriate teachers in the secondary schools declined from 68 to 56 per cent, but they

21. See Appendix 12.

increased numerically from 670 to 785.[22] The duplication of this type of case elsewhere underlines the fact that, despite the strenuous efforts of African countries to Africanize their schools, many of them will continue to have a sizable need for expatriate teachers for many years to come. This applies particularly to many of the French-speaking African countries.

We have thus far considered the implications of prevailing teacher salary structures for the future costs of educational systems, and we saw that for developing countries especially they imply very sizable increases. But now shifting the focus, what can be said about their implications for recruitment? Will they help or hamper the recruitment of good teachers?

The answer is a mixture of good and bad, sprinkled with a variety of 'ifs.' The typical provisions in teacher salary structures for automatic increments based on years of service, for retirement benefits, and generous vacations, and for permanent tenure in some circumstances, all work in a favorable direction for recruitment—*if* competing types of employment do not offer even more favorable terms. The wide spread in teacher salaries between different levels of qualification provides an incentive for able and ambitious young people to work their way up—*if* they have ready access to good in-service training programs. Similarly, the wide spread between primary, secondary, and university salaries should be appealing to such young people—*if* a reasonable chance really exists for promotion from one educational echelon to the next. All these 'ifs' are crucial. How they are resolved will vary from place to place, as will their net effect on recruitment.

But now a qualifying reality must be imposed on this apparent bit of optimism. In most countries a teacher rarely breaks the chain which binds him to his peers and jumps ahead of them up the promotion scale. Special promotion is more likely to come—if it comes at all—by leaving classroom teaching and entering administration, at the same echelon in the system. Meanwhile, those of similar 'qualification' who stay behind in the classroom—outstanding and mediocre alike—continue to ride up the salary escalator at the same speed, solely because they got on it at the same time. Excellence in classroom teaching is not rewarded by these mechanistic salary structures, nor is mediocrity discouraged. The implied assumption which underlies them—and which everyone knows to be false—is that all teachers are equally good and will remain so, except for the few who are more equal than the rest and escape to a higher paying administrative post.

22. See Appendix 13.

It would be hard to conceive of a salary structure better calculated to discourage the ablest and most ambitious students from considering a teaching career, or more likely to induce the best teachers to get out of teaching and into administration. Saying this, however, we must also confess that there is no easy alternative arrangement. The issue of 'merit promotion' has been debated in many countries, with teacher organizations usually stoutly opposed, and not without some good arguments. Some systems have tried the principle of promotion based on merit and claimed success, but they are in a decided minority. Many universities have found a partial way around the problem, with their system of diversified professional ranks, but often this has led to problems of its own. The plain fact is that as long as schoolteachers are all assigned essentially the same job, it is difficult to discriminate in their rewards—however much they may vary in quality and results. We will return to this matter at a later stage.

There is another and special respect in which the teacher salary structures of most countries, developing and industrialized, militate against solving the most serious types of teacher shortage. As the general teacher shortage begins to ease in any country, relief can be expected first in the case of 'general' teachers and in such fields as the arts and social studies. Shortages will endure much longer, however, in the fields where they have been most acute all along—in science, mathematics, and technical fields. A kind of vicious circle is at work here. Education's policy of paying teachers uniformly, regardless of subject, imposes a severe competitive handicap in bidding for these particular categories of teachers, who are usually rewarded much better elsewhere. A striking illustration comes from Austria, where a 1967 report predicted that in the future 'mathematics, especially geometry, will be the discipline for which it will be most difficult to find enough [secondary] teachers.' The report goes on to note that 'a university graduate in mathematics starts as a grammar school teacher in 1967 with 3450 Austrian schillings a month. In one of the international firms which have subsidiaries in Austria, his beginning salary would range between 6000 and 6500 schillings a month.'[23] This is called an extreme case, yet disparities of this order exist in many countries today, including the United States.[24]

23. OECD, *Austria: Study on the Demand for and Supply of Teachers* (Paris: Directorate for Scientific Affairs, 1968).
24. See Appendix 14.

What are educational systems to do about this type of problem? They lack the means to pay *all* teachers what it would cost to get enough good mathematics, science, and technical teachers. On the other hand, they cannot get enough of these types of teachers at the uniform price which they can afford to pay. Failure to solve the problem simply aggravates it further, by retarding the increase in output of students in these fields who would eventually relieve the shortage. Two experts who examined the impact of education's uniform salary policy on recruitment of mathematics, science, and technical teachers in the United States came to this conclusion: 'We know of no other industry that pays so little attention to the market situation when establishing salaries.'[25]

The general teacher shortage—and not merely these special cases—is further aggravated by conditions prevailing at the root source of supply, the teacher training colleges. Neglected earlier in the enrollment 'boom,' teacher training capacity now seems to be expanding more rapidly. The numerical output can be expected to grow considerably, but again we come hard up against the issue of quality. If there is to be an improvement in respect to quality as well as numbers, there must be an increase of input into the teacher training colleges of first-rate trainers and of good trainable human material. That, precisely, is the blistering rub in many countries. There is a dearth of able professors for training teachers, partly because training colleges are so often isolated from research and from the mainstream of education. The consequent low standing that teacher-training institutions have in the eyes of those who might make the best teachers, deters them from a personal association with the enterprise of education. The deterrence can be removed only by a sustained counterattack on the conditions which induce good students to avoid the teacher training institutions, and hence to bypass the teaching profession as a career. Some countries, such as France, do not appear to suffer from this problem, but a great many countries evidently find it a most serious problem.

Yet another factor complicates the question of teacher supply. It is the high 'loss rate' among trained teachers in some countries (though, fortu-

25. '. . . It is quite general, particularly in unified school districts but not only in them, for unified salary schedules to prevail. That is to say, for teachers with the same amount of training and experience, salaries are identical. The first grade teacher, therefore, is paid the same as the 12th grade physics teacher. All teachers get salary increases automatically as they gain experience (or as time passes), and they also improve their incomes as they take more courses . . . ,' from J. Kershaw, and R. McKean, *Systems Analysis and Education*, Research memorandum no. 2473-FF (Santa Monica, Calif.: Rand Corporation, October 1959), p. 59.

nately, not in all). A recent study in Norway finds 'indications that dropout from the teaching profession has increased in recent years.'[26] In the
United Kingdom, 'out of every 1000 women who enter teaching, only 193
are still doing school work six years later—out of 1000 men who start teaching, only 677 are still doing so after six years (which is perhaps the more
startling figure).'[27] This in turn is part of a larger story. Specifically, the
manpower shortage of recent years, along with shifts in social policy,
prompted some educational systems to turn more heavily to *woman*
power. Women comprise three-fifths of Austria's primary teacher staff,[28]
three-quarters of the United Kingdom's (two-fifths at secondary level),[29]
and they play a comparable role in United States schools. But the merit in
the arrangement is diminished by the fact that education loses out heavily
in the competition with marriage and children.

There is a further complication when a country's social policy provides
that men and women teachers should be given equal pay for equal work.
This would seem a highly desirable social policy. But suppose the rest of
the economy is not bound by that policy? Suppose it pays men substantially higher salaries than it pays women for similar work? Then it follows
that the teaching salaries which are high enough to attract able women
may not be high enough to draw equally able men into teaching, or to
hold them once they are in it. There is an irony here. By taking the lead
in actually applying what most people would agree *in principle* to be a
desirable social policy, education—and hence pupils—may end up with a
self-inflicted wound.

We come lastly to a geographic problem of teacher supply which will
continue to plague many countries, even after they have achieved a good
over-all teacher supply-demand balance. It is symbolized by the rhetorical
question asked in an old American song: 'How are you going to keep 'em
down on the farm?' Educational systems in heavily rural countries face
the perennial human problem of getting enough qualified teachers to staff
the schools of rural areas where they are urgently needed, but where the
rural life holds little appeal for teachers; so little in fact that the best
teachers tend to congregate in the cities, while the education of rural
youth is often left in the hands of inferior teachers. Here again the salary
structure and status symbols often work against a solution, by attaching

26. OECD, *A Case Study in the Application of Teacher Demand and Supply
Models in Norway* (Paris: Directorate for Scientific Affairs, 1968).
27. *Times* (London), 20 June 1967.
28. See OECD, *A Case Study . . . , op. cit.*
29. See Appendix 15.

the highest rewards and status to urban teaching, rather than giving special incentives to rural teaching.

Most of the problems we have just reviewed regarding 'teacher inputs' finally translate into one overarching question: Will educational systems be able to *afford* more and at the same time better teachers? To this question we now turn our attention.

## Money: Education's Purchasing Power

COMPETITION AND PRIORITIES · KEY FACTORS AFFECTING
EDUCATION'S FINANCIAL POSITION · RISING EXPENDITURES PER STUDENT
· EDUCATION'S RISING 'SHARE' OF TOTAL RESOURCES · TRENDS IN
INDUSTRIALIZED NATIONS · FINANCIAL AGONIES FOR DEVELOPING
NATIONS · IMPLICATIONS OF THEIR POPULATION GROWTH.

The issue of financial resources has lurked in the background of almost everything said up to this point. We come now directly to the matter and ask: Is money—or the lack of it—at the root of the educational crisis? How much will be needed, where will it come from, what are the chances of getting enough, and what happens if getting enough proves impossible?

We can approach these questions with a clearer head if we promptly brush aside the old cliché that 'nothing is wrong with education that more money won't fix.' This half-truth too easily diverts people from digging deeper to the other sources of education's problems. There are, in fact, important constraints besides money which can limit the speed at which an educational system can expand, change, and improve—and sometimes these prove even more unyielding than the money factor. This said, however, we are still left with the fact that money is an absolutely crucial input of any educational system. It provides the essential purchasing power with which education acquires its human and physical inputs. With too little money, education can be helpless. With an ample supply, its problems become more manageable even though they do not vanish.

The questions about financial resources posed above cannot be divorced from their environment; education is but one part of a seamless web of things that make up life in a society. At any given time, the society's economy has just so much income to deploy. The amount that goes to education is subtracted from the amounts available for other purposes. For these reasons, the claims of education on national resources encounter the competitive counterclaims of important material needs, such as investment in agriculture and industry, roads and housing, and important social needs, such as health, old age security, and unemployment relief. Regrettably, education's toughest adversary in more than a few countries is the military budget. But education even divides against itself in a competition for resources—where the rivals may be primary education versus secondary, or secondary versus university; expanded teacher training versus expanded construction of classrooms; and, of special importance, formal education versus nonformal.

This competition demands the formulation of an order of national priorities, whether explicitly or implicitly. The settling of national priorities, however, especially where equally strong arguments produce a deadlock in reason itself, is a notoriously painful affair. The matter can be greatly aided by solid facts, rationally analyzed. But in the end the priorities are finally set, not by a planner's slide rule, but by a political process —a process sometimes marked by rough-and-tumble budget battles among ministries, or between them and legislatures, or within legislatures. What finally emerges usually reflects a blend of the values of the society, and the comparative strengths and strategies of contending pressure groups. Indeed, precisely on this account, it is important for educational leaders to master not only their own field but the language and techniques of economists as well, in order to be better armed for the defense of their own proposals in the annual 'battle of the budget.' Good rhetoric is no substitute for facts and analysis in winning these battles.

Because every case of national priorities is a distinctive case, the answers to the questions asked above will not everywhere be the same. These differences, with their nuances, must be noted. But in any context, the financial dimensions of the educational crisis can come into sharper focus if three key indicators form the lens trained on what has been happening and what is likely to happen. These indicators include: the trends in expenditures and costs per pupil; the trend of over-all educational expenditures; the trends in the percentage of total national product, and total public revenues, spent on education.

Let us take the first of these. 'Hard' evidence on the behavior of educational costs per student is sparse. More research is needed here, and could pay high dividends. But, hard or soft, all the evidence we have been able to collect points mainly in one direction. In the industrially advanced and developing nations alike, educational costs per student, at every level, whether measured in current or constant prices, seem to have been rising in the past fifteen years. The main reason for this is the upward trend of teacher costs noted previously.

An economist would infer from this that education is 'a rising cost industry'—that its input costs (at constant prices) for each similar unit of output follow an upward trend line over the years. If this is the case, as it seems to be, the implications are serious and far-reaching. It means, in effect, that each year, ad infinitum, an educational system needs more finances simply to accomplish the same results as in the previous year. If it wants to do more, and to do it better, it will need a still larger budgetary increase—all this apart from keeping up with inflation. We shall return to this matter later on when discussing the inner workings of educational systems. Right now we turn to a closer examination of the evidence at hand.

The industrialized countries offer the most consistent evidence of the upward trend of expenditures per pupil. This is indicated in Chart X. Some of these increases doubtless reflect an improvement in the quality of education's product from year to year. But there are clear cases where falling quality and rising costs have gone hand-in-hand. Either way, it seems fairly clear that a net increase in quality by no means accounts for the full rise in the real costs per student.

Does anything on the horizon indicate that the past upward trend in unit costs will be halted or reversed in the industrialized countries? The answer, regrettably, is no. In theory it could be slowed down by a growing abundance of manpower qualified to teach, coupled with a slackening demand for such manpower by other employers. But as long as labor productivity in other fields continues to rise, as it promises to do, education will have to maintain a reasonable parity between its salaries and those paid by others if it is to win an adequate share of well-qualified manpower. Meanwhile, if the productivity of teachers is not rising apace with teacher salaries—and there is little reason to believe that it is—costs per student will keep rising. This expectation is reinforced by a recent pioneering—if controversial—study in the United Kingdom, which concludes that education's productivity in England has actually been declining.[30] Its author makes no claim to infallibility or to the universal applicability of the

30. See Maureen Woodhall, 'Productivity Trends in British Secondary Education, 1950-1963,' draft paper presented at the Seminar for Professors of Educational Planning (Economics), 5-16 June 1967, IIEP, Paris (mimeographed).

Chart X.  Expenditures per pupil (in constant prices) in industrialized nations

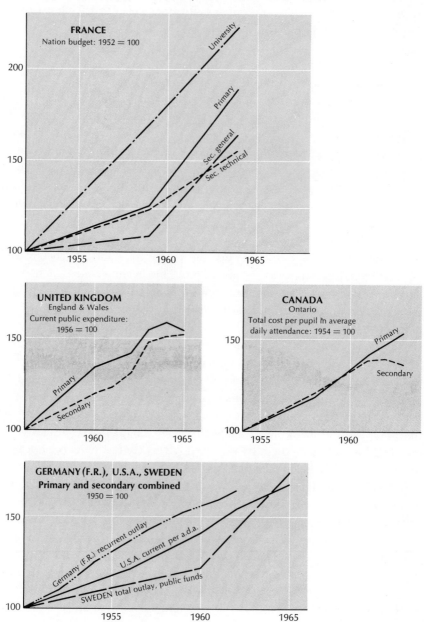

*Source:* See Appendix 16.

findings. But there is good cause to suspect that if similar studies were made elsewhere, they might reach similar conclusions.

In the case of the developing nations, the scattered evidence available adds up to a mixed and confusing picture, as will be seen in Chart XI. The weight of this evidence indicates rising costs per student, but in certain situations the evidence, taken at face value, indicates declining costs, at least over a short period. Unfortunately, we can find little solace in such instances. From what we know of them, it appears that the *apparent* decrease in costs per student is traceable in the main to five factors: (1) the lag of teacher salaries behind a rampant price inflation; (2) the extensive use of unqualified teachers whose salaries are well below those of qualified teachers; (3) an increase in the pupil-teacher ratio, reflecting the overcrowding of classrooms; (4) a shift in the educational 'mix' toward a higher proportion of lower-cost types of education, such as fewer secondary boarding schools and more day students; and (5) the double-shift system. Given the nature of most of these five factors, it seems fair to conclude that in most cases where unit costs appear to be falling, the decline is illusory. What is being measured over a period of time is not the self-same object, but a declining quality of product or a changing product 'mix.'

This conclusion, however, now needs to be qualified by noticing some scattered instances where there appear to be genuine cost reductions for the same or a better quality of product. Perhaps the clearest cases of this kind are to be found in a few new African universities, whose costs per student are reported to have fallen as low initial enrollments rose toward the planned capacity of these institutions. This, however, is a one-time-only kind of economy, not the onset of a trend destined to continue downward. And even with respect to these reductions, the per-student cost of most African universities are still strikingly high when judged by two criteria: first, the economic ability of the African countries concerned to support them; and second, the costs of a comparable education in Europe.

In the future, developing countries could conceivably fight off rising costs per student, as they have to some degree in the past, by several expedients—providing they were willing to pay a heavy price in quality. They could do it, for example, by maintaining a high proportion of unqualified teachers in the lowest salary brackets, by avoiding general teacher salary increases, by forgoing expenditures on textbooks and other essential learning materials, by continuing to overcrowd their classrooms, and by extending the double-shift system. But all these expedients, apart

Chart XI.   Mixed trends of recurrent expenditures per pupil in developing countries

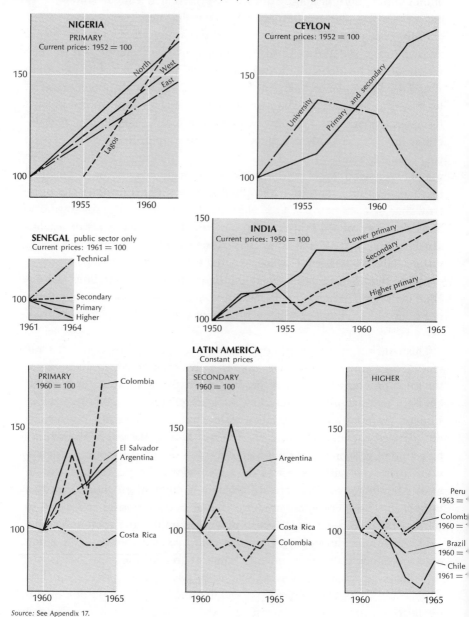

*Source:* See Appendix 17.

from their adverse implications for quality, have practical limitations. The crowding of classrooms reaches a physical maximum when literally not another student can be squeezed in. Likewise the double shift can be extended just so far, before it breaks into a triple shift. If there are few textbooks to begin with, little can be saved by not doubling the number. Keeping unqualified teachers will be difficult to justify when teacher training institutions and universities are turning out better qualified teachers in larger numbers. And resisting the powerful demands of teachers for salary increases—to keep even with inflation or with increases granted to other parts of the public or private sector—will be no easy matter. Organized teachers in developing countries can be a more potent pressure group than in the industrialized countries, precisely because they comprise a large fraction of the small and powerful educated elite. The conclusion would therefore seem to be that developing countries have already largely exhausted the main conventional escape routes from rising unit costs.

A larger conclusion forced upon us, especially when we recall our earlier discussion about the built-in cost increases in teacher salary structures, is that in the years ahead, unit costs and expenditures per student in developing countries are destined to rise even more rapidly than in the industrialized countries. Alternatively, quality, instead of rising, may tumble to the point where the educational 'investment' will in fact be disinvestment.

On these grounds, we believe that a responsible educational planner in any country faces a moral imperative. He must have the courage to allow for marked increases in unit costs when he computes the financial price of reaching bold future targets for educational expansion, especially when these are coupled with a policy for improving quality. To assume that costs per student will be held at a standstill by far-reaching economy-producing innovations still to be introduced is to indulge in fantasy. Such fantasy can produce a further decline in quality; it can dangerously mislead higher authorities and the general public, and be followed by disenchantment and cynicism.

The unpleasant forecasts we have felt obliged to make are based on the assumption of educational 'business-as-usual.' It is conceivable, on the other hand, that there could be great cost-reducing educational innovations that would make our forecasts read like a giant misprint. If so, we would be the first to hail the happy event. Regretfully, however, we as yet see no great thrust of innovation which promises to rescue educational systems from the serious financial plight facing them in the next ten years.

This plight becomes even clearer when we look at the second and third indicators—the trend in the growth of educational expenditures and in their relation to economic output and public budgets. Virtually everywhere, educational expenditures have been rising sharply for the past ten to fifteen years, not only in absolute amounts, but as a percentage of GNP, national income, and total public revenues.

The bright side of this picture says that all nations and peoples have come to assign a greater value and a higher priority to education. But the dark side tells us that educational expenditures cannot continue to grow at this pace indefinitely. National budgets must meet other important needs as well. Education cannot continue to command a rapidly increasing share of available resources without producing serious stresses and distortions in the whole society and economy. This is not a question of philosophy or viewpoint; it is a matter of elementary arithmetic.

The arithmetic does not insist, of course, that educational budgets must cease to rise altogether. Rather, it says that there is a stage when the rate of education's budgetary increase must be set more closely in line with the over-all rate of growth of the economy and of total public revenues. As this slackening occurs, educational systems will receive smaller annual budget increments than earlier—and the more so if the nation's economic growth rate is slow. Moreover, a large fraction of each year's budget increment will be committed in advance to cover inescapable cost increases in on-going programs. Educational managers will thus have a smaller area of maneuver for expanding and improving education, and for redeploying educational resources to improve the balance and productivity of the system.

It is impossible to generalize about the point at which this flattening-out process will set in. There will obviously be great differences in timing and levels among countries, depending on their respective traditions, values goals, and, above all, on their stage of development and rate of economic growth. But that a point will be reached by all, sooner or later, is inevitable. Indeed, it has already been reached in a number of countries, both developing and developed.

A cross section of what has been happening to educational finance in *industrialized* countries is shown in Chart XII. The countries included are fairly representative. Most have moved from a point where they were spending between 2 and 4 per cent of GNP on education in 1955 (a considerable increase, for many, over 1950), to the point of spending

Chart XII.   Over-all educational expenditures by industrialized nations

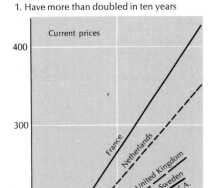

1. Have more than doubled in ten years

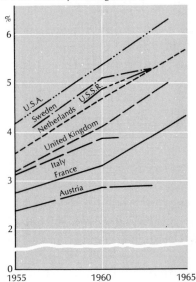

2. Have risen as percentage of GNP

3. Have risen as percentage of total public budgets

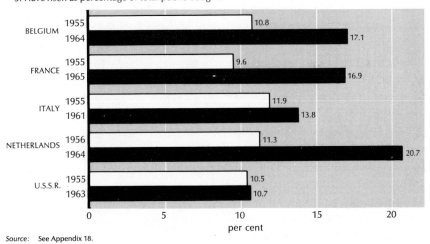

| | | per cent |
|---|---|---|
| BELGIUM | 1955 | 10.8 |
| | 1964 | 17.1 |
| FRANCE | 1955 | 9.6 |
| | 1965 | 16.9 |
| ITALY | 1955 | 11.9 |
| | 1961 | 13.8 |
| NETHERLANDS | 1956 | 11.3 |
| | 1964 | 20.7 |
| U.S.S.R. | 1955 | 10.5 |
| | 1963 | 10.7 |

*Source:*   See Appendix 18.

between 4 and 6 per cent by 1965. There is reason to expect that these percentages in industrialized countries will continue to climb for some years to come, though at a slower pace, if their economic growth remains strong.

This expectation is consistent with recent projections made for several developed countries. The phenomenon in France is perhaps in some measure transitory. France has been—and still is—undergoing an extraordinary expansion of facilities for education at all levels, costing each year about 1 per cent of the GNP. Although these capital outlays may later decrease, they will be more than offset by the increased outlays required to operate and maintain all these new facilities. To an outside observer, therefore, it seems inevitable that over-all French educational expenditures will reach or exceed the mark of 6 per cent of the GNP soon after 1970.[31] Recent projections for the Netherlands—which may well be on the low side —imply a rise in educational expenditures from 5.7 per cent of GNP in 1965 (up from only 2.9 per cent in 1950) to 6.3 per cent by 1970.[32] In the United States, enrollment forecasts published by the Office of Education imply an increase in total educational expenditures from 6.3 per cent of GNP in 1965 to 6.7 per cent or higher by 1975.[33]

The foregoing and other evidence points to the likelihood that by 1970, or soon thereafter, a majority of western European and North American countries will find themselves spending 6 to 7 per cent of their GNP on education. Because of sizable differences in definition and measurement of GNP as between Western countries and the Soviet Union, comparisons are difficult and can be misleading. But from the available evidence of past trends, it appears that Soviet outlays on education, in relation to total national income and output, are at present roughly comparable to the United States and to the highest levels in western Europe. As with other industrialized countries, it would seem reasonable to expect a gradual further increase in the Soviet Union's educational effort, despite its already high level.

Most industrialized countries should be able to negotiate this further upward climb of educational expenditure, but not without considerable difficulty in some cases. The United Kingdom, for example, is in serious trouble right now. Until its economic growth speeds up and its balance-of-payment difficulties untangle, it will be hard pressed even to maintain its present educational services, much less to enlarge and improve them in line with announced goals.[34] Several continental European countries have lately announced major primary and secondary school reforms

31. See Appendix 18.
32. See Appendix 19.
33. See Appendix 20.
34. See, for example, *Times* (London), 22 June 1967.

and bold plans for university expansion, only to discover, when they tardily 'costed' them, that they would have to be postponed because of financial stringencies. More such unpleasant surprises are doubtless in store for other countries.

Still, even though industrialized countries may be delayed and inconvenienced by financial constraints, the crux of their educational crisis is not their shortage of resources. It is, as we observed earlier, the overpowering inertia of their traditional educational systems, fortified by some sectors of public opinion, which slows their adaptation to their environment, making them progressively obsolete and irrelevant.

The story for *developing* countries is very different. Their educational authorities increasingly find that they are moving onto rougher and rougher financial ground, which for some may soon become impassable. The economic growth rates of these countries, though they vary widely, have on the whole been disappointing.[35] Against the 5 per cent growth target set for the United Nations Development Decade—which many criticized at the time (1961) for being too modest—the actual performance has averaged out at an estimated 4.25 per cent, but with many well below this level.[36] Even small percentage variations in their economic growth rates can make an enormous difference—in either direction—in the ability of developing countries to strengthen their educational systems. This crucial fact cannot be overstressed. On the one hand, they must improve their educational performance in order to accelerate their economic growth, but on the other, they cannot greatly increase their investments in education until and unless their economy grows. It is a 'chicken-and-egg' situation. Regrettably, only a small minority of the nations facing this problem have yet reached the 'take-off' point, from which self-sustained economic growth can be reasonably assured.

The situation for many such countries looks even grimmer when one examines what has been happening to the pattern of their general budgetary expenditures and to their accumulated financial commitments. The 'social services' sector of their public budgets has proliferated rapidly, leaving precious little room for essential development investments. Civil service establishments have similarly proliferated and become very expensive. Their debt service obligations on foreign loans have grown steadily and in many cases have already reached ominous proportions. A

35. See Appendix 21.
36. United Nations, *The United Nations Development Decade at Mid-Point. An Appraisal by the Secretary-General* (New York, 1965).

Chart XIII.    Enlarging youth population increases school costs— the example of primary education in Uganda

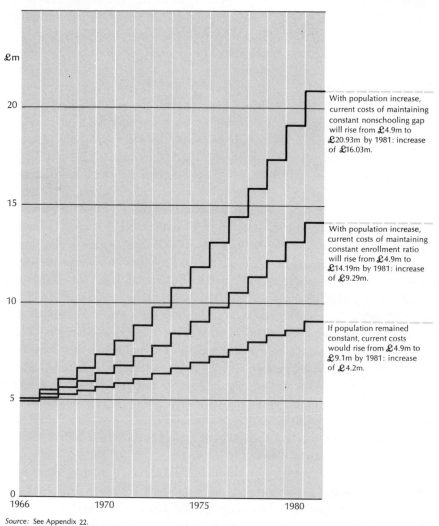

£m

20    With population increase, current costs of maintaining constant nonschooling gap will rise from £4.9m to £20.93m by 1981: increase of £16.03m.

15    With population increase, current costs of maintaining constant enrollment ratio will rise from £4.9m to £14.19m by 1981: increase of £9.29m.

10    If population remained constant, current costs would rise from £4.9m to £9.1m by 1981: increase of £4.2m.

5

0
1966          1970          1975          1980

*Source:* See Appendix 22.

growing number of countries have become tragically saddled with large military and police costs. And lately the critical food problem has pushed dramatically into the foreground, demanding urgent attention.

With these facts now in full view, one needs no crystal ball to see that most developing countries will find it more and more difficult to enlarge the share of their total resources going to education. Many will find it increasingly difficult even to maintain the present share. Their leaders will need great wisdom and courage to make a successful passage over the difficult economic terrain ahead. And they will need more than this. They will need even more help from the outside than they have already been getting. The alternative for many is a worsening crisis, the repercussions of which could send shock waves all around the world.

Apart from the *general* financial stringency of developing countries, their educational systems have some additional special problems. The first is the effect of their population explosion on their budgets. We have already alluded to the example of Uganda and have indicated the race its elementary schools must run in the next fifteen years just to stay abreast of their expanding clientele. Chart XIII shows estimates of what this population growth, by itself, can do to Uganda's primary school budget. (The underlying assumptions and methods used in this chart[37] may suggest a method by which other countries may diagnose their own situation in this regard.) One estimate for Uganda shows the cost of maintaining the recent 'participation ratio' (about 47 per cent) in coming years. The other (labeled the 'nonparticipation gap') shows the cost of maintaining constant the absolute number of children *not* going to school at all.

Another thorny problem for developing countries—which applies with special force to Africa—involves the relationship between teacher salaries and the average per capita income. In the latter average we have a rough indicator of a nation's economic ability to support education and other services, since the means for paying for these services must come in the main from the incomes of the whole population. A picture of how this indicator stands in various places can be seen in Table 4. But the general point can perhaps best be illustrated by a single contrast. In the United States, the typical primary or secondary school teacher earns just over twice the average per capita income. Thus when one more teacher is added, the school budget must be expanded by an amount roughly equal to the average income of two members of the population. In an African country, however, adding one more teacher means expanding the school budget by an amount equal to the average income of anywhere from 20 to 30 members of the population. Adding a university professor costs considerably more. Or, stated another way, relative to what the average of their countrymen receive, teachers in Africa are much better paid than teachers in the most advanced industrial countries. Yet, at the same time,

37. See Appendix 22.

their standard of living is typically lower. Though to a lesser degree than in Africa, the same applies in many other developing countries.

TABLE 4

*Ratio of schoolteachers' salaries to per capita income*

| COUNTRIES | SALARY LEVEL | PRIMARY | SECONDARY |
|---|---|---|---|
| Africa | | | |
| Ghana (1961) | at midpoint | 4.2 | 14.0 |
| Madagascar (1965)a | after ten years | 18.2 | 23.7 |
| Niger (1961)a | at midpoint | 46.2 | — |
| Senegal (1961) | average | 8.1 | 17.3 |
| Southern Rhodesia (1961) | at midpoint | 6.3 | 18.5 |
| Asia | | | |
| Burma (1962) | at midpoint | 3.9 | 15.1 |
| India (1966) | average | 2.5 | 4.6 |
| Korea, Rep. of (1962) | at midpoint | 9.8 | 12.4 |
| Pakistan (1962) | at midpoint | 2.9 | 7.8 |
| Latin America | | | |
| Argentina (1963) | after ten years | 1.7 | 3.0 |
| Chile (1963) | after ten years | 2.7 | 4.8 |
| Ecuador (1963) | after ten years | 5.3 | 7.6 |
| Mexico (1963) | maximum | 5.6 | 15.7 |
| Panama (1963) | after ten years | 3.6 | 9.0 |
| Industrialized nations | | | |
| Austria (1962) | at midpoint | 1.1 | 1.6 |
| Japan (1963) | average | 1.9 | 2.8 |
| United Kingdom (1964) | average | 2.6 | 3.0 |
| U.S.A. (1965) | average | 2.1b | 2.1b |

*Sources:* United Nations, *Monthly Bulletin of Statistics* (May, 1967); World Confederation of Organizations of the Teaching Profession (WCOTP), *Survey of the Status of the Teaching Profession in Asia* (Washington, D.C., 1963); WCOTP, *Survey of the Status of the Teaching Profession in the Americas,* prepared by Margarita Davies (Washington, D.C., 1964); WCOTP, *Survey of the Status of the Teaching Profession in Africa* (Washington, D.C., no date); P. Guillaumont, D. Garbe, P. Verdun, *Les Dépenses d'enseignement au Sénégal,* Monographies africaines, no. 5 (Paris: Unesco/IIEP, 1967); J. Hallak, R. Poignant, *Les Aspects financiers de l'enseignment dans les pays africains d'expression française,* Monographies africaines, no. 3 (Paris: Unesco/IIEP, 1966); OECD *Educational Planning and Economic Growth in Austria, 1965-1975* (Paris: Directorate for Scientific Affairs, 1968); United Kingdom, Department of Education and Science, *Statistics of Education, 1965* (London) pts. I and II; United States, *Digest of Educational Statistics* (Washington, D.C., 1965).

a GNP per capita.
b Average for primary and secondary combined.

These extreme income ratios between teacher salaries and average per capita income have no doubt helped to draw people into the teaching profession. But they cannot last. They cannot last, that is, if education is going to keep expanding. For one thing, educational systems simply will not have the means to keep hiring more teachers at these rates, while continuing to upgrade present rates. Moreover, as education expands, its extreme scarcity value, on which these high salaries are based, will gradually diminish. All this, however, does not alter our basic point. Education will remain a very expensive commodity in developing countries for a long time to come—relative to the population's ability to pay for it.

This same point can be seen from another angle, through the prism of population figures. These figures show that developing countries are much 'younger' than developed countries. Typically, half of their population is 19 years or younger, whereas the median age for most industrialized countries is 30 to 35 years. This means that the working-age population in developing countries, being proportionately smaller, must carry a much larger burden of support—including educational support—for those below working-age. To illustrate: in France and the Federal Republic of Germany there are about five working-age people for each school-age child. In Ghana, India, and Morocco, there are only half this number; or two and a half working-age adults for each school-age child.[38]

Yet, despite the heavy burden, educational expenditure trends have moved up even more dramatically in the developing countries—relative to their resources—than in the more advanced countries. Chart XIV offers a sample of the evidence. Many of the figures shown have a wide margin of possible error, but the general picture they convey is reasonably reliable. A majority of these countries have doubled or even trebled their educational expenditures within a period of only five to ten years.[39] Many Latin American countries that were devoting only 1 to 2 per cent of GNP to education in the early 1950's are today spending between 3 and 4 per cent. Some, like Mexico and Honduras, are now spending as much as 25 per cent of their total public revenues on education. At the same time, some African countries have reached the remarkable point of spending on education, including substantial foreign aid, the equivalent of 6 per cent or more of their GNP, and one-fifth or more of their public funds. Even so, they are still a very long way from meeting their educational needs and goals. One cannot help wondering how long they can keep this up, while at the same time desperately hoping that they can.

The leaders in many developing countries are by now well aware of the formidable facts of economic life facing them. They realize that it will take a longer time to reach their educational goals than was earlier hoped, but they are undaunted in their determination to reach them. It requires a full measure of personal and political bravery for these leaders to speak candidly to their peoples, saying that educational aspirations must be

38. See Appendix 23.
39. See Appendix 24.

Chart XIV.   Over-all educational expenditures in developing countries

1. In absolute amount

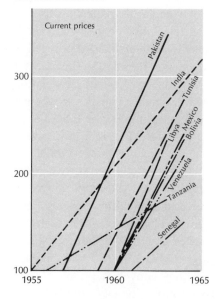

2. As percentage of GNP or national income

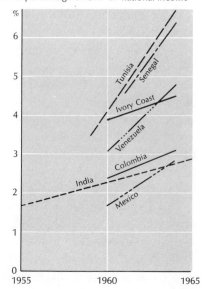

3. As percentage of total public budgets

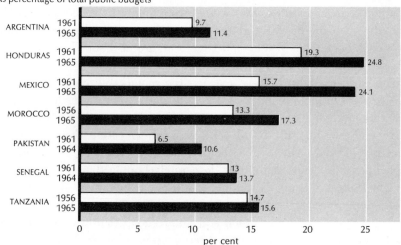

*Source:* See Appendix 24.

adapted to more realistic levels and to a more realistic time schedule for their fulfillment.

For its bearing on what has just been said, it is worth examining for a moment the ambitious regional educational targets which were adopted a few years ago by Unesco conferences of the ministers of education in Latin America, Asia, and Africa. These regional targets have unquestionably helped to spur the educational efforts of many countries. Statistically, much progress has already been made toward achieving these long-term enrollment goals. In the case of secondary education, the progress has even run ahead of schedule. Recently, however, Unesco statisticians estimated the financial requirements involved in keeping on schedule toward these targets up to 1970. The analysis showed that to meet the schedule African nations as a group (though with variations among them) would have to spend nearly 7 per cent of GNP on education by 1970. To the same end, the Latin American group would have to spend 5.43 per cent of GNP and the Asian group 4.26 per cent. By then, primary school participation would be 71 per cent of the total age group in Africa, 74 per cent in Asia, and 100 per cent in Latin America.[40] But even these imposing figures may understate the case, because the economic assumptions underlying the estimates just cited favored the optimistic side. It was assumed, for example, that there will be a sustained annual growth rate of 5 per cent in Latin America and Asia, and of 4.39 per cent in Africa. It was further assumed that economy-producing innovations and various other educational adjustments would in the main keep unit costs from rising (except for moderate rises for primary education in Africa, and primary and higher education in Asia). These estimates, of course, do not predict what will happen nor do they pretend to be a plan of action. But they strikingly reveal the magnitude of the economic and the economizing tasks required in order to achieve the targets set several years ago.

We cannot resist citing once again the case of India, which all along sheds much useful light on the problems being considered in these pages. The recent Indian Education Commission not only had the boldness to set forth the large enrollment increases and quality improvements which it considered essential up to 1985 but it had the courage to spell out their formidable financial implications. These are summarized in Chart XV. To achieve the Indian goals will require an estimated sixfold increase in

40. See Appendix 25.

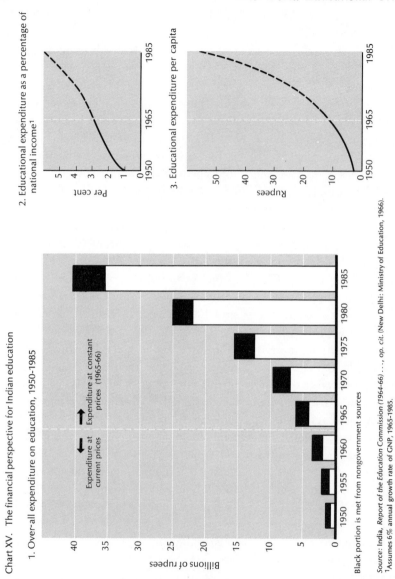

Chart XV. The financial perspective for Indian education

1. Over-all expenditure on education, 1950-1985

2. Educational expenditure as a percentage of national income[1]

3. Educational expenditure per capita

Black portion is met from nongovernment sources

*Source:* India, *Report of the Education Commission (1964-66) . . ., op. cit.* (New Delhi: Ministry of Education, 1966).
[1]Assumes 6% annual growth rate of GNP, 1965-1985.

total educational expenditures (at constant prices) from 1965 to 1985, and a fivefold increase in per capita expenditures. On the favorable assumption that India's economy will grow at 6 per cent annually throughout this period, educational expenditures will have to expand from 2.9 per cent of GNP in 1965 to 6 per cent by 1985. A nation aware of these hard facts must be animated by a passionate conviction, courage, and confidence to set itself so ambitious an educational course.

The evidence that we have been able to collect and assess on the crucial matter of financial inputs and cost trends, has led us, regrettably, to a disturbing picture of the future, especially as it applies to developing countries. If enough people become aware of these difficulties and become determined to do more about them, then this somber picture could acquire a brighter cast. This would be the case, for example, if the following combination of developments were to occur: a sharp rise in external assistance to developing countries, plus a vast cutback everywhere of present high military expenditures and their redeployment for peaceful uses, plus a quickening of economic growth, plus great improvements in the efficiency of educational systems. But given the looks of things at the present time, such a happy conjunction seems only a distant dream. It is not a realistic basis for immediate educational planning and policy.

So much for the input side of educational systems. We turn now to an examination of what has been happening—and is likely to happen—on the output side. Later, we will inspect the process that lies in between.

# III

## The Outputs of Educational Systems:
## Fitness for Needs

---

*Finished versus Unfinished Products*
DIFFICULTIES OF MEASURING EDUCATIONAL OUTPUT · GREATER RISE
IN NUMBER OF UNFINISHED PRODUCTS · FAILURES AND DROPOUTS ·
CONSEQUENCES OF DIFFERENT POLICIES OF ADMISSION · THE OUTLOOK.

It is impossible to measure with any presently known gauge the full output and eventual impact of an educational system. Some sense of what is involved can be grasped if we imagine a school whose whole output consists of a single student. On the day he graduates, what kind of an output does he embody? The answer is that he embodies a multiplicity of outputs—represented, for instance, in the facts and concepts he has learned, the style of thinking he has acquired, and also such changes as may have occurred in his outlook, values, ambitions, and personal conduct. If one then asks how all this will affect the future life of this student, his family, and society, the difficulty is several times compounded. Such cause and effect relationships are often as indistinct as a line drawn through water. But if these matters are hard to get at in the case of a single student, they are infinitely more elusive when the matter to be judged is the output represented by multiple streams of individuals, flowing through different educational channels for different lengths of time.

A full and precise judgment on the outputs of any educational system is next to impossible; however, an approximate and useful judgment can be formed. The useful, though imperfect, basis we choose here is a combination of several possible indicators of the output, fitness, and productivity of an educational system, which will be dealt with below.

The easiest measure of output is the number of students emerging from the system. Some make their exit prematurely, before completing a standard cycle. These are the dropouts and the failures—depending on whether they have left voluntarily or been rejected by the examination and marking mechanism of the system. Other students struggle through and complete the cycle, then either depart into 'the real world' or stay on through the next cycle.

It is important to distinguish between 'finished' and 'unfinished' products. Granted, the nonfinishers are not a dead loss. They carry something useful away, more or less in proportion to how long they stayed in the system, even though the system has not given them all that it intended to. But the important point is that societies and educational systems themselves make a sharp distinction between finished and unfinished products. In many developing societies, of course, even to have gone to school at all, to have learned to read, sets a person apart, puts him in the modern world and gives him a special status. To have attended secondary school or a university, even without finishing one's course, may bring one within the privileged fold of the small 'educated elite.' And, in a society where educational attainments—symbolized by certificates and degrees—are closely linked to preferred categories of employment and to social status, the student who finishes has much more promising career prospects. The one who drops out or fails, on the other hand, burns important bridges to the future. When so much is at stake, including the whole family's social status, there is little reason to wonder why anxieties mount high as examination and admission times approach, whether in Dar-es-Salaam or Paris or Oak Park, Illinois. These very anxieties and aspirations, as we saw in our discussion of social demand, were the main force that sent enrollments and educational output soaring all over the world in the past ten years.

The rise in 'finished' outputs in recent years is shown for a sample of countries in various regions of the world in Charts XVIa-d. As would be expected, primary school output rose steeply in the developing regions, for they started the decade with something far less than universal schooling, and still have a long way to go. But in all the regions, secondary and higher level output rose sharply. In many countries, the 'educational pyramid' which planners speak of became more full-bodied, and the middle and upper heights began to resemble more closely the slopes of a real pyramid, in contrast to their previous resemblance to a narrow spear perched upon a broad, low box.[1]

1. See Appendix 26.

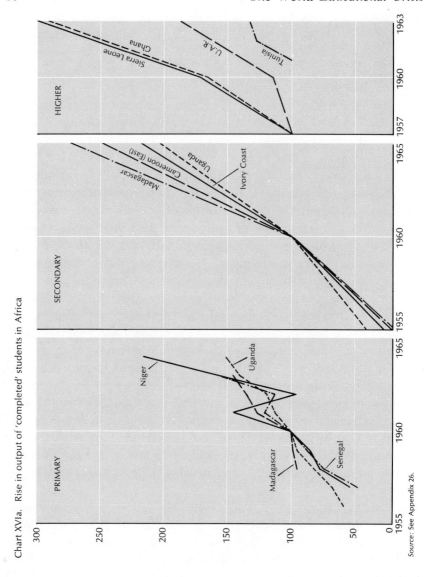

Chart XVIa.  Rise in output of 'completed' students in Africa

*Source:* See Appendix 26.

This greatly increased outpouring of graduates has already had a
marked impact on the 'educational profile' of the labor force in most
countries, raising considerably its potential productivity for the years
ahead. However, most educational systems, as near as we can judge from
the imperfect evidence, have had an even larger increase in output of
'unfinished' products in this period. This fact comments in its own way on

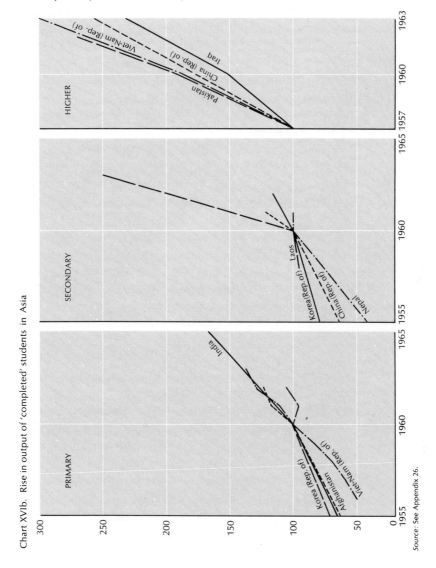

Chart XVIb. Rise in output of 'completed' students in Asia

Source: See Appendix 26.

the disparity between educational systems and their environment. The matter deserves attention.

It will be recalled that when we discussed student inputs, we contrasted the 'wide open' and the 'highly selective' types of systems. It must here be added that while both produce large numbers of unfinished products, they do so with a different psychic and physical impact.

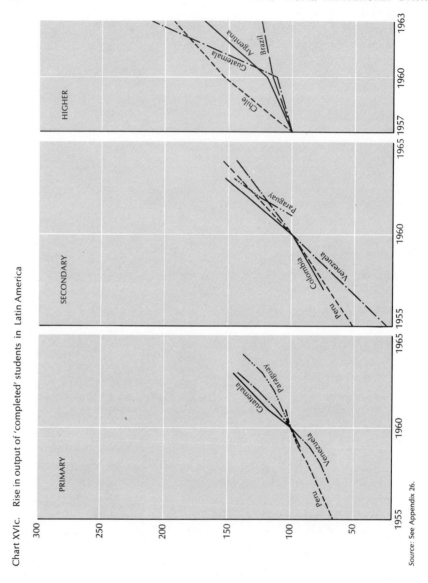

Chart XVIc.  Rise in output of 'completed' students in Latin America

*Source:* See Appendix 26.

First, the selective system. This system is inclined to worry less about those who leave prematurely, because, as we noted, its traditional mission, above the primary level, has been to winnow out the most promising and form them into an educated elite which will guide the affairs of society. Through its screening and rejecting process, it stamps large numbers as 'failures' before they even have the chance to choose for them-

Chart XVId.  Rise in output of 'completed' students in various industrialized nations

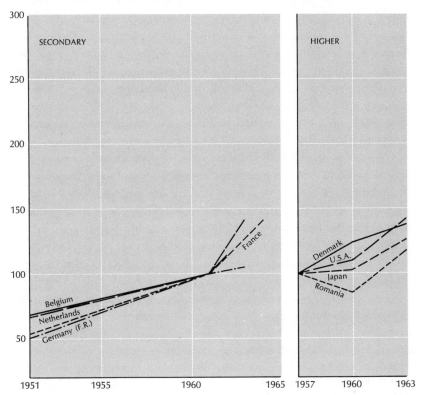

selves whether they will struggle on or become dropouts. In such circumstances, a 'failure' may be crippled for life.

Second, the 'wide open' system. This system has far fewer failures but many more dropouts. Its stated mission is to give every child a chance to develop his potential to the full, whatever it may be. But when the dropout rate is high, the managers of such a system can be tormented by a sense of guilt, suspecting that they may have been the hand that cut off the dropout's future chance.

Western European countries such as France and England are making the difficult transition from what was once a highly selective system to a more open one. So far the social philosophy and goals have changed more than the educational system's structures, examinations, and practices. The

French system illustrates what this can lead to. In recent years almost half the lycée students who took the *baccalauréat* examinations to enter the university failed. On top of this, about 40 per cent of those who conquered the 'bac' and gained entry to the university failed to get beyond the first university year.[2] These high and cumulative failure rates, and all that they manifest, have rather naturally been the target of severe criticism by students, parents, and not a few educators. The problem, however, is by no means confined to France. In its different versions it can be found in most of Europe.

The version in the United States may be exceptional. For many years, American educators have worried about the numerous dropouts among secondary school students, just beyond the age of compulsory attendance. They have worried also about the low academic motivation of the same students in the final throes of their 'improvement,' just prior to 'freedom.' Whether it has been mainly a result of the strong efforts of the schools to ameliorate this situation or of environmental factors, the earlier high dropout rate among secondary school students has fallen steadily over the years. Only 30 per cent of the students entering the fifth grade in the United States forty years ago went on to complete high school; today more than 70 per cent do.[3] Ironically, however, as the dropout problem eased at this level, it has become a matter of concern at the next level. American educators are now worried over the fact that apparently more than half of the students who enter junior colleges do not finish.[4]

Turning from the developed to the developing countries, one can often find a magnified form of the same conflict between social goals and educational realities. Most of the developing countries have as their ultimate goal the attainment of an open system of education which will serve each youngster to his fullest potential. They know they cannot have such a system overnight, and so each is pursuing one or another long-term strategy for getting there.

India and many Latin American countries, for example, started early with a liberal approach to admissions. The result was that their classrooms became severely overcrowded, the proportion of nonfinishers has been high, and criticism is widely made of the 'poor quality' of education. There are in these countries important exceptions—particularly the

2. See R. Poignant, *L'Enseignement dans les pays du Marché commun, op. cit.*
3. See Appendix 27.
4. See Burton R. Clark, *The Open Door College: A Case Study* (New York: McGraw-Hill, 1960), and L. L. Medsker, *The Junior College: Progress and Prospect* (New York: McGraw-Hill, 1960).

older 'prestige' secondary schools and the newer technical, scientific, and medical institutions—where admission has been sharply regulated, numbers held down and quality sustained. These prestige institutions constitute what is virtually a separate system within the educational system —islands of excellence in a sea of mediocrity. A good case can be made, of course, especially in the light of United States experience, for having a diversity of institutions of widely differing quality. But when quality drops below a tolerable minimum, on a vast scale, the case loses its force. In the instance of the East African nations, we have already noted how some are trying to hold back elementary enrollments for the time being in order to build up the secondary and higher levels of their educational systems. At these post-primary levels where a selective policy is pursued, quality seems to have held up well, while the rate of dropouts and failures is relatively low, thanks to the rigorous screening beforehand. Their 'losers' are not so much rejected from the system; they simply fail to get into it. This, of course, is statistically interesting, but no solace to the unlucky ones whose educational aspirations have thus been thwarted.

Available data on school dropouts in developing countries are notoriously unreliable. For this reason, the statistical samples given in Table 5 are presented only to suggest the order of magnitude of the problem. However, one thing can be flatly said here. In virtually all developing countries, whatever their policy of admission at the secondary and higher levels, dropouts are enormous at the primary stage and have been a widespread cause for concern. It is not at all unusual for at least half the children entering the first grade in one of these countries to leave before the end of the fourth year, without even having acquired permanent literacy. It is doubtful that the investment in their education is entirely lost, but a large portion of it certainly is, representing a substantial fraction of total educational investment made by these countries. What is worse, most of these early dropouts are sentenced to join the ranks of permanent adult illiterates at the bottom of the social-economic heap. They are 'the wasted generation.' It remains to be added that the aggregate figures about them, such as those in the statistical sample given in Table 5, conceal the socially important fact that dropouts tend to run a good deal higher in rural than in urban areas. The rate is also often higher for girls than for boys, depending on the traditional local attitudes toward women.

What does the future look like? In the case of finished educational products, it is safe to predict a continuing increase in their number virtually everywhere, because of the large numbers of pupils already in the pipeline, and the even larger numbers waiting to get into it. The rate of increase will depend, of course, on such large variables in each situation as finances, population trends, expansion of educational capacity, and the types of admission and examination policies adhered to.

TABLE 5

*Estimated primary school dropouts in certain developing countries*

| COUNTRIES | GRADE I | GRADE II | PER CENT GRADE III | GRADE IV | GRADE V |
|---|---|---|---|---|---|
| *Africa* | | | | | |
| Cent. Afr. Rep. | 21.8 | 11.7 | 9.6 | 7.1 | 8.0 |
| Dahomey | 24.5 | 12.8 | 10.7 | 11.0 | 5.7 |
| Madagascar | 18.1 | 10.6 | 13.6 | 23.4 | 9.2 |
| Niger | 12.6 | 4.8 | 12.0 | 5.0 | 11.9 |
| Togo | 3.1 | 1.9 | 1.0 | 2.0 | 10.9 |
| Upper Volta | 19.2 | 17.3 | 7.3 | 16.7 | 8.2 |
| *Asia* | | | | | |
| Afghanistan | 4.0 | 1.5 | 2.0 | 7.0 | 4.0 |
| Ceylon: Urban | 15.6 | 7.5 | 9.7 | 10.6 | 8.1 |
| Rural | 17.4 | 11.4 | 11.7 | 12.8 | 9.8 |
| Philippines | 9.2 | 6.8 | 7.6 | 10.0 | 8.5 |
| Thailand | 12.0 | 5.0 | 6.0 | — | 6.0 |
| *Latin America* | | | | | |
| Argentina | 13.4 | 5.6 | 7.6 | 10.0 | 10.1 |
| Costa Rica | 7.1 | 10.7 | 10.6 | 11.5 | 10.7 |

*Sources:* (Africa): IEDES, *Les Rendements de l'enseignement du premier degré en Afrique francophone,* III (Paris, 1967); (Asia: Afghanistan and Ceylon): Unesco, 'The Problem of Educational Wastage at the First Level of Education in Asia,' in *Bulletin of the Unesco Regional Office for Education in Asia,* Vol. 1, no. 2 (Bangkok, 1967); (Philippines and Thailand): Ministry of Education, Japan, in co-operation with Unesco, *Education in Asia* (Tokyo, 1964), p. 63; (Latin America: Argentina): Consejo Nacional de Desarrollo, *Educación, recursos humanos y desarrollo económico y social* (Buenos Aires, 1966), p. 42; (Costa Rica): unpublished data.

The outlook for unfinished products is less clear. If the experience of the United States is any indicator, many western European systems can anticipate a growing problem of dropouts and failures at the secondary and higher levels, as their participation rates rise and their educational pyramid fills out. But they can help counter this if they speed the adaptation of their educational structures, practices, and examination procedures to their new clienteles. The United States, for its part, will no doubt continue to grapple with the problem of high school and college dropouts; by natural extension it will worry increasingly about the already numerous cases of abortive Ph.Ds.

As for the developing countries, it is hard to foresee any rapid decline in their heavy elementary school dropout rates, though for many the rate may gradually decline, particularly where a policy of 'social promotion' replaces examination barriers. We still know too little about what causes the phenomenon in each situation. How much, for example, is due to local cultural and economic factors? How much to poor, unattractive teaching, especially in rural areas? The answer to such questions beg for more local research. Meanwhile, one cannot be certain as to what measures can best be taken to correct the matter, what these measures would cost, and how effective they might be.

One thing, however, seems a fair if ironic conjecture. If any developing country should suddenly succeed in overcoming this primary level dropout problem, it would be faced with an equally formidable problem—that of staffing and financing the educational system to handle the larger number of pupils in the upper primary grades, and on up the educational ladder. If nothing else good can be said for it, the heavy dropouts low on the ladder have thus far lessened the pressures further up.

It is difficult also to see many developing countries, where previously a liberal policy of admission has been in force, applying the brakes on admission to secondary and higher education. They can succeed in applying high selectivity to newer, more specialized institutions, to keep numbers within reason and quality up. But this will put even greater pressure for admission on other sectors of higher education, which become the catchall for those failing to gain entry to more selective institutions. In Latin America and India, for example, one could make a strong case, based on experience and economic and pedagogical good sense, for a more selective policy throughout higher education. But the practical political obstacles to such a policy seem well nigh insurmountable. In most African countries, on the other hand, which have so far clung to rigorous selection, quality can be more readily preserved and a host of related problems averted. Yet, with the demand pressures steadily mounting, it may become increasingly difficult for them to sustain selective admission.

As we recognized earlier, figures on graduates and dropouts are useful indicators of an educational system's output, but in themselves they do not provide a sufficient basis for evaluating its performance. Indeed, no one type of indicator does; we must examine as wide a variety of them as we can find, then base a judgment on the combination. With the search still on, we move along to ask: How well does education's output fit the manpower needs of national development?

## *Fitness for Manpower Requirements*

INDICATORS OF FITNESS · USEFULNESS AND LIMITATIONS OF
MANPOWER STUDIES · THE ILL-FITTING 'MIX' OF GRADUATES IN
DEVELOPING COUNTRIES · THE PERVERSE RATIO OF PROFESSIONALS TO
SUB-PROFESSIONALS · EFFORTS TO REMEDY IMBALANCES · POTENTIAL
FLEXIBILITIES · THE MISFIT OF RURAL SCHOOL PROGRAMS.

A central assumption underlies the conviction—now widely shared by educators and economists—that education is a good investment in national development. The assumption is that the educational system will produce the kinds and amounts of human resources required for the economy's growth, and that the economy will in fact make good use of these resources. But suppose the opposite happens? Suppose the educational system turns out the wrong 'mix' of manpower? Or suppose it turns out the right mix, but the economy does not use it well? What then? Doubts then arise about education's productivity and the efficacy of the investment made in it.

This is exactly what seems to be happening today in many countries. Educational systems are falling far short of turning out the right numbers and combinations of manpower needed for optimum development. To an equal degree, their employment structures and incentives are poorly geared to make the best use of educated personnel, and hence to serve the real needs of development. We must again admit that our measuring tools are inexact. Still, it is nonetheless possible to spot a number of practical indicators of the disparity between what the educational system is turning out, what the economy can use at the moment, and what it will need for future growth. The correspondence between these can never be perfect, any more than can the forecast of manpower requirements, to be mentioned in a moment. But it need not be perfect. It is enough, or at least it is a big step forward, to identify the major respects in which the match between education and the economy is conspicuously poor, or is likely to be so in the future. What is thus identified can then serve as a practical basis for altering the educational system's course in order to enhance its future contribution to national development.

As for manpower surveys and requirement projections, these are not the equivalent of revealed truth. In the present state of the art, they are inescapably shot through with limitations, uncertainties, and imperfections. Further, as is true of many diagnostic indicators, manpower studies are often more helpful in showing what an education system is doing wrong and should correct than in showing what it is doing right and should keep on doing. Subject, however, to an active awareness about the negative aspects of the matter, manpower surveys and requirement projections can be very useful, indeed indispensable, to educational planning.

In recent years wherever manpower studies have been made in developing or industrialized countries, they have almost invariably revealed large discrepancies—both current and prospective—between the pattern of educational output and the pattern of manpower needed for economic growth. In symphony orchestra terms, they reveal the presence of too many oboe and tuba players and not enough violinists. Specifically, on the 'long' side, the studies have usually shown a relative abundance of secondary school graduates with a classical university preparation, and a corresponding abundance of arts and law graduates from the universities, relative to need. In some Latin American countries, there were also too many medical doctors who seemed unlikely ever to practice medicine, or, if they did, would not practice in rural areas where the need was greatest. On the 'short' side, the studies show that, both absolutely and relatively, there are current and prospective shortages of middle-level technicians of various sorts, relative to the output of university engineers. There is also short supply in health, agricultural, and other types of specialized manpower—mostly in the maths-science based fields—that are urgently needed for national development. The issue here is not whether liberal arts graduates are important to these countries—they clearly are. The issue is one of balance between these fields and others. To swing too far in the opposite direction could be just as serious.

The existence of such evident discrepancies is underlined without the help of sophisticated statistical techniques. Their presence is visible to any informed observer. But to correct the existing situation by rational planning, it is advantageous to get as good a measurement as is possible of their order of magnitude. This, in any event, is the conclusion reached by the IIEP after looking at manpower studies in several countries in Africa, Asia, and Europe.[5]

Evidence and testimony from many other scattered sources bear out the serious discrepancy—not just statistical but qualitative—between educational systems on the one side, and national and local manpower requirements on the other. Viewing the Indian situation broadly, a member of the Indian Education Commission recently gave this personal assessment:

> We [in India] have developed a kind of education which is not related to the needs of a nation that is trying to transform a traditional society into a modern society, to make use of science and technology, and of all the techniques that are available for national development.[6]

A developing country can land in deep trouble by slavishly adhering to the educational forms and rituals of industrialized countries, in a context where they simply do not fit. The phenomenon crops up in varying degrees at all levels of education and in all sectors of the curriculum. But a particularly troublesome sector is technical and vocational training at the secondary or post-secondary level. For a variety of reasons, these kinds of formal technical training have often been conspicuously unsuccessful and unsuitable in industrialized countries. Yet, despite their miscarriage in their countries of origin, they are nonetheless exported and imported at great expense into less developed countries, side by side with shorter and more flexible nonformal training schemes, delivered by a different breed of advisers.

There are many sad stories whose common plot tells of technical training schemes, embraced by all parties with good intentions, yet rendered irrelevant in their application. One African country, for example, with outside help, has been training cabinetmakers in compliance with established European standards. Right now, however, that country does not need cabinetmakers. It needs and has plenty of people who can saw rough boards for concrete forms. That, in fact, is what many of the expensively trained cabinetmakers end up doing, side by side with young men who

5. G. Hunter, 'High Level Manpower for Development,' *Higher Education and Development in South-East Asia*, III, pt. 1 (Paris: Unesco/International Association of Universities, 1967); ILO, *Rapport au gouvernement de la République Tunisienne: l'évaluation et la planification de la main-d'oeuvre* (Geneva, 1965); G. Skorov, *op. cit.*; G. Skorov, 'The Absorptive Capacity of the Economy,' in *Manpower Aspects of Educational Planning: Problems for the Future* (Paris: Unesco/IIEP, 1968); R. Poignant, *Education and Economic and Social Planning in France, op. cit.*

6. IIEP, *The Qualitative Aspects of Educational Planning*, IIEP/Unesco. Scheduled for publication in 1968.

never went to school, and at the same low rate of pay. Their wages, in fact, are so low that the total income of a lifetime would perhaps not repay the cost of their unusable technical training. Another country is reported to be turning out well-trained stonemasons. The trouble here is that there is no commercially usable stone in the country.

Not all efforts at technical training are by any means as unproductive and uneconomic as those just cited. On the contrary, one finds many authentic 'success stories.' But they are usually cases where a strong effort was made to *adapt* training forms to a local need, and not simply to *copy* a foreign model indiscriminately.

There is another aspect to technical training which should be noted, which involves the unsuitability of the university 'mix.' The figures given in Table 6 of the distribution in selected countries of university graduates by major fields of study reveal, for example, that in most of the developing countries shown, fewer than 4 per cent of the graduates have studied the field of agriculture (and there is cause to believe that most of these become administrators). Indeed, many of the universities do not even include faculties of agriculture.[7] Yet the need to raise agricultural productivity is one of the main imperatives of economic development in most such countries.

In many developing countries also—though fortunately not in all—engineering and the natural sciences, as shown by Table 6, still account for only a small fraction of total graduates. Usually, social ·sciences do better, but the lion's share goes to humanistic studies and law. While the latter studies have an undeniable value and importance, national development requires a good many other things besides, and thus there is an unquestionable need for a better balance in the student outputs of universities.

Another common source of difficulty is the imbalance between the output of sub-professionals and full professionals in associated fields. The proper ratio may differ by countries and by fields, yet it is still a universal problem. If the trained professional is to be fully productive, he must be backed by sufficient paraprofessionals and technicians who can perform appropriate supporting tasks. Guy Hunter suggests that the optimum

7. 'The universities in Senegal and the Ivory Coast are wholly French in structure, content and tone . . . Faculties of agriculture, for example, do not yet exist, though it was possible in Dakar in 1961 to take a course entitled, "History of French agriculture in the Fourteenth Century" . . . ,' Elliot J. Berg, 'Education and Manpower in Senegal, Guinea and the Ivory Coast,' in F. Harbison and C. Myers, eds., *Manpower and Education: Country Studies in Economic Development* (New York: McGraw-Hill, 1965), p. 265.

TABLE 6

*Percentage distribution of university graduates in selected developing countries, by fields of study[1]*

| COUNTRY | YEAR | SOCIAL SCIENCES | NATURAL SCIENCES | ENGINEERING | MEDICAL SCIENCES | AGRICULTURE | ARTS, LAW, AND OTHER |
|---|---|---|---|---|---|---|---|
| Ghana | 1963 | 4.0 | 0.5 | 3.0 | a | 0.8 | 92.7 |
| Sierra Leone | 1963 | 2.0 | 1.3 | 0.5 | a | a | 96.2 |
| Tunisia | 1963 | 1.3 | 1.2 | a | b | 1.1 | 96.4 |
| Brazil | 1963 | 17.0 | 3.8 | 10.6 | 21.0 | 3.5 | 44.1 |
| Mexico | 1963 | 2.6 | 3.1 | 5.4 | 12.3 | 0.5 | 76.1 |
| Venezuela | 1963 | 20.9 | 1.4 | 9.1 | 27.4 | 2.6 | 38.6 |
| Ceylon | 1963 | 9.3 | 7.8 | 2.4 | 6.8 | a | 73.7 |
| Lebanon | 1962 | 9.7 | 9.7 | 7.9 | 10.8 | 3.7 | 58.2 |
| Thailand | 1963 | 21.1 | 4.6 | 6.4 | 10.4 | 6.3 | 51.2 |

1 The fields of study considered respect the Unesco definitions.
a Zero or almost zero.
b Included with natural sciences.
*Source:* IIEP estimations based on data given in: Unesco, *Statistical Yearbook, 1965, op. cit.*

ratio of technicians to university graduate specialists is between 3 : 1 and 5 : 1, depending on the country and the subject.[8] Against this norm, he and other investigators have found that in many developing countries this ratio is often 2 : 1 at best and sometimes only 1 : 2. In these circumstances full professionals end up doing the tasks which sub-professionals should be doing.

A good example of this is provided by Chile, in the field of health, where an investigator reports three doctors for each nurse, in contrast to Sweden's ratio of five nurses for every two doctors and the United States ratio of seven nurses for two doctors. To make matters worse, the number of nurses graduating in Chile has recently been about half the number of doctors. And a high proportion of these nurses soon depart from the hospital to marry or migrate to the United States for better pay (since the United States also has been underproducing nurses).

The impression should not be left that educational systems have ignored these problems of imbalance—they have not. A number of countries—Sweden, the United Kingdom, Nigeria, and India are cases in point—have created multipurpose secondary schools (akin to American comprehensive schools), designed to prepare some students for the university and others for jobs through vocationally oriented 'terminal' programs. Likewise, many nations are endeavoring to strengthen and modernize their secondary level mathematics and science courses in order to prepare more and better qualified candidates for higher level technical and scientific studies, and to make other students scientifically literate in order to live more effectively in a scientific era. At the university level also, many nations have sought to strengthen their technical and scientific faculties, or have created new high level institutions in these fields. None of these efforts has been easy, and not all have succeeded, owing to such obstacles as shortages of specialized teachers, adverse student and parent attitudes, and prejudices of teachers and administrators in old-line fields and institutions.

A few more points remain to be made about the disparity between education and manpower needs. First, on the encouraging side, the discrepancy is not always as bad as the statistical gaps would suggest. The job classifications and corresponding educational qualifications typically used in manpower studies are, after all, rather artificial. Even where they conform reasonably well to the realities in advanced economies (which often they do not), it by no means follows that they are appropriate for

8. G. Hunter, 'High Level Manpower,' III, pt. 1, p. 20.

less developed economies—whose training needs are typically less sophisticated. Yet, when these countries pay too much attention to the procedures of industrialized countries, they often overtrain people for jobs which bear the same label in both types of economy, but which in fact are very different.

In any event, people and jobs are usually not as rigidly positioned as is implied by these conventional employment classifications and their 'official' educational equivalencies. If they were, many economic systems might come to a grinding halt. It seems reasonable to assume that if a person has a good basic education, is well motivated and reasonably intelligent, and has been endowed by his education with a measure of flexibility, he can adapt quite quickly to a wide range of jobs, regardless of what the 'book' may prescribe in the way of educational qualifications. For this to happen, however, rules for specific academic requirements for particular jobs must be made more flexible, and the content of the required training must be made commensurate with the functions actually to be performed. In this respect, developing countries are often more rigid than industrialized countries—to their considerable disadvantage.

But there is a reverse point that is less encouraging. People who emerge from educational systems bearing the proper *label* of educational qualification for a particular type of work often are not in fact well qualified to perform it. Either their education was poor and misdirected or their attitude toward work was poor, or something of both elements affected them. A complaint to this effect is often sounded by employers in developing countries and, one should add, in industrialized countries as well.

Most of our discussion up to this point, as it applies to developing countries, has dealt with manpower in the 'modern' sector. Indeed, this by itself reflects the greatest weakness of typical manpower studies as a guide to educational planning. They focus largely, often exclusively, on 'high-level' manpower (essentially, secondary school graduates and above) in the 'modern' sector (largely *urban*). In so doing, they ignore the bulk of the labor force in developing countries, the bulk of the potential educational clientele, and the paramount development need. As a rule, in developing countries 70 to 95 per cent of all people live and work in the rural areas. And it is precisely here that the process of modernization has thus far made its smallest imprint. Yet, if these countries are to pull their whole economy and society up by the bootstraps, the rural-agricultural sector, and not merely the more glamorous industrial-urban sector, is where the development process must be accelerated.

It is in the rural areas also that education—hand in hand with other development efforts—must make a vital contribution. The question thus arises: How well do the educational systems of developing countries meet this hard test of fitness? In other words, what is their contribution to bringing agricultural and rural life toward the 'takeoff' point?

Professor Fred Harbison's answer to this question, in the case of Nigeria, applies equally to a good many other countries. Nigeria's educational system, he says, is almost exclusively oriented toward filling city jobs in the modern sector.

> The values, subject matter and examination criteria at all levels of Nigerian education assume that school leavers want to become government civil servants, teachers, and employees of relatively modern and industrial and commercial establishments.[9]

Many educators might argue that this is precisely what rural schools should do—prepare youngsters to transfer to the city. This well-intentioned view, however, simply does not square with the realities facing the large majority of these rural youngsters. Harbison points out—as does George Skorov for Tanzania—that the modern urban sector simply cannot provide jobs for more than a small fraction of the total labor force, and will not be able to for a long time to come.[10] Currently the figure for Nigeria is about 5 per cent, and at best it cannot grow very fast.

Nor is Nigeria a special case. It appears that for well over a decade to come, in many highly rural countries like Nigeria, the 'traditional' sector and the 'middle' sector (making its way to the 'modern' sector) will have to absorb four-fifths or more of the nation's labor force—including a major proportion of newly educated young people. Yet almost everywhere, educational systems tend to orient and train young people for work in the 'urban' sector. In this fundamental respect, therefore, it must be said that these educational systems and their basic orientation seem grossly out of line with the future needs of their students and with the development needs of their society.

This poses yet another problem for education in its present crisis. Most people would agree that education should imbue its students with modern concepts, knowledge, and skills for life in a modern world, wherever

9. F. Harbison, *Critical Manpower Problems in Nigerian Agricultural and Rural Development,* Education and World Affairs Nigeria Project Task Force (New York, May 1967).

10. *Ibid.;* and G. Skorov, *Integration of Educational Economic Planning in Tanzania, op. cit.*

they may live. It should not simply fit them passively to accept life in a traditional, static economy. Else, why go to school at all? Yet most of today's students will in fact spend their lives in rural areas which have scarcely been touched by modernizing forces.

Is there a way out of this dilemma? One way would be for such educational systems to concentrate on fitting young people to engage constructively in the work of *modernizing* agriculture and rural life, rather than on fitting them to escape from it. In short, instead of preparing them to be sent to the modern sector in the city, they should be prepared to help bring the modern sector to their own rural area. True, like most things in education, this is far easier said than done. Yet it must be done in order to correct the present imbalance between educational systems and the realistic needs of their environment.

In a different way, the educational systems of most industrialized countries are also ill-fitted to the needs of their students and societies, despite their much more modern environment. The issue here is not primarily the unsuitability of the 'subjects' offered, but how they are taught, what attitudes and styles of thinking are instilled (or not instilled), and the kind of perceptions of the world which are conveyed to students.

The industrialized countries have a rich cultural and intellectual heritage, and it is certainly a proper function of the schools and universities to pass it on to future generations. But today, and in the future, they must do more. The reason for this is that the eighteenth and nineteenth-century legacy of world perceptions, modes of thinking, methods of inquiry and adaptation will simply not serve today's young people well enough in a world of science. Yet there is no denying that the eighteenth and nineteenth centuries still hold many European educational systems in their grip. Structural 'reforms' may be announced. But they will not attain their objective until the grip of the past is loosened from administrative forms and styles, from pedagogical aims and attitudes, from the curriculum and teaching methods, and from the very spirit which informs the milieu of these schools and universities.[11]

11. The following is taken from an article, 'Italy's Universities under Fire,' in *Times* (London), 18 July 1967:
'The clash between Italy's antiquated classical educational system and the demands of a modern industrial society which needs a highly educated and sophisticated managerial class, has been documented by a study published by Shell Italiana, a subsidiary of the international oil company. In 400 pages this criticizes the classical and technical-scientific schools and shows how badly prepared students are to choose a university course of study.
'Presenting the study, Signor Diego Guicciardi, the president of Shell, revealed that

Starting with the question of education's fitness for the manpower requirements of economic growth, we have moved far beyond the normal purview of manpower experts, and beyond the relatively simple issue of relating formal educational qualifications to the formal skill requirements of particular types of jobs. The plain truth is that fitting an educational system to these needs is comparatively simple, but fitting one to the full needs of national development (which is a much broader and more complicated thing than economic development) is a far more difficult and subtle affair. In fact, even assuming that the structure and curriculum of an educational system were to be completely overhauled to make a perfect 'fit' in these limited 'manpower' terms, there is good reason to believe that it still would not be adequate. It would not be adequate, that is, unless there were a corresponding overhaul of attitudes and status symbols on the part of students and their families, teachers and administrators, employers and the general public.

## *Employment and Unemployment*

MOUNTING PROBLEM OF 'EDUCATED UNEMPLOYED' · WHAT HAPPENS AS A NATION DEVELOPS · RAPID POPULATION GROWTH ADDS TO THE DIFFICULTIES · DISPARITY BETWEEN MANPOWER NEEDS AND MARKET DEMANDS · IMPLICATIONS FOR EDUCATION IN DEVELOPING COUNTRIES · GREATER FLEXIBILITY OF ADVANCED ECONOMIES.

Our main concern thus far has been with the question: 'Can education—in respect of its output—overcome or avert specific human resource shortages that hamper national development?' We turn now to what is fast emerging as a more serious manpower question, quite the opposite of the foregoing one. It is whether enough new jobs of the right sort can be found for the newly educated.

The point at issue has a potential political hurricane locked up inside it, and economists are not alone in being asked to deal with the matter.

---

of more than 20,000 requests for work received when Shell opened its new Taranto refinery, almost all came from applicants who were totally unqualified. "Further, most of the *Laureati* (university graduates) who come to Shell are equally unprepared for work in a modern company," he said.'

Education is also a party to the matter, with its attendant disputes over plans and budgets. The plain fact is that individuals, especially males, look on education primarily as a means of getting a good job. They are interested in the 'investment' benefits of education. Hence when an individual after hard work and many sacrifices emerges from an educational system with a certificate, diploma, or degree but fails to find the kind of job on which he has set his heart or, worse, finds no job at all, he can be expected to feel frustrated or bitter. He obtained his education in order to prevent his unemployment, and a socio-economic system that fails him in this regard may easily become the target of his hostility. This is even more the case if, during his education, he received no sound vocational guidance that gave him a more realistic set of employment expectations on which to base his academic choices.

But this graduate is not the only person to be involved in a counterreaction. The finance minister, who sits in a hot seat mediating amongst the rival claimants for bigger shares of the public budget, is also involved. The minister has been responding, but possibly with increasing reluctance, to annual demands for a larger share of available funds to be spent on education. He has been aware that other demands have an urgency of their own. So now, when part of the yield on the educational investment turns out to be a picket line of disgruntled job-seekers, he is likely to start asking searching questions.

The overt signs of this ominous problem have been clear for some time, especially in the developing nations. Here are a few examples.

In the Philippines, as far back as 1961, fewer than one-quarter of all high school graduates in the age group under thirty-five had full-time jobs; another 44 per cent were looking for work or had only part-time jobs; the rest had stepped out of the labor market. It seemed to make little difference whether they had taken general, academic, or vocational courses; the unemployment rate dealt evenhandedly with all. *University graduates* were doing relatively better, yet still not too well. Two-thirds had full-time jobs—but over one in four were unemployed and looking for work, or had only part-time jobs.[12]

In the United Arab Republic, a research study reports that, as of the mid-sixties,

> about 70 per cent of the university enrollment is in the Faculties of Arts, Law and Commerce, and for the vast majority of these there is no demand

12. See Appendix 28.

. . . [such] graduates . . . constitute a large and rapidly growing group whose skills are largely substandard and unwanted.[13]

In India, between 1956 and 1962, the number of job-seeking 'matriculates' and 'intermediates' on the live registers of employment exchanges (which tend to understate the real case) rose from about 217,000 to over 644,000.[14] In the same seven years, university graduates on these registers rose from under 27,000 to over 63,000. The Indian Education Commission recently estimated that the total of educated unemployed in all categories was one million in round figures.[15] From this pool of one million, of course, some were constantly being drained off to employment. But they were just as constantly being replaced by the next crop from the schools and universities. It is especially noteworthy in India's case that there is now significant, and rising, unemployment in such a specialized 'shortage' category as engineering.

In Burma, according to Guy Hunter,

> there was in 1962 and 1963 a 'surplus' of university graduates—that is to say, considerable numbers (up to 40 per cent in some mechanical and electrical branches of engineering)—of newly-graduated students were unable to find employment in the type of work for which they felt themselves qualified. Similarly, there was a 'surplus' of graduates from the technical institutes, of about 20 per cent, and even unemployment from the trade schools.[16]

In most of Latin America there has been heavy unemployment and underemployment for some years among secondary and university graduates. Africa has seen a heavy accumulation of unemployed among those who have left primary school (this group used to get clerical jobs fairly readily in the 'old days'). Nigerian authorities, troubled by this problem for some years, have now started worrying over the prospect of an imminent 'surplus' of university graduates. Production of graduates is sharply up, but the seemingly unquenchable demand for them of only a few years ago has eased off, especially with the filling up of government posts.

What about the industrialized countries? For most of them, the problem of 'educated unemployed' still lies mainly in the future. The exact

13. Malcolm H. Kerr, 'Egypt' in James S. Coleman, ed., *Education and Political Development* (Princeton, N.J.: Princeton University Press, 1965), p. 187.
14. See Appendix 29.
15. India, *Report of the Education Commission (1964-66)* . . . , *op. cit.*
16. G. Hunter, 'High Level Manpower,' III, pt. 1.

form it may take is not entirely clear, but is full of nuances at present. The European nations are pulling out of the postwar era of manpower shortages; their rising industrial and agricultural efficiency saves more jobs than it creates; their postwar bumper crop of babies is reaching maturity and, for each year hereafter, will add large increments to the labor force. All this points in the direction of a shift from shortages to surpluses in trained manpower, and to the fact that unemployment among the newly educated could soon appear.

What causes the paradox of developing nations who clearly need more educated manpower but who are unable to use it when they get it? Is education somehow at fault? Has it expanded *too* rapidly? Has it produced the wrong kinds of manpower? Or does the fault lie elsewhere— perhaps in the economy, or in economic development policies and plans? Where are the solutions to be found? Indeed, is there any solution?

The earlier history of today's industrialized nations sheds light on certain of the problems and prospects of today's developing countries. This does not mean, of course, that the latter countries should follow precisely the same path, or take as long to travel it. But there are certain inescapable stages and processes that must be gone through, whatever a particular country's philosophy or form, as it moves from a relatively low state of economic development to a more balanced industrial economy.

One of these processes is a gradual change in the composition of its labor force. Starting with a large component of unskilled, common labor and a very small component of skilled and high-level manpower, the profile of the labor force progressively alters as it comes to consist less and less of unskilled workers and more and more of skilled and high-level manpower. To put the same thing differently, a modernizing economy gradually moves from being a low-wage, low-productivity, labor-intensive economy, toward being a higher productivity, higher wage, capital-intensive, labor-saving economy with a better qualified manpower. It is at best a long transition process.

Education and training play a major role in the progression by developing an educated labor force that has a higher productivity than uneducated labor. And as the process continues, education moves from being a 'scarce' commodity to being an 'abundant' one, from being a relative luxury, available to only the few, to being a basic need for everyone who wants to escape the shrinking unskilled sector of the labor force.

In the early stages—roughly where western Europe and North America were one hundred years ago—the national structure of incomes has a very large spread between the bottom and top, reflecting among other things the high scarcity value of education. But with time and the expansion of both the economy and education, the bottom incomes move upwards faster than the top incomes (which may even move down as a result of very high inheritance and progressive income taxes).

Today, for example, the income spread in Africa between what a common laborer receives and the salary of a top civil servant or businessman may be in the ratio of 1 to 100 or higher. The income spread in the United States has never been as large as it is in Africa, but the distance between the take-home pay of an average factory worker and that of a fairly high-level business executive has now narrowed to a ratio of something like 1 to 5. The western European income spread is moving toward a similarly narrow band.

The relevance of all this to our discussion of employment and unemployment is that as more and more people become educated, the supply of new *top* jobs becomes scarcer relative to the number of educated people seeking them. These educated people then adapt to the situation (though not always gracefully) by stepping down on their 'job preference scale' until they find a job they can actually get, something less than their first choice. If the preferred civil service posts are filled, for example, they may turn to teaching, and education starts getting a better quality manpower. Eventually, as happened in Japan, for example, high school graduates overcome what reluctance they may have had for manual labor and take factory jobs. *But they become more productive factory workers* because of their education. They produce more, and eventually get paid more, and the bottom of the income pyramid moves upward.

The key to this adjustment process is that the jobs become upgraded. They may be called by the same names, but they are no longer the same jobs because they are now filled by better educated people who make something more of the job, and make a better living from it. This long 'job-upgrading' process, we hasten to add, was not, in the case of today's industrialized nations, a smooth and well-planned affair in which nobody got hurt. It was far from that. There were rough bumps along the way and no small amount of human misery. It is to be hoped that the journey will be somewhat smoother and quicker for today's developing nations. But it would be naive to expect that it will not have many serious problems and discomforts. One of the worst will be unemployment, for the uneducated and educated alike.

It is important to be clear that the development programs of the world did not *create* the unemployment problem, nor did the rapid expansion of education. What they did do was to make an ancient problem more visible, and more vocal. Vast hidden unemployment, and more particularly, vast underemployment, have been the hallmark of static, traditional societies all through history. This curse has now been brought to the center of conscious attention. Unemployment has become a matter of public concern. With the better (though still imperfect) statistics now available, it is even possible to make caliper-fine calculations on the problem. And on the behavior of these statistics, governments may stand or fall, especially if a good many of the unemployed turn out to be educated unemployed congregated in the cities. For educated unemployed are not inclined to suffer in silence, hidden in the bush. To this extent, and in a special sense, it can fairly be said that education has contributed to the noise level of the problem, but not to its quantitative level.

The problem, however, is much worse than it might have been, and the reason for this lies in three important facts. The first forces us to qualify what we have just said about development programs not creating the unemployment problem, because it was already there. Paradoxical as it may sound, the fact is that modernization tends to generate more unemployment than employment, at least in the initial stages. This is because, in the economic sense, modernization means raising human productivity—doing more work, producing more output, with fewer man-hours of effort. Translated into practical terms, this means that a given increase—say of 10 per cent—in a nation's total output is accompanied by a lesser increase in employment—the more so if much of the increase in the GNP comes out of the industrial sector where labor productivity is rising most rapidly. In fact, at the early stages of the development process, the GNP may be *rising*, while paid employment may be *falling*. This is precisely what happened in Tanzania and Kenya in recent years, though it is hoped they have now turned the corner of this 'wringing out' process.

The second fact compounds the difficulty of the first. If, at the time a nation is making its painful initial adjustments to the modernization process, it is seized by an abnormally rapid population growth, its unemployment problem becomes much larger. This is because its labor force grows much more rapidly than the economy can absorb new employees. And if, on top of this, the educational system's output has expanded considerably, then many of the newcomers onto the labor market who cannot find jobs will have had an education of some sort. It then begins to look, at least on the face of things, as if the nation had somehow got itself 'overeducated.' Such a conclusion is patently absurd when one takes into consideration the probability that the bulk of the population is still illiterate and that a majority of youngsters are still not in primary school. Nonetheless, there is a strong temptation at this point for someone in high authority to push the panic button on the educational budget. From a long-range view, nothing could be more self-defeating. Yet, it can happen.

The third fact points directly at a major, ubiquitous cause of employment difficulties. It is the unhappy fact that for many historical reasons, the employment structures of many developing countries, their labor market mechanisms, wages and salary structure, and the resultant deployment of their educated manpower are all seriously at odds with what is necessary to encourage optimum economic growth. More specifically, there is a wide disparity in most developing countries between the manpower *needed* for economic growth and the manpower *actually demanded* by the market. Likewise, there is a wide disparity between how the economy should use its available supply of educated manpower in order to promote economic growth, and how it actually uses it.

The main causes of these costly disparities include: (a) inappropriate wage and salary relationships, which tend to draw scarce manpower in the wrong directions; (b) inappropriate and overly rigid relationships between particular types of jobs and the 'official' educational qualifications for them; (c) traditional prejudices and concepts of status (opposed especially to manual labor) that repel young people from the very types of work most needed for development, drawing them instead to relatively less productive jobs; (d) a traditional 'caretaker' and 'supervisory' concept of government—in contrast to the 'activist' concept needed to spur development; this leads to an inflation of the civil service establishment and chains many of the most competent people to paper work when they should be released for positive development action.

If this is a fair statement, what are the conclusions for education? One is that unemployed engineers, for example, are not necessarily a sign that the educational system has produced too many. For many countries it is more likely a sign that the economy and the government have not yet learned how to use engineers—or agriculturists, or architects, or public health specialists—in the best interests of national development. The chances are that too many of these often well-trained specialists are behind desks, 'administering' instead of out building roads and schools, producing more food, improving public health. The chances are, also, that the pay is too high for 'administering' and too low for 'doing things.'

Should educational planners under these circumstances 'follow the market' and retrench their engineering program? Or should they follow the nation's true manpower needs and produce still more? There is no simple answer. The manpower estimates of need can sometimes be as wrong as the market, and in some cases mirror it. Still, to cut back educational output just because the economy and the system of public administration are not in harmony with national development would seem a strange way to foster development. The answer must obviously be left to those on the scene most competent to judge from all the circumstances. But one thing is clear—educational authorities have a strong interest in seeing that the noneducational bottlenecks to development get attention, even though such matters lie largely beyond their own official jurisdiction.

All this, however, does not relieve the educational system of responsibility for integrating itself, even with an imperfectly functioning economy or system of administering development. To spin off on its own and produce however much it wishes of whatever mix of students would be irresponsible and ultimately self-defeating. An educational system *can* produce too many engineers, and too many of other sorts of specialists, at a very high cost per unit—thereby greatly prejudicing other forms of education and injuring national development.

There are no general solutions to the problem of education and unemployment in developing countries; solutions can only be devised in each individual context. It will be at best a very troublesome problem for a long time to come. It is one of the inescapable difficulties of taking the passage to modernization. But the problem can be kept from being made worse than it needs to be if, by understanding its nature, those in positions of responsibility avoid the panicky decision to cut back education at the sight of some educated unemployed—a decision which, in the clarity of hindsight, could prove to have been a serious error.

If we dealt only in a glancing way with industrialized nations, it is not because they will have no problem of unemployment among the educated but because they have far better means for dealing with it. Their economies are larger, more diversified, and more resilient. They need to worry relatively less about matching manpower needs closely, partly because their employment markets come closer to reflecting these needs, and even more because there is greater flexibility, mobility, and convertibility within their labor force. Their educational systems will do well, however, to be far more vigilant than they have been in watching for evolving shifts in the employment pattern and for the emergence of new types of jobs that will call for quite different educational qualifications. Above all else, they will do most to minimize this problem of adjustment to employment if they give priority to producing people who are trainable and adaptable, and who have the capacity and motivation to continue to learn and grow. The factor of motivation forms a bridge to a matter that will be considered next.

## Attitudes and Social Change

INFLUENCE OF ATTITUDES ON EDUCATIONAL AND CAREER PREFERENCES · BIAS AGAINST SCIENTIFIC AND TECHNICAL STUDIES · INFLUENCES OF SCHOOLS AND TEACHERS · WHAT EDUCATION CAN AND CANNOT BE EXPECTED TO DO.

The baffling question of attitudes has run beneath the surface of many points made in these pages and occasionally has broken into the open. However many other casual factors are examined in the context of education and its relation to national development, sooner or later one finds that attitudes are a major cause behind many of these other causes, and behind many happenings and non-happenings. We pause, therefore, to consider the matter here.

In approaching it, we are conscious of the old warning that a subject should not be forced to assume a greater degree of precision than the nature of the subject warrants—that a picture of reality is distorted when naturally imprecise things are dealt with as though they were being precisely measured. Because this warning applies with special force to human attitudes, what is to be said next should be read principally as an hypothesis except where evidence can be cited in support of the claims made.

The first question we wish to consider is this: Insofar as a student has a free choice in the matter, how does he in fact choose an educational program to follow? It is our hypothesis that in the act of choosing he is strongly influenced by what he thinks will do the most for his economic and social future. He surveys that future in the light of the facts, gossip,

prejudices, and informed advice he may have picked up. He has a scale
of job preferences and he assesses, rightly or wrongly, what his chances
are of getting a type of job corresponding to his first preference. He then
makes these preferences the principle according to which he selects his
educational program.

If this hypothesis is correct, a second question follows from the first.
What, if anything, does the educational system itself do to reshape the
student's attitudes and choices, to make both more compatible with his
real employment prospects and with the development needs of the nation?

There is a great mass of impressionistic evidence which bears on the
answer to this question, and it comes from many regions and sources.
But the more concrete evidence is visible in the career choices students
actually make. It seems clear that, relative to needs, too many of the
ablest European students prefer the kind of employment they can qualify
for with a general, humanistic type of secondary and higher education,
while they shy away from careers requiring maths-science based studies.
To say this is not to discount the importance of two factors which are
often overlooked. One is that the attitudes of students toward the maths-
science based studies may be conditioned by their natural aptitudes; a
talent for one mode of human expression does not imply a talent for all
modes. The second important factor is that students who may have natural aptitudes for maths-science based studies may have had teachers who
were incompetent to handle such studies, and therefore failed to encourage the student.

But once these two points are taken into account, we are left with a
worrisome residual phenomenon. Good academic performers—who, for
reasons stated elsewhere, tend to come disproportionately from the educated and more affluent sectors of society—seem as a group to show a bias
against maths-science studies. This is not to suggest an absolute linkage
between such an attitude and a socio-economic background. Nor is it to
suggest indirectly that the entire sphere of the maths-science studies goes
by default to students with a less favored socio-economic background.
Lines of mental ability, regardless of background, crisscross like streaks
of light on a photograph taken at night of city traffic. But our observations
remain as stated—namely, that a heavy majority of academically able
students from the favored sectors of society, presumably because of their
employment preferences, generally choose to pursue a humanistic type of
secondary and higher education. This does not entirely explain why edu-

cational authorities in Europe have found it so difficult to channel a higher proportion of students toward fields of study in the sciences and technology in order to achieve a better balance. But it seems to explain at least a fair part of their difficulties.

We have already cited the difficulties encountered in France and the United Kingdom of trying to strengthen the flow of students into the sciences and technology. To these experiences can be added the comparable difficulties Sweden has had in directing more students into educational channels other than the 'theoretical' ones, with their heavy accent on a humanities-based curriculum (though they can also lead to maths-science studies). Thus a recent Swedish report states:

> One striking trend in the upper department has been the excessive inflow into the five 'theoretical' 9th grade streams that are supposed to lead to theoretical upper secondary education in the 'gymnasium' and 'fackskola' i.e. 9g, 9h, 9t, 9m and 9s. More than 75 per cent of all the students have been selecting these streams. In 1964 the corresponding figure was 74 per cent, and, in 1965, 78 per cent, as against 54 per cent in 1960. This trend may well continue.[17]

In the case of the developing countries, there is more empirical evidence which shows a strong student bias in favor of white-collar 'desk' or 'inside' jobs, because a traditional association has been made in those countries between manual labor—whether in field or factory—and low social status. Moreover, there is some evidence that, instead of trying to modify these attitudes, the schools and teachers tend to reinforce them. A typical result appears in a study by Marshall Wolfe, who concludes that the rapid growth of secondary education in Latin America in the 1950's was entirely unplanned with any view to serving the development needs of the region, and did little to equalize opportunity. He says:

> What the urban middle class successfully pressed for was the kind of secondary education that would lead . . . to the university and a step up on the social ladder, or at least a certificate giving access to public or private white-collar employment.[18]

This situation is well illustrated by the Indian village teacher in Kasum Nair's *Blossoms in the Dust*, who voiced a widely held attitude when he told his students:

17. OECD, *Educational Policy and Planning. Sweden, op. cit.*, p. 101.
18. Marshall Wolfe, 'Social and Political Problems of Educational Planning in Latin America,' *Problems and Strategies of Educational Planning: Lessons from Latin America* (Paris: Unesco/IIEP, 1965), p. 22.

Only education makes men of us. But education and cultivation [of the soil] cannot be combined. The two must be kept separate. How can a boy who has been to school do the hard labour which cultivation requires?[19]

Even when the authorities seek to re-orient their educational systems toward national development, their efforts can be undone by the opposing values widespread in their respective societies. The situation in Burma, as reported by Manning Nash, is a case in point. He observes that

For the Burmese educational planners, the object of education is not in doubt: education is to serve as one of the means of transformation from a raw material producing society . . . to a diversified, somewhat industrialized society—a modern nation, a socialist democracy made up of responsible and informed citizens.

But the Burmese villages, Nash adds, see it differently. To them,

education should lead to economic success (the village boy will go beyond the fourth standard to be a clerk, a teacher, or civil servant); it should lead to a display of refinement, of common knowledge [for that is how a common man earns *gon* (virtue and respect)]; and it should help get *kuth* (spiritual merit).[20]

One instinctively sympathizes with those in the developing countries who view education as an escape route from the low social status of manual labor. Unfortunately, there is another side to the matter. Nations can only be developed by the kind of strenuous labor that often entails getting one's hands dirty in the fields and factories, including many who are 'highly educated,' such as construction engineers and agricultural experts. It is true that able and hard-working people are also needed behind desks in indispensable administrative roles. But if education simply takes bright people away from hand-soiling labor and deposits them behind desks in excessive numbers, and if that is the destiny of a large majority of people with secondary and university training, how can education promote economic growth and earn a good yield on its investment?

Governmental structures in many developing countries are heavily laden with well-trained specialists of the sort desperately needed to make economic development move. But the specialists are occupied largely with administrative work, while the manpower studies flash warnings of

19. K. Nair and G. Myrdal, *Blossoms in the Dust: The Human Element in Indian Development* (London: Duckworth, 1961).

20. M. Nash, *The Golden Road to Modernity: Village Life in Contemporary Burma* (New York: John Wiley and Sons, 1965).

shortages in their specialist categories. A dramatic picture of this reality is contained in a report which makes the following observation:

> Of India's 2,600 agricultural scientists, 90 per cent are in the public sector (i.e. civil servants mainly in offices of the Ministry of Agriculture), whereas the country's agricultural production is almost entirely in the hands of private cultivators. Hardly 1 per cent of the scientists are engaged in farming or farm management, while less than 3 per cent are in these occupations in the food and dairy industries combined, fields where knowledge of agriculture can be directly applied.[21]

This vignette of Indian experience is given broader dimension by Philip Foster's studies in Ghana and the Ivory Coast of student occupational aspirations and expectations, and by an official study in the Philippines of student attitudes toward manual labor. All tend to confirm the more impressionistic reports of the way education is widely viewed as a road whose hoped-for terminal point is a white-collar job.[22]

To take note of such attitudes is not to scoff at them. It is important to understand them better so that educational systems can more effectively cope with them in the interest of national development. But what, actually, can education do about them? Even under ideal circumstances, it would be enormously difficult for school systems to instill in their students a set of attitudes, motivations, and career preferences that would promote national economic and social development—in defiance of so many family and other environmental forces which incline individuals in directions which often run contrary to national aims and needs. In the particular case of the developing countries, the difficulty is all the greater. Their schools, and especially those staffed by teachers who, themselves only a few years away from work on the land, are but one jump ahead of their pupils, cannot at a stroke reverse what has been bent by centuries of tradition and misery.

If the schools cannot be expected to wipe away these attitudes that are so unhelpful to national development, at least they can be expected not to entrench them further. With this beginning—albeit a negative one—it may be possible in time to take more positive steps. With the aid of improved teacher training, a more knowledgeable system of voca-

21. Unesco Research Center on Social and Economic Development in Southern Asia, *Sociological Considerations in Educational Planning for Economic Development* (New Delhi, 1965) (mimeographed).

22. P. J. Foster, *Education and Social Change in Ghana* (London: Routledge and Kegan Paul, 1965); see also Appendix 30.

tional guidance, a strategy of education for girls who will bear and rear the next generation, and with progress in the development and diversification of job opportunities, the schools may actually reverse the bent of the twig and point it toward modernization and progress. But they will never do it alone: it will require strong parallel efforts by others in society.

Students are not born with a preference for one kind of education or employment as against another. Nor are the able ones simply unconscious dupes of traditional prejudices that lead them to make irrational educational and employment choices. On the contrary, the brighter they are, the quicker they realize where society places its rewards, both economic and social, and where it does not. If society arranges its rewards unsuitably in terms of what is best for national development, if it perpetuates old patterns of incentives, employment, and prestige—when a new situation calls for change—then young people can hardly be expected to follow the preferences of abstract planners, or the advice of idealistic teachers. The preferences of the market place speak more persuasively to them.

In a society in transition, an educational system cannot shift student flows toward fields essential to national development as quickly as manpower planners might wish and as national interest requires, unless society itself (including above all the government) supports the shift with its social and economic incentives. Schools cannot get far ahead of public attitudes on these matters, nor can they conscientiously encourage students to get too far ahead.

The positive proof of this is found in certain developing countries where real efforts have been made to give new prestige to scientific and technical careers (as in India), and where this has been reflected in the salary structure. In these cases there has been little difficulty in attracting the best students into such careers. In this respect, some developing countries may be ahead of some industrialized ones. Unfortunately, however, in some of the same countries, comparable remedial steps have not yet been taken with respect to the prestige and rewards of sub-professionals who are essential to boosting the productivity of full professionals. This helps explain the lopsided supply relation between engineers and technicians cited earlier. One suspects that in most, if not all, of these traditional societies, the younger generation will rather quickly lose its alleged antipathy toward skilled manual labor as soon as society makes it worthwhile. A reversal of some of the wage relationships between skilled manual jobs and low-level white-collar jobs might produce some remarkable results and make education's job a good deal easier.

In any event, it is clear that education and society must continue to play back and forth on this matter of attitudes for a good while to come, and it is hoped that out of the interplay there will gradually emerge the kinds of social change and economic growth that presently proclaimed goals call for. But one thing can never be overlooked. An educational system and its students cannot be asked to do what society itself—and the government, by its incentive and prestige scales—is not prepared to do to implement the proclaimed goals. At a minimum, education can be asked to refrain from reinforcing antidevelopment attitudes and choices. It can try, in addition, to keep one step ahead of society in this respect, in an effort to accelerate the pace of social change and economic growth. But we repeat that education by itself cannot take on the whole job of reforming society, its attitudes, and its reward structures. Education is too much a creature of society and too much an *expression* of its society for this to be possible.

Still, within limits, an educational system is also its own creature and an expression of its own predelictions. This becomes clear as we look into its internal affairs and behavior, as we propose to do next.

# Inside the Educational System

*Aims and Priorities: The Road Map of the System*
EXPANSION OF EDUCATIONAL AIMS · DIFFICULTY IN ACHIEVING ALL
AIMS SIMULTANEOUSLY · PROBLEMS INHERENT IN DEMOCRATIZING
RIGHT OF ACCESS TO EDUCATION · CROSS-TENSIONS BETWEEN
'MODERNISTS' AND 'TRADITIONALISTS' · HARD CHOICES INVOLVED IN
ESTABLISHING PRIORITIES.

We have thus far looked at the educational system from the outside, first
from the standpoint of popular demand and inputs, and then from the
opposite standpoint of education's outputs and their impact on society.
We have now reached the door leading to an examination of what lies
between, namely, the inner life of the educational system.

The inner life of an educational system is shaped in no small degree
by its internal logic, dynamics, and habits. It is also very much influenced
by the pressures, constraints, and challenges bearing in upon it from the
outer environment. This being the case, before we pass through the door
and get inside the educational system, one comment about the environmental setting seems in order here.

An educational system, as we observed in the beginning of these pages,
is not a rigid thing. It has a potential internal flexibility and an internal
power of choice among alternative responses to external pressures or to
creative internal forces. In the past decade, however, it seems that
changes inside many of the world's educational systems have been
wrought probably more by external intervention than by internal initiative. This, by itself, need not be a cause for concern. An educational system can be served well by a running debate between its internal elements
and its external clients, sponsors, well-wishers, and critics. A system,
however, shows signs of malaise when there is a disproportion between

the strength of the external and internal forces—when the internal forces seem too weak to initiate changes of their own accord, and when the external forces, as someone said, seem to be dragging an educational system kicking and screaming into the twentieth century.

Since the inner workings of an educational system make up a very complex organism, poignantly human and shaped by many hands, let us first look at the aims which educational systems have set for themselves, or which societies have set for them. At the same time, let us try to re-construct the way those aims have evolved in the turmoil of recent years.

Since the 1950's, the aims of education, like other aspects of the edu-cational picture, have expanded to a revolutionary degree. A world of people, previously immobilized, got hold of a liberating idea: that knowl-edge is the key to a whole family of powers—political, social, economic; that a monopoly of knowledge in the hands of the few is but another name for the rule of the few over the lives of the many; that any people who wish to be the authors of their own history and to develop in their own way must break up the existing monopoly of knowledge. They must make the right of access to education the common property of everyone and, by extension, must also democratize the right of access to progres-sively higher levels of instruction.

The idea, of course, was not a new one. In an American context, for example, it was given currency during the American Revolution when Thomas Jefferson, as the wartime governor of Virginia, submitted to the state legislature *A Plan for the Diffusion of Knowledge.* Later, in a Rus-sian context, and still later, in an Indian one, Lenin and Gandhi, re-spectively, though with quite different versions of the ideal in mind and of how to attain it, joined in Jefferson's conviction that the wide diffusion of knowledge was an essential part of any plan to move any society to new heights. But it was not until after World War II, when old trading empires based on European metropolitan states were being liquidated, that educational aims, democratized in form, began to take hold of the consciousness of the newly named 'developing nations.' As the number of new or reborn nations multiplied, and as their developmental needs be-came apparent, Unesco responded to the new situation much as a skilled archer does who aims his arrow above the target he intends to hit, making due allowance for the downward pull of gravity. To its credit, Unesco spurred the developing nations to raise their sights and actively seek the democratic aims of education. As a result, there is now an almost universal educational consensus, supported by almost all nations, at all stages of development, with diverse political and social systems, and with equally diverse cultural backgrounds. All agree on what the broad democratic aims of education must be: universal primary education; universal literacy; equal educational opportunities for women; increased secondary and university participation; and broader adult education.

But a statement of broad aims is not self-executing. There has always been, and no doubt will always be, a great gap between the rhetoric and the deed. If, therefore, we want to get at an educational system's real aims, we must look beneath its precepts to its practices. Frequently, the two do not coincide. This does not say that the announced aims were a contrived deception. Rather it is a sign of how long it takes to alter the course of an ongoing educational system, to redeploy its energies in new directions and to marshal new energies and resources to take on new tasks and to do old ones better.

Among other things, a newly stated set of educational aims presupposes a cadre of teachers willing and competent to pursue such new aims. Yet many teachers in an educational system may have had no such orientation or training. Or again, a formal statement of a system's aims by its managing authorities can be upended by independent social pressures. It has happened more than once that educational leaders have laid out a new path to be followed, but that students and parents have chosen to head off in quite another direction. These two points, standing alone, underline the difficulty of implementing educational aims. And there are other difficulties. The managers of a system may ardently subscribe to its educational aims. The system, nonetheless, can be torn from within by arguments over a mass of specific issues where any one answer or group of answers can affect the prospects of attaining the educational aims agreed to. The arguments can be about priorities and planning, costs and resources, structure and curriculum, quality and methods, facilities and staffing, research and innovation, the language of instruction or 'student power.' More often than not the internal debate is really about means rather than ends. In the process of argument the two become badly confused.

What has just been said describes actual conditions prevailing within educational systems everywhere. Further, almost everywhere the systems are divided from within by a resurgence, in a new context, of the old arguments about who shall decide the various matters in dispute, and thereby have the final say in setting an educational system's order of march toward its aims. Should the final say be entrusted to the educators or to society? If to the educators, which ones? If to society, which of its members? What voice should students themselves have in the matter, and how should they exercise their franchise?

Each nation must find its own answers but, in some, the argument over what the answers should be has revealed deep fissures either within the society or within the educational fraternity. A narrow-based elite, governing a caste-bound society, may honor in words the democratic aims of education, but in practice may show a marked lack of enthusiasm for actually 'giving education to the masses,' fearing that this will lead in time to the dilution of the elite's own power. Conversely, a governing elite, genuinely anxious for social change and growth, may bravely march at the head of the drive for expanded educational services for the mass of the people. Yet the educational experts they depend on for help may be divided from within by arguments about how soon educational aims can be reached, or about how one can best build a mass educational system which will meet a given test for quality and efficiency.

The shape of these arguments can be seen by focusing on a matter already alluded to, namely, what has happened since secondary education was opened to a wider range of young people than had previously had access to it, who represented a wider range of family background, native ability, motivations, and career aspirations. The event occurred comparatively early in North America and in the Soviet Union, and in both places the consequence was a necessary diversification in the nature of secondary education, still in process of perfection. But for most of the world, including most of western Europe, secondary educational systems opened to a wide range of young people are in the main a phenomenon dating from a short two decades ago. The result is what we now see. It is a head-on clash between new needs and the pre-existing aims of secondary schools that had dominated their role in most places, to the virtual exclusion of everything else.

That role, as we have noted, had been to prepare students for entry into the university, by the route of a classical curriculum. As long as the students themselves represented a favored minority of the total school-age population, the school role seemed suited to the future prospects for their products. But this was no longer true when secondary education was democratized. There was a new insistence that the children of workers and peasants and shopkeepers have an equal opportunity to enter the prestigious academic route to the university. But since only a fraction of the whole age group could in fact go to the university, it became necessary to provide socially 'reputable' programs—alternative to those oriented toward entrance into a university—for the majority of students to whom a secondary education would, in all probability, mark the end of their formal education.

This reality precipitated a debate—which still rages—over the kind of educational experiences that should be provided for terminal students. Should the aim be to provide them with a marketable skill, plus an added increment of general education? Alternatively, should general education continue to be the main object, plus the development of *the skills required to learn a skill*—while relying on future employment experiences and in-service training to act as sources for the acquisition of specific skills? If the latter aim was to prevail, what kind of general education should be provided? Should it be a pale facsimile of the old pre-university school program, papering over a mass of students with a common cultural face? Or should it be a new kind of general education? And whatever the content, how could this reformed educational system be made to spread respectability, quality, and prestige evenly among its various parts, so that its student body would not be sharply divided between first-class and second-class citizens?

Even under static circumstances there would be sharp divisions of opinion among educators about how to give concrete expression to educational aims where the object in view is to train students for specific practical jobs. There would also be sharp divisions about the ways in which to establish a system of student counseling (or orientation) that would help build a reliable bridge between students and their natural talents, and between both the latter and realistic employment prospects. But the current case has been made more complex because of the increasingly dominant role of science and technology in the life of individuals and their societies. Can any job-oriented kind of training which the schools are capable of providing keep pace with a world that is rapidly and ceaselessly being transformed by the impact of revolutionary developments in science and technology?

The question not only haunts educators concerned with vocational and technical education in the secondary schools. It has forced a reconsideration of new and enlarged educational aims with respect to general education itself and the proper role of mathematics and science at every level of education, including adult education.

What is at issue here is not merely the production of scientists and technicians but the production of a scientifically and technically literate people who can live safely and sanely in a new kind of world. Indeed, man's great achievements in science have added a new dimension to the controversy among educators about the aims of education. The camp of the 'modernists' argues for a wholesale revision of the earlier classical concepts of humanism and 'culture.' They observe that, along with the great humanistic achievements of the past in the spheres of the literary arts and the plastic arts, the human animal has now expressed himself with stunning power in the creativity that has marked his development of science and technology. These, therefore, should be accorded their rightful place and value in any humanistic curriculum. The camp of the 'traditionalists,' on the other hand, resists this argument. They insist on maintaining the older concepts and spirit of humanism both of which have been frozen in the content of a curriculum and in a faculty structure which predate by many generations the recent onset of a new scientific and technological revolution.

The cross-tensions in educational aims are well illustrated by the increased emphasis in many nations on the teaching of modern foreign languages, arising because these nations meet more and more frequently in the world arena at many different points of contact—economic, political, military, scientific, and technological. The new need for precise intercommunication is acutely felt among the industrially advanced nations. But it is perhaps even more acutely felt among the developing nations, who face the need to communicate in the languages of the industrially advanced nations—in whom they see the arbiters of their fate. Thus there rises a clash between the traditionalists—who would continue to teach both an ancient and a modern foreign language as a key to the understanding of their own or another culture and to the appreciation of its finest literature—and the pragmatists, who would teach a foreign language first and foremost for its practical utility.

There is a strong case to be made for most if not all of the specific new tasks that fit into an enlarged frame of educational aims. But is it possible to achieve them all? Is it possible to pursue a multiplicity of educational aims, while spreading educational opportunities to a larger portion of the total population—and to do this without suffering an erosion of quality which will impair all the aims? Is there not a grave risk that in seeking to adjust its old aims and priorities to accommodate new ones, and in its anxiety to please everyone, an educational system may find itself with a confusion of aims, with no priorities at all, and forced to resort to papier mâché to conceal its bare spots? We cannot pretend to have answers for such questions, but hopefully what follows will shed a little light upon them.

To say this is not to anathematize the systems. Rather, it is to sympathize with their plight. One of the greatest difficulties facing an educational system and the community it serves involves the task of defining its aims and setting its priorities in operational terms that are clear and meaningful. The second and equal difficulty involves the task of determining how well the system is really doing when its actual output is weighed against its professed aims.

The system is always subject to a strong temptation to bury its real difficulties about aims in a compromise among rival views—a compromise that seems on the surface to be a fine work of group diplomacy, but actually dodges the hard but essential business of making clear decisions about priorities. Part of the same temptation is to assume that all educational subjects are of equal importance, that no single one should be subordinated to any other, that all are indispensable components of an educational system, that the system is capable of sustaining the accretions of new subjects without cutting into the old, and that all, therefore, should be granted equal time and resources.

In the practice of medicine, surgeons, when forced to choose, will sacrifice a limb in order to save a life. Yet in the case of educational systems, a concept of 'horizontal priorities,' where equal time and equal resources are to be allocated to all the aims of education, can reverse the order of values common in medicine. It can find the systems sacrificing their own life in order to save one of their limbs. Common sense would naturally protest against such a topsy-turvy choice. Yet there are disturbing signs that many educational systems appear to be making it in the day-to-day pursuit of their educational aims.

### Quality and Content: The Main Object of the System

OPPOSITE CLAIMS ABOUT RECENT CURRICULUM CHANGES  ·  TWO WAYS OF VIEWING EDUCATIONAL QUALITY  ·  NEW PEDAGOGICAL PROBLEMS POSED BY NEW CLIENTELES  ·  IMPEDIMENTS TO FLOW OF NEW KNOWLEDGE INTO CLASSROOMS  ·  INFLUENCE OF PRESTIGE PATTERNS ON QUALITY OF TEACHER INPUTS.

If educational systems were to be judged solely by the size of student enrollments, the question of a crisis in the content and quality of these systems would not arise. But if we agree, as we obviously must, that educational systems exist to teach students, not produce statistics, then in judging the content and quality of the systems, we must ask: What have the students actually been learning? How much have they learned, how well and how fast? Is there any difference between what and how well students are now learning, and what and how well their predecessors learned before the 1950's?

These are among the most difficult questions that arise in pedagogy. In trying to come to grips with them, we can easily go astray if we over-simplify, overgeneralize, overreact—or if we seek only what we want to find, and find only what we seek. It is far better to admit straight-off, as we here do, that the truth probably lies in a union of two contradictory statements which bear on the questions just asked.

One of the two statements goes like this: In many places, the structure, methods, and content of the curriculum have been changed more thoroughly in the past decade than in any previous decades. They have been updated and made more efficient by being made more relevant to the student and his environment. A great many students, therefore, are learning more and learning it better than ever their predecessors did. More has not meant worse. The talk about a decline in quality should therefore be met with some skepticism, for a good deal of it emanates from oligarchical circles as part of their general polemical war against the modernization and democratization of any aspect of the education they knew.

The second statement, which directly contradicts the first, comes from front-line veterans of educational wars, who deserve a hearing if only out of a decent respect for their battle scars. The full sweep of their criticism of educational systems exceeds in pitch anything heard before. In essence, they argue that much of the present content of education is obsolete and irrelevant, that it does not serve the purposes of students who will live in the twenty-first century. These critics, it should be added, do not say that more inherently leads to worse. They say it has led to worse —in the industrialized and developing countries alike—principally because of a critical confusion in the standards that educational systems have invoked in trying to provide for more education.

We can draw a little closer to the common frontier of truth in the contradictory views just sketched in, if we first try to clarify the meaning of the two widely used—and abused—terms, 'quality' and 'standards.'

The International Institute for Educational Planning put that task of clarification to a symposium it convened on the subject 'The Qualitative Aspects of Educational Planning.'[23] In their response, the participating

23. IIEP, *Qualitative Aspects of Educational Planning, op. cit.*

experts found it useful to distinguish between two different ways of viewing quality. One way involved a view of quality from within the educational system in the light of its own *internal* criteria. An example might be a profile of student performance based on a standard examination such as the Cambridge or the West African School Examination Certificate, the French 'bac,' or the United States 'college boards.' The other way (as we have noted already in our discussion of educational outputs) is to view the qualitative performance of an educational system by *external* criteria, such as its fitness and relevance to the needs of its environment.

These two different angles of vision for assessing a school system can lead to quite different conclusions. The quality and efficiency of a school may be high according to its own internal standards. But if its teaching, judged by external criteria, is obsolete and irrelevant for its place and time, then its quality and efficiency must be considered poor.

By the route of this analysis, the experienced educators and assorted social scientists who took part in the IIEP symposium moved on toward a number of related questions. Were the educational 'standards' of 1900 the right ones for today? Were the educational standards of an industrialized country fit to be exported to and embraced by a developing one? Should standards be 'universal,' or should they be geared to the special circumstances confronting a given country or region at a given moment in time? The symposium participants unanimously answered that educational standards—if they are to make any sense and serve any useful purpose—must be viewed as being relative to the particular purpose, place, and time of the student clientele. Any other basis for judging standards and quality was pointless in terms of a nation's development.

We are persuaded that the view which dominated that symposium is right. We are further persuaded that an action-corollary follows directly from it. The managers of educational systems must set their sights on adapting the educational curriculums and standards to the realities of the situation they face, and, in doing so, they must try to harmonize the internal and external criteria of quality. This does not mean the substitution of 'second-class' for 'first-class' educational aims and curriculums. It means raising a standard of excellence, which may take different forms as among nations but in which the common criterion for excellence is the extent to which the education being offered fits the real needs and values, currently and prospectively, of a given country.

What is the alternative to this view? It is to cling dogmatically to yesterday's curriculums and standards—to treat them as absolutes when they are really contingencies. Or worse, it is to borrow a curriculum and standards from another nation—already outmoded there, and all the more unsuited to the situation of the borrowing nation. The idea of 'international standards' is a necessary and proper guide to education in special cases where universal norms do in fact exist—as in the training of solid-state physicists or of pilots for commercial jets. With respect to the first of these, anything short of the 'best' would result in sheer waste; with respect to the second, the result would be a disaster. But leaving such special cases out of account, what is the inexorable result when a nation angles the whole of its primary or secondary school curriculum to another nation's pattern, either in the name of progress, or to ensure that a fraction of its students will qualify for entry into the universities of the other nation? The inexorable result is to divorce the educational system of the imitating nation from the real needs, conditions, and aspirations of its society. It is to pursue an abstraction which draws that nation away from an education strategy that can help its development. It is to waste the scarce resources invested in education, and thus make it a concealed saboteur of national development.

To say this is to describe what has actually been happening in many developing countries, particularly the newly independent ones. They have not looked squarely at themselves in order to frame their educational measures in the light of where they stand and where they are heading. Instead, they have too frequently tried to engraft on themselves the educational doctrines, forms, content, rituals, and indicators of quality and standards of other countries. It is far easier, of course, to point to what is irrelevant and wrong in such situations, than to say what would be right and better. To find out the right and better things to do requires enormous exploration and discovery. But be that as it may, the hard fact remains that until these nations extend their declarations of independence to their educational systems, the latter will remain in a condition of crisis, while the productivity of their educational investment will remain considerably lower than the levels that can and must be attained.

The developing countries of Africa and Asia which derived their 'founding' educational models from European systems now share with them a further challenging aspect of educational content and quality. The challenge, touched upon previously, arises from the current efforts of virtually all educational systems to open their doors wider than before and to serve larger numbers than ever before of young people who come from families of lower educational, economic, and social status.

As we have already noted, schools and universities have a simplified task when the students they serve have a relatively homogeneous educational and social background and when they have been filtered through successive fine-meshed academic screens designed to filter out a residue of the 'best performers.' But enormously complex problems arise when a vest-pocket, 'high-quality' educational system, whose main function has been to produce an elite, is asked to enlarge itself in order to serve a mass of students who are diversified in almost every respect. It is as if a specialized gift shop for the well-to-do was summoned to convert itself into a massive department store for consumers of every description, including a thrift basement for those in straitened circumstances.

A small, 'high quality,' elitist-oriented educational system which must expand and democratize itself cannot cling to the old logistics, curriculum, and hallowed monolithic standards. Unless these are sharply altered to meet new demands, the system is bound to perform badly while enrollments expand rapidly. Dropouts and failures will mount unconscionably high, quality will decline (by the old standards), and frustrations will rise. The whole system will then come under heavy fire from standpatters and reformers alike, including especially the students. Indeed, all this is occurring in many of the educational systems of western Europe, and in those of the developing nations that took their earlier educational models from European systems. They have not made sweeping adaptations congruous with the new needs of a new era. While they mean to become more 'democratic' by serving the rich and poor alike in rapidly growing numbers, they have remained bound to the educational patterns and norms appropriate to an earlier age and purpose.

How to make necessary educational changes, and what forms these should take, will be questions destined to nag the industrialized countries for years to come. And it must be emphasized that present pedagogical knowledge and research shed but a wan shaft of light on what the proper answers to the questions should be. But the prospects of the industrialized countries in this respect seem smooth compared to the plight of the developing nations. Their educational systems, charged with the task of helping to bring their ancient societies suddenly into the last third of the twentieth century, do not have the advantage of rich environmental supports for education such as the industrialized countries enjoy. They lack, for example, a broad base of adult literacy, or elaborate systems of information-bearing mass media, or an atmosphere irradiated by living examples of high culture and modern science. In rural areas especially, their schools are called upon to launch a child from a static, ancient, and impoverished environment into a dazzling new world of modern ideas, outlooks, knowledge, and gadgets. At the same time, however, they are cautioned not to alienate the child from his own cultural heritage, or from the practical development needs of his own neighborhood. How can they meet these diverse and often clashing expectations? To do so would tax the wisdom of the world's finest teachers in its best-endowed schools. But these are not found in the rural areas of the developing countries.

As if the difficulties just described were not enough to create a crisis in the content and quality of education, there is a further difficulty. In form, it is the straightforward problem of how to keep the content of classroom education up-to-date with the rapidly advancing frontiers of knowledge.

In theory, the classrooms of the world should have ready access to the great and growing stockpile of human knowledge. In fact, however, a barrier stands between them and knowledge. What seeps through, usually tardily, comes mainly through two 'knowledge conduits'—textbooks and teachers. (Students themselves, of course, are an important third conduit of knowledge into the classroom, but the knowledge they bring often does not conform to what the official curriculum calls for.) In an age when the quantity of human knowledge is doubling every decade, the textbook and the teacher, for all too familiar reasons, inevitably become purveyors of obsolete knowledge. The obsolete, moreover, not only perpetuates itself in the content of education, but in the methods for conveying knowledge—or to add a further point, in the very architecture of the school. Yet all the while, in the world beyond the school, everything moves at a swift pace—changes in knowledge, changes in technologies, changes in job requirements, shifts in population.

The obvious inference to be drawn from these many changes has been stated in a previous place, but warrants repetition here. Educational systems must undergo a shift of emphasis. The new stress must be not so much on producing an *educated* person as on producing an *educable* person who can learn and adapt himself efficiently all through his life to an environment that is ceaselessly changing. If an educational system itself is not adaptable to changing environmental conditions, how can it expect to produce people who are?

What has just been asked forces us to reconsider the question of teacher input into the school systems, and to do so because of its bearing on the subject of educational content and quality. Education does attract a considerable number of highly creative, adaptable, and dedicated people. On the whole, however, most educational systems attract a teaching force which at best is at the average level of general competence of the system's total graduate output. They can hardly be expected to be creative, innovative, and ingenious people, especially when the nature of their workload seldom gives them time to reflect, to renew their own knowledge, to experiment, and to evaluate the results of their efforts. Nor can miracles be expected of school systems, given the way they are organized and staffed, and their working time and tools.

Further, the sociology and prestige patterns of educational systems are a major obstacle to achieving good quality in the 'newer' branches of learning, especially in the 'terminal' and technically oriented programs of newly diversified secondary school systems. The old classical 'pre-university' course remains king. The best teachers gravitate toward its throne, and the best students are drawn to it with them, even though their real first choice may lie elsewhere.

The often unhappy experiences with educational reforms of recent years, aimed particularly at a diversification of education at the secondary school level, make one thing very clear. The need to deal with the problems of educational content and quality posed by a changing environment will not be met merely by restructuring the educational systems in a formal way. That is, it will not be met merely by making room for new traffic patterns of student flows and new branches of learning, expressed in new programs reached through new channels. There must also be a change in the teachers and their methods. Every means must be used to end the old 'pecking order' of status which tends to insist, automatically, that everything new in education is 'second class.' Students must also be more effectively guided into those educational channels that hold the greatest promise to them personally, besides serving their nation's needs. With this in mind, let us consider next the issues of educational technology, research, and innovation.

## Technology, Research, and Innovation

CLASHING VIEWS ABOUT NEW EDUCATIONAL TECHNOLOGIES · MEANING OF EDUCATIONAL TECHNOLOGY ILLUSTRATED · ANCIENT ORIGINS OF EDUCATION'S TECHNOLOGY · ARCHITECTURAL IMPEDIMENTS TO NEW TEACHING PROCESSES · ROLE OF EDUCATIONAL RESEARCH · SIGNS OF PROGRESS.

A reference to technology made in the course of a discussion about education often conjures up either a utopian or a cataclysmic vision among members of the audience. In the utopian vision, technology means a machine with magic powers. Turn on a switch, apply the machine to the child, and the obstacles of traditional pedagogy melt away. The child in a twinkling of an eye is infused with knowledge whose quantity and quality will lead to greater marvels when he comes of age. Even better, since the machine costs so little on a per capita student basis, yet can do so much for so many on a grand scale, it makes possible a sharp reduction in school costs.

In the cataclysmic vision, technology also means a machine—but a malign one where education is concerned. Geared to work in a self-regulating way, it kills in students the intuitive value judgment, the leap of the imagination, the wayward but luminous question. It stuffs the student only with facts and allows for no dialogue. It thus denies him precious educational qualities—attitudes of mind, styles of thinking, depths of appreciation—that can be acquired only by a continuous and direct exposure of the pupil to the teacher over long periods. Worse still, the machine means that teachers will be put out of jobs.

There is a connection between the utopian vision and real-life episodes where educational systems have made hasty, wasteful, and even harmful investments in 'gadgets.' There is also a connection between the cataclysmic vision and other real-life episodes marked by strong opposition to any suggestion for critically re-examining education's customary ways of doing things, or for developing and testing new educational methods with the object of improving both the educational and economic efficiency of the existing order.

In our own view, however, both visions conceive of educational technology in too narrow a way. Educational technology, broadly conceived, includes all the different methods, materials, equipment, and logistical arrangements employed by education to further its work. These range from the lecture method to the Socratic dialogue, from the seminar to the drill session. They include the blackboard, desk, and textbook; the pupil-teacher ratio and the layout of classrooms and corridors; the chronological grade system, the academic calendar, and the school bell that punctuates time into modular units; the examinations and grades that influence the students' futures. Each of these is an integral part of a 'system' and a 'process' whose ultimate objective is to induce learning.

From this description, it should become apparent that a dispute about the technology of education which is confined to the question of whether or not to use the 'machines' comprising the 'new media,' poses the wrong question. The real issue is whether all the ways of doing things carried over from the past are still relevant and sufficient to education's needs, or whether certain subtractions and additions would improve the situation. In short, the issue is whether it is necessary, desirable, and possible to recast fundamentally the whole of education's technology, combining the best of the old and the modern in ways that will form an essentially new, integrated 'system' of teaching and learning, capable of yielding better results for any given level of effort.

We can deal with this issue with more élan if we realize that the basis for education's technology was not decreed by a voice sounding out of a burning bush. Today's technology of education is mainly the product of a great historical stream made up of trial and error, occasional outbursts of great individual ingenuity and persuasion, of long practice and imitation, and of sheer habit. Take the pupil-teacher ratio as an example. It is one of the most sacrosanct of education's articles of faith. It has withstood the repeated siege of research results which suggest no fixed relationship between the size of a class and how much is learned. Other variables obviously have more to do with what is learned—variables such as the quality of the teacher and the parents, the supply of teaching materials, the style and tone of the school, the health and nourishment of the pupils. Where, then, did the concept originate that a one to twenty-five or one to thirty pupil-teacher ratio was the 'ideal' to be aimed at? An enterprising historian finally traced the matter back to a doctrine derived from the Talmud Baba Bathra which contains this instruction:

> One teacher is to have twenty-five pupils; if they be fifty, then two teachers must be appointed; if they be forty, the teacher has to have an assistant.[24]

The talmudic doctrine, an oral tradition to begin with, was laid down long before printed textbooks, blackboards, films, radio, television and other modern teaching aids were heard of. It apparently made a grand tour of educational systems elsewhere and persisted in its influence despite all subsequent changes, including the invention of movable type and the penetration of schoolrooms and universities by the book.

Still, the persistence of this doctrine is not surprising when one recalls that every new technological instrument proposed as a tool of learning has always been opposed. Even the adoption of the written word in place of the tutorial oral tradition of instruction through a dialectic was strongly opposed, and by no less great a teacher than Socrates. In warning about the dangers of written knowledge, Socrates said:

24. Sir Eric Ashby, F.R.S., 'Reflections on Technology in Education,' The Joseph Wunsch Lecture, 1966 (Haifa: Technion, Israel Institute of Technology, 1967).

For this invention of yours will produce forgetfulness in the minds of those who learn it, by causing them to neglect their memory inasmuch as, from the confidence in writing, they will recollect by the external aid of foreign symbols and not by the internal use of their own faculties.

He objected to written work on another ground:

And so it is with written discourses. You could fancy they speak as though they were possessed of sense, but if you wish to understand something they say, and question them about it, you find them ever repeating the one and the self-same story.

Given this tradition of resistance to change, it is not surprising that, while fantastic revolutions have occurred in the last fifty years in the technologies of industry, agriculture, transportation, communications, and weaponry, this has not been the case with education's technology. It is true that new things have been added, and old things improved. But for the most part, these have been superimposed like geological strata on the bedrock methods and logistics that have prevailed for generations. There has been no fundamental reshuffling and reordering of available technologies to create a new synthesis of educational methods.

Even when there has been a clear sign of change in one matter, a close look at it usually reveals that the change proceeds on the assumption that nothing else will change. This is the case, for example, when films, or workbooks, or television lessons, or language laboratories, are simply added to what is already going on, the latter being perpetuated with little if any change. Another case in point is the state of school architecture. There has been an energetic search for ways to build satisfactory school buildings more cheaply, through applying modern industrial methods of prefabrication and modular dimensions, and a greater use of basic designs that can be repeated with appropriate modifications. Many of these innovations in architecture and construction, however, have implicitly assumed that teaching methods and the internal logistics of schools will remain much the same in the future. What is actually needed is not simply less expensive buildings, but buildings sufficiently flexible to permit new ways of teaching and learning to go on within them, rather than buildings which will blockade new methods.

Some wise person once observed: 'First we shape our buildings, then they shape us.' This is education's whole history. There are beginning to be interesting departures from the old norms, but the self-contained classroom still rules. With its rigid walls, the self-contained classroom has for generations been the monk's cell of the educational process. It was and is still designed, even in the newest schools, to accommodate one teacher (at a desk before a blackboard), a prescribed number of pupils (arranged geometrically at desks facing the teacher), wall space for a few exhibits, a cabinet in which to keep precious books and other teaching aids. At the sound of the opening bell, the process gets under way. A whole school of these cells, resembling the space modules of an egg crate, first fills up with youngsters, and soon the familiar teaching-learning process begins. At another sound of the bell, the cells flush out their 'learners,' who sweep down the wide corridors to other cells and other subjects. Each subject gets equal time. The corridors cost a great deal and are used but a fraction of the time. The same applies to the auditorium and the lunchroom.

Once this building is built to fit education's traditional technology, it stands firmly for at least two or three generations to thwart any serious changes in the traditional deployment of space, time, and students. This fact adds a note of urgency to the innovative efforts now going on, particularly in the United States (with encouragement from the Ford Foundation-backed Educational Facilities Laboratory) and through Unesco's advisory program on school construction, to circumvent these brick and plaster impediments to new educational technologies—by designing buildings which foster learning and invite innovation rather than hampering them.[25]

Yet an improvement in the architectural shell encasing the educational process cannot, by itself, bring about needed changes within the process itself. The triangular disconnection between education's technology on one side, the tidal wave of new students on a second side, and a teacher shortage on the third side, is a deeply disturbing reality. Thoughtful leaders of education have not only taken notice of it but have criticized the disconnection in the strongest language. Thus in speaking of 'methods of teaching and forgetting' to a conference of educators in India recently, Dr. Malcolm Adiseshiah, the Deputy Director-General of Unesco, said:

> Looked at as a business enterprise, the school and the college present a woebegone spectacle. We find in education an antediluvian technology which would not survive for an instant in any other economic sector. The teaching methods and learning techniques . . . are rusty, cranky and antiquated.

25. J. Beynon, 'Educational Architecture *v.* Educational Change,' in *Educational Costs and Productivity* (Paris: Unesco/IIEP, December 1967) (mimeographed).

Nor was this all. Dr. Adiseshiah stressed the linkage between a stand-still technology and a low-grade quality and content of education, found especially in many developing countries:

> The learning techniques . . . remain the same: the rote method, the technique of cramming, and, once the examination menace is passed, of forgetting all these useless impedimenta. The examination system is not an evaluation of a student's personality and intellectual equipment, his powers of thinking for himself, reflection and reasoning. It is a challenge to resourceful deception and display of superficial cleverness.[26]

The solution often advocated for conditions such as these is 'more educational research.' Yet, ironically, the absence of a strong innovative spirit in educational systems is traceable in part to the very nature of traditional educational research. Not only was it starved for resources, both money and talent, but for years it tended to stagnate in quiet intellectual backwaters isolated from the main stream of scientific research and development. The dominant character of educational research in Europe for a long time was more philosophical than experimental, more humanistic than scientific, more theoretical than empirical. In North America, a new breed of 'educational researchers' who grew up in the graduate schools of education, chased there by the older disciplines, sought to emulate the social sciences, especially in the quantitative measurement of things. In fact, however, the researchers were mainly ignored by and isolated from the major social scientists of the university community, and their research was also, to a considerable extent, isolated from the practical problems and environment of ordinary schools themselves.

Thus, much of 'educational research' until very recently, though bearing the superficial hallmarks of scientific research, was essentially philosophical or descriptive in nature. It was not within the modern scientific tradition of rigorous analytical, experimental, and developmental research that was producing notable results elsewhere. Further, educational research for the most part was a fragmented collection of sporadic and ineffectual attacks—especially by Ph.D. candidates—either on problems which by their very nature required a broad-scale and sustained attack, or else on trivial but manageable topics of little basic significance. Little wonder, then, that for many years educational research was not held in

26. Malcolm Adiseshiah, 'Education and National Development,' in *Unesco Chronicle,* XIII, no. 2 (Paris: Unesco, February 1967).

high regard, even by practicing educators. Little wonder, also, that it had difficulty attracting talent and resources and, with some notable exceptions, had little impact on the practices and course of events in educational systems.

The irony is that the educational system, which has been so much the home and mother of the modern scientific method, has applied so little of it to its own affairs. The point here is underlined in a recent OECD survey (see Table 7) showing the magnitudes of total research expenditures in several of its member countries, the relation of these expenditures to the GNP, and the proportion of research conducted within educational institutions (though most of the latter has had little or nothing to do with educaion per se).

TABLE 7

*Total research and development expenditure*

| COUNTRY | MILLION U.S. DOLLARS | PERCENT OF GNP | PERCENT OF TOTAL RESEARCH PERFORMED IN EDUCATIONAL INSTITUTIONS |
|---|---|---|---|
| Austria (1964) | 23.2 | 0.3 | 26.0 |
| France (1963) | 1 299.1 | 1.9 | 13.4 |
| Germany, Fed. Rep. of (1964) | 1,436.3 | 1.6 | 20.5 |
| Japan (1963) | 892.0 | 1.6 | 19.5 |
| Netherlands (1964) | 314.4 | 2.1 | 16.5 |
| Spain (1964) | 27.4 | 0.2 | 7.1 |
| United Kingdom (1964-65) | 2 159.9 | 2.7 | 7.6 |
| U.S.A. (1963-64) | 21 323.0 | 3.8 | 11.0 |

Source: OECD, *International Statistical Year on Research and Development, Statistical Tables and Notes,* II (Paris, 1968).

The bare-bones picture is more strikingly revealed by glancing at the state of affairs in the United States, a country which leads all others in the recent growth of available research funds. Thanks mainly to the heightened interest of United States private foundations and the federal government's entry into the field of education on an extensive scale, total expenditures on educational research in the United States are estimated to have trebled between 1960 and 1965 (from less than $33,000,000 to over $98,000,000).[27] Even so, the amount is minor when compared with the evident need and the vast sums spent on education itself. There have been numerous and long-standing proposals to the effect that support for educational research and development should be at least 1 per cent of total educational budgets. Yet the 1960 figure for the United States was only 0.12 per cent and the 1965 figure 0.22 per cent. By contrast, the more

27. Estimated figures from United States, *Digest of Educational Statistics, op. cit.,* 1966.

dynamic industries in the United States spend up to 10 per cent of their turnover on research and development, to improve their products and production processes. Indeed, a single major chemical firm is reported to be spending $110 million a year on research—which is more than is spent in the entire nation on educational research.[28]

As education and its problems come increasingly to the fore in public budgets and debates, we must hope that the pressures generated by a public concern will pierce the inner world of education itself and make that world more predisposed to accept the need for change. By the same token, we must hope that the external constraints of parental and public opinion which often inhibit desirable educational changes will be relaxed. In both respects, recent signs are favorable, at least in some nations more prone toward innovation.

In such countries, the manifest inability of conventional approaches to provide answers to the heightened problems of education has been the prod behind moves in new directions. A number of key subjects—for example, mathematics, the sciences, and foreign languages—have been given modern formulation and content, new orientation and new and more effective learning aids. The initiative is spreading to the social studies, and more recently to the humanities (which many educators consider to be the last stronghold of resistance to 'heresy'). In addition, attempts have been made in many countries to try out the 'new media'—films, radio, television—and to develop 'programmed learning.' The IIEP recently examined a number of these efforts to determine their effectiveness and the practical economic and administrative feasibility of using them, especially in developing countries.[29] It turned out that most of these experiments are small scale and at best can have only a fringe effect. Most are being superimposed upon the previous pattern rather than integrated into new and more efficient learning systems. Most have been *ad hoc*, with little careful planning in advance, careful evaluation in process, and reporting of results in a scientific manner. Still, the lessons of these initial endeavors are important; the cumulative evidence clearly shows that these 'new media' and new technologies, when properly used, can have a salutary—sometimes a dramatic—effect on educational quality, quantity, and costs.

Again, on the research front, the complex but intellectually challenging problems of education are increasingly attracting the curiosity and energies

28. *Time*, New York, 30 June 1967.
29. W. Schramm, *et al.*, *The New Media: Memo to Educational Planners* (Paris: Unesco/IIEP, 1967).

of workers in related fields, such as economics, psychology, sociology, anthropology, and public administration. In the context of university status hierarchies, education is at long last becoming a 'respectable' area of inquiry for scholars in a variety of disciplines. The isolation of educational research is thereby being diminished; a new and fruitful dialogue has sprung up among the related disciplines; new educational problems, along with many older ones, are being attacked from new sides; and in consequence, new insights and useful guides to policy are beginning to emerge.

It must be emphasized, however, that these new tendencies in research have established only a small bridgehead on the banks of education. The old resisting tradition of descriptive research remains strong. One has only to make a quick 'content analysis' of leading journals of educational research to see that this is so. It is encouraging, to be sure, to find more new articles than ever before addressed to the urgent preoccupations of today's educational managers and the critical planning and development problems they face. Yet they are still in the minority; the preoccupations of educational research of a former age continue to dominate many journals as if in layers of overprinting.

If, as seems likely, there is a further expansion in the flow of funds for educational research, several things must follow. It will be necessary to evolve an effective strategy, a new orientation, and a clear order of priorities that will link research more productively to the basic and practical problems which underlie the educational crisis. Above all, if larger funds are to be well used, it will be necessary to reform and strengthen the institutional infrastructure for getting relevant educational research done, for mobilizing more good talent for the purpose, and for ensuring that the results are quickly communicated and put to practical use.

Meanwhile, there has been encouraging evidence that the rate at which new educational content and practices are being adopted has been stepped up. Professor Paul Mort of Columbia University, many years ago showed empirically that when a useful new educational practice had been invented, it would take about fifteen years before 3 per cent of the American school systems adopted it, and fifty more years before it was completely 'diffused.'[30] The latter figure was the equivalent of two full generations of students passing through the teacher training colleges—or —on the basis of a two- to four-year curriculum—between twelve and fifteen training classes. A recent study suggests that the rate of change has quickened, though is still quite slow. It dealt with various innovations that have been available for general adoption for at least the last ten

30. *Today*, Chicago, North Central Association, 72nd Year, XI (March 1967).

years. Of the twenty-seven specific innovations that were singled out for examination, the survey showed that six had already been adopted in the typical American high school. That left twenty-one innovations—or roughly three-fourths of the total—still waiting in the wings after ten or more years.

Without venturing to pass judgment on the substantive merits of the innovations, or on their general applicability in the light of special local conditions, the figures cited are of a piece with remarks made elsewhere about progress in technology and research. They show that energetic new approaches to education (even when promising) are small and tardy, and that they spread slowly relative to the urgent need for change all along the educational front.[31]

Recalling the potential lessons cited earlier which education might draw from agriculture's experience with its technological revolution, we might close this particular discussion with the following hypothesis. Before the creation and adoption of innovations can be greatly speeded up, there must be, first, a widespread transformation of the attitude toward change in education—by the public and educators alike; second, the creation within education of new institutional means and personnel whose prime concern is to seek improvements and innovations; and third, the fostering within teacher training colleges of attitudes that help make future teachers more receptive to innovations, thereby enabling education to engage in a vigorous and continuing process of self-renewal and advancement.

## *Management: The Operation of the System*

A CRUCIAL ASPECT OF THE EDUCATIONAL CRISIS · HEAVY GRIP OF
THE PAST · LACK OF MANAGEMENT TRAINING AND RESEARCH ·
INBREEDING PROCESS OF RECRUITMENT · NEED FOR MANAGEMENT
TEAMS · LOW REWARDS OF EDUCATIONAL EXECUTIVES · SOME BRIGHT
SPOTS.

Any productive system, whatever its aims and technology, requires management. It must have leadership and direction, supervision and coordination, constant evaluation and adjustment. In the case of an educational

31. P. H. Coombs, 'The Technical Frontiers of Education,' 27th Annual Sir John Adams Lecture at the University of California, Los Angeles, 15 March 1960.

system, as we said much earlier when we analogized it to agriculture, its problems of management are extraordinarily difficult, partly because its over-all size is divided into many small and scattered parts.

A host of organizations and people have a hand in managing at least some aspects of an educational system. They include government agencies at all levels, churches and other private bodies, politicians and civil servants, administrative heads of universities and local schools, professors and teachers, students and parents, and endless critics of every stripe. Here, however, we are less concerned with the foregoing people than with the management milieu within which they function. The issue for us is not the individual ability and moral worth of educational administrators, their devotion to duty, or their taste for hard work. These are often of a very high order. The issue instead is whether the basic managerial *arrangements* of educational systems are adequate to the tasks before them. Are they well oriented to these tasks? Do those responsible for major decisions and direction of the system have the right kinds of specialized help and information flows? Do they have the appropriate analytical concepts and tools to know what is going on within the system, to assess its performance both internally and in relation to its environment, to size up its options and plan its future, and to monitor the implementation of such plans? Does the management process of the system draw on all the available resources—both within and outside the system —for maximum strength and effectiveness? Are the arrangements for recruitment and career development of various sorts of management personnel well suited to the needs? Are there adequate means for seeing where changes are needed in the system, for determining the best sorts of changes, then getting them adopted?

The questions echo their own answer. The managerial arrangements typical of educational systems are grossly inadequate to deal with a crisis-ridden set of new challenges and are, themselves, a crucial part of the educational crisis. The main features of these arrangements were cast during an earlier era when education and the world outside were moving slowly by today's pace, and when the size and diversity of education's tasks were much smaller. They were not designed for planning in today's sense of the term, or for implementing such planning, or for critical evaluation of the educational system's performance, or for a rigorous promotion of innovation. They have neither the spirit, nor the tools, nor the personnel for these purposes. Nor have they the necessary means of consultation, communication, and co-ordination. This is true in both industrialized and developing countries; in great measure the latter borrowed their administrative practices from the former. Thus, many newly independent countries are still clinging to an old colonial-type school administration which was designed primarily to serve a caretaker, regulatory, and supervisory role—whereas what they need is a more dynamic, development-oriented form of administration, calculated to take initiatives, to unleash ingenuity throughout the system, and to bring about growth and change.

The consequence here—to cite but one example—is reflected in a recent official Indian report, which charged that

> antiquated and unimaginative administration procedures did great damage to schemes of science education in secondary schools; imperfect co-ordination between the objectives of the junior technical schools and the needs for lower level technical manpower made of that project a wasteful and expensive scheme; absence of appropriate action at various levels hampered programmes of teacher-training which should have enjoyed a very high priority in schemes of qualitative improvement[32]

The implication in the whole of what has just been said is obvious. The needed revolution in education must begin with educational management. Many able educational administrators are acutely aware of this need; if they were given half a chance, they would readily lead the revolution they know is called for. But the same administrators are hard pressed and harried, trying to make the old machinery serve new purposes and carry new workloads it was never designed for. They scarcely have time even to court a new idea, much less to marry it into the system. The conservative nature of the system, moving by the momentum of its own mass, thus grinds down even a would-be bold administrative innovator until even he is absorbed into the conservative mass and reflects its conservative behavior.

A recent study of the legal framework of educational planning in East Africa, and another in Nigeria, both show how thoroughly the administrative tools of a previous era have been carried forward and applied to a vastly altered set of aims and circumstances, often with poor results.[33]

32. Asian Institute of Educational Planning and Administration, 'Educational Planning and Administration,' a working paper for the National Seminar, Srinagar, 12-25 June 1967, New Delhi.

33. J. R. Carter, *The Legal Framework of Educational Planning and Administration in East Africa: Kenya, Tanzania, Uganda,* African research monographs, No. 7 (Paris: Unesco/IIEP, 1966), and A. C. R. Wheeler, *The Organization of Educational Planning in Nigeria,* African research monographs, No. 13 (Paris: Unesco/IIEP, 1968).

Yet the case here is not confined to developing countries alone; styles and methods of school administration, now inadequate or obsolete in many respects, remain deeply imbedded in many industrialized countries.

Universities in many countries are in even worse administrative shape than the schools, some coming close to being totally devoid of managerial machinery with which to plan, make decisions and implement them. In Latin America, for example, the chronic preoccupation of most universities with safeguarding their autonomy—as if it were an autonomous end in itself—has caused them to neglect their role of leadership for the whole educational system, and their obligation to society and its development goals. France, on the other hand, presents the picture of universities suffering cracks in their internal administration, because of the countless constraints and pressures flowing automatically to and from a highly centralized external administration. The results did not escape sharp comment at a recent conference of French university administrators and professors held at Caen. A passage in the conference report reads:

> If . . . a professor has to spend two days in Brussels or London to work with a colleague there, according to the letter of the law, he must request leave of absence—at the ministerial level—six weeks in advance. Faced by the realities of research, and of administrative delays, such a rule can mostly never be applied.

Indeed, said the report, the central administration itself

> is crushed by the burden of detailed 'information' which it cannot handle and its energies are dispersed by trifling details with which it was never designed to cope . . . a system crippled by delays in communication and often rendered ludicrous.[34]

One root of the difficulty is the absence in most educational systems of strong institutional provisions for doing creative research on problems of educational management, and for the continuous development of personnel to serve various managerial functions in the system. A closely related source of difficulty is the fact that most such systems have an inbreeding process for selecting and developing management personnel. In primary and secondary education, the top manager has worked his way up from being a teacher, which means that his main professional

34. A. Lichnerowicz, 'Structures des universités,' General report submitted to the Caen Conference, 1966.

training has been teacher training. And, because of this, the result is a relatively closed system of ideas and practices. At the university level in many countries, the 'top manager' is a professor, elected by the faculty, usually to serve for a limited time and then get back to teaching. The last thing he is expected to do is manage the institution. If he tried, the results might be disastrous. This inbreeding process, at whatever level, cuts the educational system off from potential sources of creative leadership, executive talent, innovators, and specialists—represented by able people who did not decide at an early point in their lives to become teachers, but who may turn out to be well suited to help manage school systems.

It is worth recalling here that hospitals in many countries used to operate on a similar theory. They once assumed that only a trained doctor was qualified to be a good hospital administrator. The way matters actually worked out bore no resemblance to the theory. The professional services of the doctors in their own specialities were lost to the hospitals when the doctors were installed in administrative posts. What the hospitals frequently got in return was poor administration. When enough hospitals sank into the mire of financial troubles, this system was changed, at least in some countries, beginning with a change in the traditional assumption that underlay the whole thing. A new breed of specially trained hospital administrators was put in charge of the institutions, and they began to show significant improvements after that.

The foregoing does not argue by indirection that good teachers are not a satisfactory source for good educational managers. They often are. Nor is the argument being made that, because someone can ably manage a given enterprise lying outside the sphere of education, he can with no further preparation be shifted into the sphere of education and manage it just as ably. A well-grounded knowledge of what goes on in education is obviously indispensable to its effective administration. Indeed, precisely for that reason, the main burden of our argument is as follows.

First, because educational systems have grown so complex, they need carefully recruited, well-trained modern managerial personnel of many sorts. Second, since there is a world-wide shortage of such people, an educational system suffers from a self-inflicted wound if it denies itself a potential source of managerial talent lying beyond the products of its own inbreeding process. Third, because of the complex tasks now facing educational systems, they need not only 'administrators' in the narrow meaning of the term, but a diversified 'management team.' Among others, such a team should include good analysts and research directors—who are not necessarily best produced, or only produced, in teachers' colleges and graduate schools of education.

An educational system, therefore, must call upon a wide assortment of its constituent parts to produce the kinds of skills, knowledge, and management instruments required for its effective functioning. The managers of space programs draw on and orchestrate knowledge from all the physical and biological sciences, and skills from all the technologies, just to put one man within reach of the moon. How much more must education draw on all the sources of learning to equip itself with men and instruments capable of managing school systems that can bring millions of young people to a place in the sun.

A further word to be added about recruitment recalls our earlier discussion of education's competitive disadvantage in the talent market. Education is big business these days. The chief local school administrator is often the biggest businessman in town—presiding over the largest budget, the most employees, and the largest bus system and restaurant chain, not to mention the destinies of the community's most precious asset, its children. Such responsibilities would logically call not only for the best executive talent anywhere available, but for rewards commensurate with these responsibilities. Yet salaries of most educational administrators—above all in the wealthiest countries—are typically more in line with the earnings of a medium-sized local merchant than with the earnings of important executives elsewhere in the economy. The wonder is that school systems and universities get as many first-rate administrators as they do. But they may not continue to do so, especially as the school administrator's job grows ever more demanding.

Some matters shine more brightly against a dark background, and on this account, one can take heart from the promise of things to be seen against the sombre background picture drawn of the general state of the managerial arts in education. In the United States, for example, there are these representative bright spots: leading graduate schools of education, working in concert through the Council on Educational Administration, are breaking new ground by experimenting with new practices in training school administrators, by conducting research on the problems and new techniques of administration, and by fashioning new instruments with the object of improving school administration. Significantly, they are exploring for the first time the potential management lessons for education by examining other fields where management practices have leaped ahead. And they are devising channels for lateral entry into school administration from the outside. Then, again, a few universities are developing new internal information flows and mechanisms for 'operations research' and 'systems analysis' to improve their decision-making, efficiency, and general performance. Numerous colleges and universities, with help from private foundations, have formulated and applied comprehensive long-range plans for their future development. Nor are these stirrings confined to the United States. Their counterparts, or movements in other pioneering directions, are visible in the Soviet Union, Canada, France, England, and the Scandinavian countries.

Still, the fact remains that while these signs of a much-needed managerial revolution in education are indeed hopeful, they are nevertheless exceptional. Taking matters in a world-wide aggregate, the management side of educational systems is entangled in a shroud of attitudes and methods carried over from the quiet, simpler past into a turbulent, seething present where new demands branch and flare on all sides. The great majority of nations have yet to establish their first programs for the professional development of managerial personnel and for research to improve managerial practices for education. The majority of universities in the world have yet to install a modern system of internal management in which administrators, teachers, and students all play appropriate roles. And most of the world has yet to take the matter seriously enough to treat top educational administrators on a parity with other top executive talent.

## Costs and Efficiency: Where the System Pinches

MEANING OF EDUCATIONAL EFFICIENCY AND PRODUCTIVITY · LACK OF INCENTIVES TO IMPROVE · REASONS FOR RISING COSTS · ILLUSTRATION OF THEIR IMPACT · NEW BUILDINGS COMMIT FUTURE BUDGETS · DROP-OUTS AND REPEATERS · EFFICIENCY PROMOTED BY SYSTEMS ANALYSIS · SEVEN BASIC PRINCIPLES · SOME ENCOURAGING EXAMPLES · NEED FOR UNCONVENTIONAL APPROACHES.

Our earlier discussions of teacher and financial inputs and fitness of outputs to the environment showed that it is imperative for educational systems to improve both their internal efficiency and their external productivity—in short, to get bigger, better, and more useful results from their available resources. It will help our further discussion if we pause here briefly in order to define these important terms more precisely.

Adverting to the schematic view of education as a 'system' given in Charts I and II in the opening chapter, we can here define the *internal efficiency* of the system as the *relationship of its output to its inputs*. Efficiency increases when any change is introduced in the process which causes this ratio to improve. Even though it is impossible, as we have said earlier, to get a full and precise measure of a whole educational system's output, this manner of looking at the matter can lead to new insights about how to improve the system's performance. In practice, it is much easier to assess the efficiency of particular sub-systems, whose objectives are more limited and definable, and whose results are more susceptible to evaluation. These might include the sub-systems for learning arithmetic, a foreign language, spelling, reading, or a science at one or another school level, or the sub-system for learning mechanical engineering at the university. If, for instance, some new method or some improved learning materials are introduced into the process which result in more learning, without a proportional increase in costs, the sub-system has been altered and its efficiency increased. In this context, it should be noted, unit costs become an important indicator of efficiency.

*External productivity*, meanwhile, can be defined as *the ultimate benefits accruing to students and to society from earlier educational investments (inputs)*. These benefits, of course, are even less precisely measurable than the immediate learning 'outputs' which students carry away from the system on the day they leave it. Yet the concept itself is useful in making a common-sense search for ways to improve external productivity. A change in the curriculum, for example, which substitutes something relevant for something irrelevant to the student's life and society, or which puts up-to-date content in place of obsolete content, has a high probability of raising external productivity. It should be noted that in this case, although the action taken was internal to the system, the ultimate effect was external to it. In practice, then, changes made inside an educational system—provided they are the right changes—can benefit *both* internal efficiency and external productivity.

What we have just said applies to the system's productivity, viewed from an external vantage point. But there is another meaning of the productivity concept which applies to the way in which any *particular* type of input of the system is used—such as its teachers or its buildings. This is analogous to the economist's meaning of 'factor productivity' (referring to the different 'factors of production'), when he speaks of the 'productivity of labor,' or of capital. In this sense, we may define the productivity of a particular educational input as the total output of the system relative to the amount of that particular factor used. The productivity of the various factors combined, obviously determines the efficiency of the system as we have just defined it.[35]

To keep all this from sounding too abstract and theoretical, let us show how it applies to the case of 'teacher productivity.' If teachers are given better tools to work with—such as more and better texbooks and other teaching materials, or language laboratories, or a teacher's aide to handle clerical and housekeeping chores, or good quality instructional radio or television programs—they may be able to teach more pupils, and the pupils may succeed in learning more in a given hour or academic year than under the previous combination of factors. The teacher himself may not 'work' any harder. However, he may enjoy his work a good deal more. With better tools, his professional capabilities are more fully utilized and he accomplishes larger and better results. His 'productivity' increases.

It is precisely in this way that the productivity of workers and professionals in other fields has been increased over the years, permitting them to enlarge their output per hour and to earn better salaries. Consider how many fewer patients today's doctor could handle if he were denied a car to make his rounds, and how much less he could do for their health if suddenly he were without his modern instruments, laboratory services, and prescriptions. The farmer, the factory worker, the engineer, the architect, the business executive have all increased their productivity—and their incomes—in the last two generations by adopting new tools and methods, and by subdividing tasks between themselves and their subordinates or others.

This modernization process has not yet gone far in education. No one who has objectively observed the educational process at work, or who has actually worked in it, can doubt for a moment that every educational system—including the most 'modern'—has abundant room for improvement of its efficiency and productivity. Improvement, of course, is far easier called for than achieved. As we observed in connection with management, educational systems lack the institutional means and the

35. Economists will recognize, we hope sympathetically, that in the interests of conveying the essential concepts of efficiency and productivity to noneconomists, we have simplified the matter by avoiding questions such as *marginal* productivity. We have also tried to define these concepts in ways which educators will see as relevant to their own enterprise.

modern analytical tools for identifying potential improvements of this sort and then taking advantage of them. Moreover, such improvements often involve changing familiar routines and adopting new techniques and new divisions of labor. Such changes, affecting many participants in the system, easily inspire resistance among many people who tend to see in a proposed innovation either a device for extracting more work from them for the same pay, or one for making their own job obsolete.

This points up the great importance of incentives to change. It also underlines another profound difference between education and other 'industries.' These other industries ordinarily sell their output on a market —the farmer his potatoes, the manufacturer his shoes. The farmer or manufacturer thus has a simple means for checking his efficiency: he can measure his 'earnings' by the difference between his input costs and sales receipts. Since his object is to maximize his 'earnings,' he has a strong incentive to introduce whatever changes of process or product promise to improve his 'output-input' ratio.

Education, unfortunately, has no such handy yardstick of its efficiency. Nor does it have any such built-in incentive to change. Such indirect incentives as one might conceive for an educational system, to improve its efficiency and productivity, are easily outweighed by the dis-incentives and the sheer inertia of the process. A good example of this has already been referred to in another connection. It is the fate of various attempts to adopt 'merit' systems of teacher pay and promotion, aimed at providing more individual incentive. While there are practical difficulties with any such schemes—and while particular 'merit pay and promotion' schemes have been favored by teachers' organizations in a few places like Yugoslavia—teachers' organizations in general have strongly opposed 'merit' systems. They claim that there is no objective way to judge a teacher's merit, or that the particular scheme being contemplated might be abused by administrators, or in any event, is 'undemocratic.'

Whatever the pros and cons of the 'merit pay' approach, teachers' organizations everywhere could greatly serve their profession and students if they resolutely searched for ways to create strong incentives to improve educational efficiency—and yet to protect other legitimate aims of the teaching profession. The suggestion, we think, is not farfetched. In a quite different context—namely, that of the United States coal-mining industry—precisely such an improvement scheme was supported by the United Mine Workers' Union, which helped restore health to the sick coal industry by collaborating with the mine owners on introducing innovations to increase the efficiency and labor productivity of the mines. The analogy should not be pressed beyond its natural limits. Yet if innovations raised teacher productivity and incomes as dramatically as they did in the case of coal miners, the educational crisis would be well on its way toward a solution. But, of course, producing good students is a good deal more complicated than mining coal.

Saying this, let us here recapitulate the main reasons why education now faces its greatest crisis of efficiency and productivity, as revealed in the way rising costs threaten to undo the fondest hopes of educators. What is to be read into the reasons is nothing more or less than what the words say. They do not say, for example, that larger classes are a cure for all ailments. Nor do they say that the particular causes of rising costs are either good or bad per se. They simply state the following objective realities:

Education is a 'labor-intensive' industry, using large amounts of high-level, high-cost manpower. In competing with less labor-intensive industries whose efficiency and labor productivity are steadily rising, education will continue to lose the race, badly, until it does more to improve its own efficiency and the productivity of the human talents it employs.

On the foregoing grounds, if education is to maintain a competitive position in the manpower market, educational salaries must keep on rising, even though educational efficiency and productivity do not. When education fails, for budgetary reasons, to maintain such a competitive position, it receives poor teachers instead of good ones. Then the educational 'Gresham's Law' goes to work, and the system sinks lower into mediocrity.

The need to strengthen teacher training, plus the substantial 'leakage' of trained teachers from the system, impose high 'capital costs' for each teacher who actually enters teaching and stays on.

Automatic salary increments and retirement benefits, which have their own justification, can nonetheless keep pushing up costs as the average age of the teacher corps rises, which it does when the expansion of the corps slows down.

The extreme spread between lower and upper salary scales in teacher pay structures, based on formal qualifications and the vertical echelons of the system, causes large increases in unit costs per student whenever poorly qualified teaching staff are upgraded or replaced by better qualified staff.

Costs per student enlarge quickly as overcrowded classes are brought back to normal size, and as the more costly secondary and higher levels of the system's 'pyramid' flesh out in relation to the primary level.

Increased emphasis on scientific and technical studies at the secondary and higher levels, which have inherently higher unit costs, further accelerate the rise in the over-all average of costs per student for the whole system.

TABLE 8

*Impact of rising costs on the elementary school budget of a hypothetical developing country over ten years*

A country of 5 million inhabitants, with a national income of $200 million ($40 per capita income)

|  | INITIAL YEAR | TEN YEARS LATER | |
|---|---|---|---|
|  |  | CASE A | CASE B |
| 1. Primary school age population | 1 200 00 | 1 536 000 | 1 536 000 |
| 2. Primary school enrollment ratio | 33% | 33% | 50% |
| 3. Primary school enrollment | 400 000 | 512 000 | 512 000 |
| 4. Over-all pupil-teacher ratio | 50/1 | 40/1 | 40/1 |
| 5. Number of teachers | 8 000 | 12 800 | 19 200 |
| of which: Qualified | 1 200 (15%) | 3 456 (27%) | 5 184 (27%) |
| Half-qualified | 2 000 (25%) | 6 144 (48%) | 9 216 (48%) |
| Nonqualified | 4 800 (60%) | 3 200 (25%) | 4 800 (25%) |
| 6. Annual salaries: (dollars) |  |  |  |
| Qualified | 1 800 | 1 800 | 2 304 |
| Half-qualified | 720 | 720 | 922 |
| Nonqualified | 300 | 300 | 384 |
| 7. Total current expenditure on primary education (dollars) | 6 000 000 | 14 500 000 | 27 855 000 |
| 8. Expenditure Index | 100 | 241 | 464 |

The combined effect of a few (not all) of the foregoing cost-increasing factors is demonstrated in the model presented in Table 8. While this model is fictitious, it is based on authentic data from several African countries. It suggests the order of magnitude of what could happen to elementary school costs alone in such situations over the next ten years, given the following assumptions:

In Case A: (1) the national student 'participation rate' stays constant at 33 per cent while the total age group in the population grows at 2.5 per cent each year; (2) the 'qualifications profile' of the teacher corps improves moderately; (3) basic teacher salary levels remain unchanged; and (4) the over-all pupil-teacher ratio improves from 50 to 1 to 40 to 1.

In Case B: the same assumptions hold, except that (1) the pupil 'participation rate' moves up to 50 per cent, and (2) the level of teacher salaries rises at an average of 2.5 per cent per year in line with incomes in the rest of the economy.

These are conservative assumptions, yet their consequence over ten years is to raise total recurrent costs of elementary schooling, in Case A, from $6 million to $14.5 million, and in Case B, from $6 million to about $28 million. And half or more of the nation's children would still not be in elementary school! These built-in forces of cost increase are like a time bomb ticking away under educational budgets. Any school system would be well advised to construct an appropriate cost model of this sort to fit its own situation.

Two further important points must be made about education's cost dilemma.

The first is the simple but often overlooked fact that a new building commits the system to sustained future recurrent costs, adding up quickly to more than the building itself costs. More research is needed on what this ratio (of initial investment costs to subsequent annual recurrent costs) actually is under different circumstances. But in France, for example, it seems at present to run in the neighborhood of 6 to 1 at the primary and secondary levels, and of about 7.5 to 1 at the university level. In other words, once a new school is built, the costs of running it each year thereafter are at least one-sixth of the original cost. A spot check in the Ivory Coast suggests a ratio of 5.8 to 1 at the primary level,[36] and in Uganda a similar ratio seems to hold for general secondary schools. Ratios in other places may well vary widely from these. But the essential point still holds. New capital investment in education—free or paid for—puts a mortgage on the system's future income. This needs to be watched with special care by developing countries, lest the new school building offered on easy terms, with the best of intentions, should turn out, as in the fable, to be a 'white elephant' which later will eat the recipient out of house and home.

The second point concerns the heavy cost impact of dropouts and repeaters, and of 'finishers' who end up never applying their extensive training to what was intended. The *average* cost per student, arrived at by dividing total enrollments into total costs, may grossly understate the actual cost of turning out one 'completed' student, and even more so the cost of those finishers who finally make good use of their training.

36. J. Hallak and R. Poignant, *Les Aspects financiers de l'éducation en Côte-d'Ivoire,* Monographies africaines, no. 8 (Paris: Unesco/IIEP, 1966).

In many developing countries, as we have said, fewer than half of those who enter primary school ever finish. Of those who do finish, more than half take more than the 'normal' time. In Gabon, Ivory Coast, and Mali, for example, of the students who completed the sixth grade, fewer than one-third made it in only six years; 40 per cent took seven years and the rest took eight or nine.[37]

The actual total cost per graduate, when the full costs of dropouts and repeaters are imputed to the *finished* products, is shown in Table 9. It contrasts the 'nominal' cost of a cycle, if each entering student actually finished 'on time,' with the 'actual' cost per graduate when total costs of repeating grades and of 'nonfinishers' are taken into account.

TABLE 9

*Unit cost by educational level in a Central American country in 1963/64*

| EDUCATIONAL LEVEL | NOMINAL COST PER PUPIL PER YEAR (DOLLARS) | NOMINAL LENGTH OF CYCLE, (IN YEARS) | THEORETICAL COST PER CYCLE (DOLLARS) | ACTUAL AVERAGE COST PER GRADUATE (DOLLARS) |
|---|---|---|---|---|
| Primary | 51 | 6 | 306 | 800 |
| Secondary (academic) | 104 | 5 | 520 | 2 970 |
| Secondary (vocational) | 217 | 5 | 1 085 | 5 285 |
| University | 391 | 5 | 1 955 | 9 739 |

*Source:* unpublished data.

Evidence of this sort makes it clear that educational managers everywhere must mount major campaigns aimed at raising educational efficiency and productivity. But how can they best go about this? What are the main points within their educational system where they should direct their attack? What options are available to them?

A two-part answer suggests itself. The first part enjoins them to plan their campaign on the basis of a systems analysis and several basic principles, and the second, to exploit the practical lessons of experience which already exist. We will look briefly at each of these.

As to the first, the same sort of systems analysis which we have used in these pages on a global scale can be profitably brought to bear on the specifics of any particular educational system. It is true that the techniques for doing so still require further refinement. This need not delay

37. J. Proust, 'Les Déperditions scolaires au Gabon,' and I. Deblé 'Rendements scolaires dans les pays d'Afrique d'expression française,' in *Etudes 'Tiers-Monde,' Problèmes de planification de l'éducation* (Paris: IEDES, 1964).

the matter, for the essential logic and method of the systems approach are already at hand. But it is necessary to apply them to the best facts already available in any given situation, while the search goes on for more and better facts and for more sophisticated techniques.

In thus applying a systems analysis as an aid to fashioning a strategy of action, it will be rewarding to keep in view the seven principles listed below. Some of these are familiar to any first-year student of economics, for they have been at the heart of all modern advancement in human productivity. Others are familiar to students of modern psychology and pedagogy, but have never been put to full use. Combined, these principles can be powerful working tools for reshaping and improving any educational system in an almost infinite variety of ways.

(1) *The principle of individual differences* tells us that students vary enormously in their individual aptitudes, rates of learning, and ways of learning; hence each will learn best when the means and conditions of learning are flexibly adapted to his particular pace and style. Conversely, when a 'teaching-learning' system is extensively used which tacitly ignores these wide individual differences, the educational efficiency in such a situation is bound to fall well below the optimum.

(2) *The principle of self-instruction* says that every student, whatever his aptitudes, has an inherent curiosity and capacity for learning a great deal on his own, provided he is properly motivated and guided, and is given access to the 'stuff of learning' in attractive and digestible form. Conversely, a youngster's natural curiosity and will to learn can be suppressed and even killed if he is exposed over long periods to conditions which cause him to associate 'learning' with fear, monotony, defeat, or irrelevance.

(3) *The principle of combining human energy and physical resources* states very simply that the 'work' accomplished by a human being (teacher or student) can be greatly increased by placing more and better tools and technologies at his disposal, and teaching him how to use these to best advantage.

(4) *The principle of economies of scale* reminds us that wherever expensive educational facilities and equipment are involved, the costs per student are likely to decline—with no loss of quality and effectiveness—as things are done on a larger scale, until the point where *dis*-economies of scale may set in. What may be prohibitively expensive on a small scale may be economically feasible on a large scale, and indeed may be the lowest cost approach.

(5) *The principle of division of labor* says that if people with differing

kinds and degrees of special competence break a complex job into its component parts, and if each person then handles the parts that best match his competence, each performs at his highest productivity, and the total result will be greater.

(6) *The principle of concentration and critical mass* says that it is wasteful to embark upon certain learning objectives unless they are going to be pursued beyond some minimum point of intensity and continuity, short of which the effort will have little if any worthwhile 'pay-off.'

(7) *The principle of optimizing* states that whenever several different components are combined in a productive 'system,' it is never possible for every component to be used to its theoretical maximum productivity, but the *optimum* over-all results will be achieved when the components are combined in such proportions as to use the scarcest and more expensive components most intensively, and the cheaper and more abundant ones less intensively. Optimizing an educational system or sub-system involves a process of 'trade-offs' designed to achieve the best combination of good learning results on the one hand, and tolerable economic costs on the other. The optimum arrangement from a purely economic point of view rarely coincides with the optimum arrangement from an educational point of view; thus in practice the most satisfactory compromise must be sought.

These principles, stated in abstract, may seem inert, but they can be brought to life and given practical meaning as we turn to the second side of the answer to the question asked above. Numerous educational systems have, in fact, made significant attempts over the past ten years to improve their efficiency and effectiveness. Their experiences warrant closer examination and wider dissemination. Here, for example, are some of the things they have tried, from which others might get useful clues:

*Reduction of school construction costs,* through the application of modern planning, engineering, and production methods, such as the well-known British and Mexican experiences; and methods now being encouraged by Unesco school construction centers in developing regions;[38]

*Redeployment and more intensive utilization of available space,* such

38. Educational Facilities Laboratories, Inc., *The Cost of a Schoolhouse* (New York, 1960); Interstate School Building Service, *Economies in School Construction* (Nashville, Tenn.: George Peabody College for Teachers, 1962); Mexico, Regional School-building Centre for Latin America, CONESCAL (Mexico, 1965 to date); United Kingdom Department of Education and Science, *Building Bulletin* (London, 1955 to date); and Unesco, various publications of the Regional School-building Centers for Africa and Asia, Khartoum and Colombo.

as year-round academic schedules adopted by certain United States universities; double shifts in primary schools in developing countries, such as Tunisia and several Latin American countries.[39] The latter is not considered a desirable long-run solution educationally, yet as an interim expedient, still heavily used by the U.S.S.R. and, in some cases, the United States, it has permitted more children to get proper schooling, evidently without serious injury to quality;

*Communication by radio and television of excellent teaching,* and of new and more up-to-date subject matter, and the extension of these means of educational services to new clients previously unserved, at much lower costs than by conventional means;[40]

*Lengthening of school hours* to provide more time for teaching and learning (in certain developing countries where school hours and the school year were much too brief to ensure satisfactory results);

*Sharing of expensive school facilities and specialized personnel* by two or more neighboring institutions (e.g., laboratories, athletic or eating facilities, auditoriums, courses of study, etc.) when this is possible without incurring heavy offsetting costs in transportation or boarding accommodations;

*Sharing of specialized high-cost university programs*[41] by neighboring states or nations, who can afford to accomplish together what they cannot afford to do alone (e.g., the University of East Africa, Central America, the Southern Regional Education Board, and several cooperating college groups in the United States, the Universities of Dakar and Abidjan);

*Use of teacher aides* in the classroom (i.e., paraprofessional 'helpers')

39. American Association of School Administrators, *Year-round School* (Washington, D.C., 1960); G. Oddie, *School Building Resources and Their Effective Use. Some Available Techniques and Their Policy Implications* (Paris: OECD, 1966); W. H. Stickler, and M. W. Carothers, *The Year-round Calendar in Operation* (Atlanta: Southern Regional Education Board, 1963); D. J. Vickery, *A Comparative Study of Multipurpose Rooms in Educational Buildings* (Bangkok: Unesco Regional Office for Education in Asia, 1964); D. C. Webb, *Year-round Operation of Universities and Colleges* (Montreal: Canadian Foundation for Educational Development, 1963); J. T. Shaplin, and H. F. Olds, *Team Teaching* (New York, Evanston, and London: Harper & Row, 1964); and J. L. Trump, *Images of the Future: A New Approach to the Secondary School* (Urbana, Illinois: Commission on the Experimental Study of the Utilization of the Staff in the Secondary School, 1959).

40. W. Schramm, *et al., op. cit.* (in particular, the summing up to Chapter 4, 'What do the new media cost?').

41. Consejo Superior Universitario Centroamericano, *Plan para la integración regional de la educación superior centroamericana* (Costa Rica, 1963); and Unesco, *The Development of Higher Education in Africa* (Paris, 1963), pp. 219, 238.

to handle clerical and housekeeping chores, thereby helping the regular teachers to do more direct teaching (e.g., numerous public schools in the United States);[42]

*Greater emphasis on well-planned self-instruction*—for example, use of programmed learning materials, 'teaching machines,' language laboratories, and good books, all of which enable students to move at their own pace and teachers to serve more students (e.g., numerous examples in North America and Europe; a few in developing regions);[43]

*Increased expenditure on textbooks and other 'learning aids,'* to enable students to learn more on their own, to raise teacher productivity, and to 'protect' students against poorly qualified teachers. (Unfortunately the reverse trend exists in many developing countries, where pressure of rising teacher costs has the counteracting effect of depressing allotments for instructional materials and school libraries);

*Application of modern management practices to school services,* including the running of bus services and cafeterias, procurement and stocking of textbooks and other supplies, building maintenance, and so forth. Simple operations analysis in a number of school systems and universities have revealed wide room for improving such services and lowering costs.

*Consolidation of undersized educational institutions* into larger, more efficient and better quality units. This applies especially to secondary schools and small teacher training institutions. (But several Latin American countries have run the other way in proliferating astonishing numbers of 'mini-universities,' which cannot possibly hope to be either educationally or economically viable.)[44]

*Rationalizing the location and size of schools* to serve a scattered student population best, at least cost (e.g., research in the Netherlands applying 'location theory' to education; the allocation of specialized sec-

42. M. Blair, and R. G. Woodward, *Team Teaching in Action* (Boston: Houghton Mifflin Company, 1964); Central Michigan College, *A Co-operative Study for the Better Utilization of Teacher Competencies* (Mount Pleasant, Mich., 1955); K. Lovell, *Team Teaching* (Leeds: University of Leeds Institute of Education, 1967); and J. L. Trump, *Images of the Future, op. cit.*

43. P. K. Komoski, and E. J. Green, *Programmed Instruction in West Africa and the Arab States,* a report on two training workshops (Paris: Unesco, 1964); A. A. Lumsdaine, and R. Glaser, *Teaching Machines and Programmed Learning,* I (Washington, D. C.: National Education Association of the United States), 1960, I; 1965, II; and Fund for the Advancement of Education, *Four Cases of Programmed Learning* (New York, 1964).

44. Interstate School Building Service, *School Construction, op. cit.;* and Unesco, 'Provisional Report of the Meeting of Experts on Higher Education and Development in Latin America,' University of Costa Rica, San José, 15-24 March 1966, in *Higher Education and Development in Latin America* (Paris: Unesco, 1966), pt. II, p. 8.

ondary vocational training facilities among different Lebanese towns, on the basis of comparative cost studies of alternative patterns).

Even this brief and assorted list makes clear that there are many opportunities for achieving improvements in educational efficiency. It also makes clear that there is no single panacea. The task must be approached from many angles, at many points, and with enormous determination.

Most of the foregoing types of action involve no striking departures from conventional practice. They can unquestionably, when imaginatively and vigorously applied, achieve considerable gains. But the question remains whether conventional measures such as these will suffice to solve the problem. Our own guess is that something more is needed. We need a fundamentally new strategic approach which breaks the shackles of convention and dares to contemplate innovations of a sort we readily accept in other realms of life but which, for lack of courage or imagination, we have scarcely yet dreamed of in the vital realm of human learning and development.

Curiously enough, it is far harder to innovate in formal education than to do the unconventional thing in nonformal education—the topic to which we now turn.

# V

# Nonformal Education: To Catch Up,
# Keep Up, and Get Ahead

A MOTLEY BUT VITALLY IMPORTANT ASSORTMENT · NO CLEAR
INVENTORY OR ASSESSMENT AVAILABLE · SCATTERED SPONSORSHIP AND
ADMINISTRATION · MAJOR 'SHADOW' SYSTEMS OF EDUCATION HAVE
PROLIFERATED IN INDUSTRIALIZED COUNTRIES · THEIR IMPORTANT
ECONOMIC AND CULTURAL AIMS · NEEDS AND PRIORITIES OF DEVELOPING
COUNTRIES ARE DIFFERENT · RURAL AND AGRICULTURAL DEVELOPMENT
MERITS A HIGH PRIORITY · SOME PRACTICAL OBSTACLES · COMMON
NEEDS OF ALL NATIONS.

Up to this point we have made only occasional reference to that be-
wildering assortment of nonformal educational and training activities that
constitute—or should constitute—an important complement to formal education in any nation's total education effort. These activities go by different names—'adult education,' 'continuing education,' 'on-the-job training,' 'accelerated training,' 'farmer or worker training,' and 'extension
services.' They touch the lives of many people and, when well aimed,
have a high potential for contributing quickly and substantially to individual and national development. They can also contribute much to
cultural enrichment and to individual self-realization.

There is, therefore, a wide general agreement that this shadowy 'other
system' of education is important and warrants greater attention. Yet one
gathers from the scanty evidence that the many bold words about the
matter have seldom been matched by equally bold deeds. One evident
reason for this is that in contrast to the relative neatness and coherence
of the formal education system, nonformal educational activities are an
untidy mélange that defies simple description, or the diagnosis and measurement of systematic planning. Few nations have even a moderately

138

good inventory of their present activities in this realm, much less an assessment of future needs and how best to meet them. (IIEP attempted such an inventory in Tanzania and Senegal.)[1]

The aims of these activities are often unclear, their clienteles undefined, and responsibility for their management and funding scattered across dozens of public and private agencies. They spring up spontaneously, come and go, at times succeed brilliantly but just as often die unnoticed and unmourned. Nobody in particular is in charge of monitoring them, of keeping their evolving pattern in over-all perspective, of identifying gaps that need filling and projecting future requirements, or of suggesting priorities and better ways of harmonizing them and boosting their efficiency and effectiveness.

The matter is further beclouded if one fails to distinguish clearly between the needs for nonformal education of the more industrialized countries and those of the less advanced ones.

### The Case of Industrialized Nations

The industrialized countries of Europe and North America have increasingly come to recognize that formal education—to whatever level—must be followed by appropriate forms of 'continuing education' throughout each person's life.[2] Life-long education is essential in a rapidly progressing and changing society for three primary reasons: (1) to ensure the employment mobility of individuals, and to make unemployable 'dropouts' of the past employable; (2) to keep already well-trained people abreast of new knowledge and technologies essential to their continued high productivity in their respective fields; and (3) to improve the quality and satisfaction of individual lives through culturally enriching their expanding leisure time. In this perspective, the continuing education of teachers, at all levels, is of special strategic significance; if they fail to keep up with the frontiers of knowledge they will be giving yesterday's education to tomorrow's citizens.

In response to these several requirements, there has evolved very rapidly in most industrialized countries an astonishing network of 'continuing education' programs. It is entirely possible that in some countries

1. See J. King, *Planning Non-formal Education in Tanzania*, African research monographs, No. 16 (Paris: Unesco/IIEP, 1967); and P. Fougeyrollas, F. Sow, and F. Valladon, *L'Education des adultes au Sénégal*, Monographies africaines, no. 11 (Paris: Unesco/IIEP, 1967).
2. See Appendix 31.

(e.g., the United States and the Soviet Union) the aggregate of economic resources and human energies already committed to these part-time programs approaches the total involved in full-time formal education.

The full truth of the matter here is unknown, but an effort by Professor Harold Clark of Columbia University to take stock of the situation in the United States led to some startling conclusions. He found that, in addition to the 'formal' education system, there were at least three 'informal' educational systems, largely hidden from view but extensively engaged in teaching many of the same things. One was run by private business, a second by the military establishment, and the third embraced a motley assortment of educational activities sponsored by private voluntary organizations.[3] Some giant industrial firms, as nearly as Professor Clark could calculate (the accounting records are never clear on these matters), were spending about as much on the high-level training of their employees and customers as the instructional budgets of some of the nation's largest universities—often on the very same subjects. He found also that the amount of 'Sunday school' space in the churches of some communities equaled the classroom space of local public schools. An incidental discovery he made was that private yacht clubs were giving the same navigation courses as the Naval Academy at Annapolis, and that their students often did better than the future naval officers in the same examinations. The military services, on the other hand, were providing such good civilian technical training to military personnel that they were rapidly losing them to private employers.

Much the same phenomenon has occurred in western Europe, though not yet to the same extent as in the United States.[4] The accomplishments of the Scandinavian countries in the field of adult education have been noteworthy. The French government has lately given increased attention to special training and retraining programs for adults.[5] Adult education

3. See H. F. Clark, and H. S. Sloan, *Classrooms in the Factories* (Institute of Research, Farleigh Dickinson University, Rutherford, New Jersey, 1958); H. F. Clark, H. S. Sloan, C. A. Hebert, *Classrooms in the Stores* (Sweet Springs, Mo.: Roxbury Press, Inc., for the Institute for Instructional Improvement, Inc., 1962); and H. F. Clark, and H. S. Sloan, *Classrooms in the Military* (New York: Bureau of Publications, Teachers College, Columbia University, for the Institute for Instructional Improvement, Inc., 1964).

4. See A. A. Liveright, 'Observations on Developments in the Field of Higher Adult Education in 1965,' limited circulation statement at the Center for the Study of Liberal Education for Adults, Boston, February 1965.

5. See 'La Formation professionnelle des adultes,' in *Notes et études documentaires,* no. 3104, 9 July 1964, Paris, Sécrétariat général du gouvernement, Direction de la documentation.

in the Federal Republic of Germany and the United Kingdom, largely through private auspices, has taken on new life since 1945. Industrial firms throughout Europe are stepping up their in-service training and career development programs (though apparently too slowly to keep pace with their needs). The military services are training computer programers, electronics technicians, and the like, who end up in civilian jobs.

The U.S.S.R. and other socialist countries of Europe have all along attached high importance to 'continuing education' and have made impressive strides in pursuit of it. They appear to have gone farther than most Western nations in breaking down the artificial barriers that have perpetuated for too long an unwholesome separation between formal and nonformal education. As a result, there is a continuing dialogue in the socialist countries between the universities and technical schools, the industries they serve, and the pioneers of industrial research. Two questions are central to the dialogue: (1) the adequacy of the existing educational programs, and how they might be improved, and (2) what new types of manpower will be needed for new types of technologies still on the horizon, and hence what innovations are needed now in educational programs in order to meet these new needs. Beyond this, the educational systems in these countries have forged an unusually close relationship between work and study. Thus about half the students enrolled in university engineering programs in the Soviet Union are part-time students with regular jobs. They do much of their learning by correspondence, and more recently by television as well, along with periodic study periods at the university.[6] There are numerous opportunities for an able and ambitious worker in the Soviet Union to advance himself by 'going back to school,' without heavy personal sacrifice. University professors, in turn, are obliged, and given time off, to keep pace with relevant new developments in their own fields, such as computer programming, in order to keep their research capabilities from growing obsolete. Other professionals, such as doctors, are obliged and enabled to keep pace with new knowledge and techniques in their respective fields.

This proliferation of shadow systems of education will surely continue apace in the industrialized countries. The need is evident, the motivation is strong, and the resources can be found. Besides keeping people up to date, these more flexible programs are compensating for the deficiencies of the formal educational system which stem from its failure to adapt rapidly enough to changing needs.

6. Nozhko, *et al.*, *op. cit.*

All this underscores the importance of evolving a more coherent view of the 'nonformal educational system' to facilitate a more effective co-ordination of its many parts with each other and with formal education.

The same conditions that created the need for 'continuing education' in these countries have also made necessary a fundamental redefinition of the role of formal education. In this new context of rapid change, the prime role of formal education—as we have several times stressed—must be to 'teach people to learn for themselves' so that they can later absorb new knowledge and skills efficiently on their own. Even the greatest universities cannot hope to turn out 'educated' people—in the sense that they have 'completed' their education. Their aim and hope must be to turn out educable people, well prepared for a life of learning—which is a quite different matter.

### The Case of the Developing Nations

The developing countries are presently in a very different position with respect to nonformal education. Because they do not have the same broad economic base or the same broad base of popular education as the developed countries to build on, they face quite another set of urgent needs and priorities. When this fact is overlooked, the well-meant efforts of 'adult education specialists' from industrialized nations to apply their own doctrines, priorities, and methods to developing countries can prove useless or worse.

The poorer countries now face a priority task of nonformal education which years ago confronted today's industrialized countries. It is to bring to the vast numbers of farmers, workers, small entrepreneurs, and others who have never seen the inside of a formal classroom—and perhaps never will—a spate of useful skills and knowledge which they can promptly apply to their own and their nation's development.[7]

Another priority task is to upgrade the competence of partially qualified people—teachers, for example—already holding jobs in the private and public sector, so that they can more effectively perform the jobs. Indeed, this kind of in-service training can be the key to improving the quality and efficiency of educational systems, government administrations, and small enterprises. Further, there is the immense task, emphasized by Guy Hunter in his Tanzania study,[8] of salvaging the edu-

7. See Appendix 32.
8. G. Hunter, *Manpower, Employment and Education in the Rural Economy of Tanzania*, African research monographs, No. 9 (Paris: Unesco/IIEP, 1966).

cational investment represented by those thousands who leave primary school, secondary graduates, and dropouts who as yet have no jobs, but who can be fitted for some kind of employment with appropriate forms of special training (the counterpart of the training tasks now being undertaken in the United States under the Economic Opportunity Program and its Job Corps).

Given the extreme scarcity of their time and resources, these nations can ill-afford to dissipate them on a wrong order of priorities. For example, they can ill-afford to dissipate them on indiscriminate popular literacy campaigns that may have little impact on development goals, or on extramural university adult education programs designed to feed the personal enthusiasms of already educated persons for 'consumption' education. As desirable as these things are, priority must go to 'investment' education at this stage, and to people who can make it pay off for the ultimate benefit of all. Unesco, for one, has recognized this necessity. It has thus urged its member states in Africa, Asia, and Latin America to direct their pilot literacy projects to *work-oriented* learning and to carefully selected groups within their active labor force whose productivity can be most quickly and substantially increased by well-tailored literacy programs.[9] The concept of literacy is thus enlarged in object to include making farmers and workers 'literate' in useful, modern techniques which they can put to practical use.

With a world-wide food shortage looming ever more ominously, and with the economic growth of many developing countries being hobbled by lack of sufficient effort to modernize their agricultural and rural sectors, it is clear that farmer training, extension services, and the training of rural leaders (innovators and entrepreneurs of several sorts) must be a major objective of nonformal education in the years immediately ahead. Fortunately, it has already been well shown—in Kenya, to cite but one example—that well-conceived short training courses for practicing farmers and their wives (even if they cannot read) can have a quick and handsome yield, provided they are followed up with effective advisory services and are complemented by the other necessary ingredients of a well-integrated agricultural development campaign.

But a special set of difficulties must be reckoned with here. The problem of training farmers and rural leaders, it appears, is less one of know-

9. See Unesco, *Literacy: Three Pilot Projects,* reprints from the *Unesco Chronicle,* XI, no. 12 (Paris, December 1965); XII, no. 3 (March 1966); and Mary Burnet, *ABC of Literacy* (Paris: Unesco, 1965).

ing what is needed than of achieving the proper organization and staff for getting it done. In this connection, the lack of economic resources is often far less of an obstacle than the tangled maze of conflicting jurisdictions and uncoordinated efforts by numerous agencies having a hand in agricultural and rural affairs. It seems imperative to redeploy human talent and energies from the least productive forms of administration to the most productive forms of farmer and rural training.

Another major obstacle that the poorer countries face (along with richer ones) is the lack of organizational means for bringing important forms of nonformal education within the purview of educational planning—since the latter has typically been confined to formal education and sometimes not even to all of that. In the absence of over-all planning there is no rational basis for setting priorities, for allocating scarce resources, or for choosing the proper balance and division of labor between various types of formal and nonformal education aimed at related objectives. One gets the distinct impression from very sparse available evidence that in most developing countries too small a share of total available educational resources has been allocated to nonformal education.[10] Furthermore, the meager resources actually allocated to nonformal education are too often wasted for lack of a clear strategy, good planning, firm priorities, and workable administrative arrangements.

Despite the wide differences noted between the industrialized and the developing countries, they nonetheless share certain important needs with respect to nonformal education. First, they must get a clearer picture of what they are already doing and how well they are doing it—this, as a basis for fashioning ways to do it better, to fill important gaps, and to cut down on the less important activities in favor of the more important. Second, they need to bring about a more effective relationship between formal and nonformal education, to break down the wall between them, and to achieve a more efficient division of labor between the two. Third, to do all these things, they need to apply effective forms of research to this largely unresearched yet vitally important sector of education.

In their efforts to meet these needs, all countries can learn from and assist one another considerably—a subject of broad dimension to which we will next turn our attention.

10. See, for example, Hunter's conclusions on Tanzania in Appendix 33.

# VI

# International Cooperation: A Key to

# Meeting the Crisis

---

## Education's World-Wide Common Market

MUTUAL BENEFITS OF EDUCATIONAL COMMERCE AMONG NATIONS ·
IMPORTANCE OF INDIVIDUALS IN FOSTERING THIS COMMERCE · MAIN
COMPONENTS.

Statesmen and their advisers are struggling hard these days to create regional common markets through which economic goods may flow in greater abundance. Educational systems, however, already have their own common market, and have had one for a very long time. It is world-wide, and its 'volume of trade' has boomed in the past twenty years—in size, diversity, and geographic scope. Even so, its potential benefits have as yet been scarcely realized.

Can this international exchange in educational and cultural goods be deployed to help solve the educational crisis which all the members of the educational common market share? The question states and frames our central concern here. Before coming to it directly, however, several intermediate questions must first be considered. How has this enlarged international exchange in recent years affected the crisis now at hand? Has it in some ways helped to precipitate the crisis? Has it in the main been a neutral force? Or has it served to keep the crisis from becoming even more acute?

A look at some key features of this exchange system may put these questions in clearer focus, as will, perhaps, a reference back to Chart III, outlining the relationships between one nation's educational system and others in the world.

Behind this diagram lie several facts of capital importance, of which the first is this: Virtually every national educational system is an integral part of a world-wide educational system, and the same can be said of the 'intellectual community' of each nation—some of whose members work outside the boundaries of the educational system yet are a major adjunct of it. This is not only true in theory but is a vibrant functional reality. Indeed, any educational system which tries to seal itself off from this world community is bound to be afflicted with gangrene, as surely as a human limb cut off from the arterial circulation of blood. And what the system suffers, its society is bound to suffer too.

A second fact explains why this is the case. Educational commerce among nations is almost always and everywhere mutually beneficial. One proof of this can be found in the fairly recent experiences of the Eastern and Western nations. In the darkest days of political tension, with economic trade between them all but dried up, these nations—including the United States and the Soviet Union—found it to their mutual advantage to maintain educational and cultural exchanges. The benefits are now beyond doubt, and the process continues. The exchange may have helped their respective economies to grow faster. But most observers would agree that a far more important benefit was to keep the channels for intellectual and cultural discourse open, even though the channels for other dialogues were frozen. An important effect was to help destroy mischievous myths and false images, harbored by each party about the other. The exchange helped to broaden and deepen authentic mutual understanding, through first-hand observation and face-to-face dialogue. The exchange also stimulated and enriched each of the educational systems involved. It did the same on an individual basis for the many creative scholars, writers, and artists who at last confronted each other in a world forum, which they sensed all along was their proper place.

Another proof of the mutual benefits of world-wide intellectual exchange is found in the realm of science and technology. Here, every nation has learned that free trade in knowledge and in scholars is imperative to the progress of each. Some barriers still impede this scientific interchange. But there is no denying the fact that the scientists in recent years—aided by Unesco, other international organizations, by governments, and by voluntary professional societies—have been exemplars of an intellectual cooperation which the carriers of other forms of knowledge would do well to use as a model. Melville said of the intellectual giants who lead such an intellectual exchange: 'For genius, all over the world, stands hand in hand with genius, and one shock of recognition runs the whole circle around.'[1]

This brings us to the third important fact behind our diagram—a fact sometimes obscured by the institutional superstructure facilitating the intellectual exchange. It is that *individuals* really make the wheels go round in the common market of free intellectual exchange. Institutions, of course, are essential. This is true above all of the universities in every land. They are—or should be—the main props of the whole intellectual structure. In the last analysis, however, it is the individual scholars, teachers, and students who come and go from these institutions that give the common enterprise its vitality, its failure or success, its poverty or richness. James Perkins summed it up this way:

> It is from the university that the intellectual emerges to join his fellows in other lands, and to which he must return to re-examine, retest and reformulate his ideas before sending them out in the world again.

Perkins reminds us also that there are ground rules in this system of international exchange which impose special demands and obligations upon its members. They include:

> an overriding commitment to the search for truth; a dedication to the objective stance; a rejection of prejudice based on a distaste for what is different; a realization that the scholarly search has no end; a willingness to examine and re-examine matters that seem to be settled.[2]

A fourth fact to be noted is that the trade which takes place among educational systems does not fit into tidy packages with clear labels. It is diffuse and many-colored. Still, for convenience of analysis and discussion, most of its assorted components can be loosely sorted into three categories: (1) *knowledge and ideas*—transported through the printed word, on films, by electronic means, or in people's heads; (2) *individuals* —teachers, students, researchers, experts, and others; and (3) *physical facilities, equipment, and supplies*—sent from one country to another and useful for the technology of the educational process.

1. Quoted in James A. Perkins, 'The International Dimension of the University,' an address delivered by the Cornell University president before the Women's Planning Committee of the Japan International Christian University Foundation, New York, October 1966.
   2. *Ibid.*

To facilitate exchange in these three forms, another ingredient is often necessary, namely, money—money for scholarships and fellowships, for sending experts and teachers 'on loan,' for acquiring supplies and equipment and for constructing buildings.

This brings us to the final important fact behind the diagram. It is that the principle of mutual benefit, the ground rules and the importance of individuals in making the exchange system work—all these apply with equal force to educational transactions between industrialized countries and less developed ones. Many such transactions these days go under the label of 'external assistance' or 'foreign aid,' and this fosters popular notions of a *one*-way flow. In reality, however, the benefits almost invariably flow in *two* directions. The point was succinctly put by Ricardo Diez-Hochleitner, a departmental director at Unesco: 'Technical assistance cannot continue to be looked at as one-way traffic. All countries need some specialized manpower from other countries, in the same way as they need material products from each other. . . . In the future, should we not perhaps replace technical assistance by a concept of technical co-operation?'[3]

Anyone who has been part of this flow—the teacher, the professor, the adviser, or the scientist who has gone abroad to 'help' another nation's educational system—will usually affirm that he came home the richer for the experience. If any such visitor has the eyes to see, the ears to hear, and the mind to learn what another culture is about, he can hardly avoid taking home a rich harvest. His new insights and knowledge will be even deeper if he goes out of his way to initiate close contact with his foreign colleagues, for they very likely see the world, the same academic subject, the educational process itself, in a very different light. And it is not only the itinerant individuals who benefit from this confrontation of diverse perceptions. Educational institutions and nations also benefit when they lend a share of their human resources to others. Their own students, faculties, and knowledge are eventually enriched by what is brought back from overseas by their own teachers and researchers, as well as by foreign visitors. The only thing they sacrifice is parochialism.

So much for the basic features of the educational common market.

Let us now examine more closely the part of the total volume of international trade in education which is called 'external assistance' or 'foreign

3. Ricardo Diez-Hochleitner, 'Technical Assistance to Developing Countries in the Field of Education,' a working paper of the Working Group on Education at the Ninth World Conference of the Society for International Development, Milan, 7-11 June 1967.

aid.' In doing so, our main object is to define the bearing the latter has on the world educational crisis, and what it can do to help overcome the crisis.

## *External Assistance and the Crisis*

THE QUANTITATIVE DIMENSIONS · STRATEGIC IMPORTANCE OF AID ·
SELF-SUPPORT BY POOR COUNTRIES · RECENT DECLINE OF AID VOLUME ·
QUALITATIVE DIMENSIONS · ATTEMPTS TO EVALUATE AID RESULTS ·
LESSONS OF EXPERIENCE · HOW AID HAS AGGRAVATED THE CRISIS ·
FUTURE NEEDS.

Perhaps because we hear so much about it, it is tempting to think of 'external assistance' between developed and developing nations as constituting the bulk of the international trade in education. In reality, it is only a small portion of the whole—though a highly strategic one. The major portion of the world's entire educational intercourse takes place among industrialized nations, with only a minor share coming under 'official' programs, such as the Fulbright Program (which has been largely managed by academic people themselves on a bilateral basis). There is no doubt, however, that official exchanges have stimulated nonofficial exchanges among industrialized nations since World War II and have added an important accent on mutual understanding and mutual benefits.

Even in the case of the greatly expanded educational traffic between industrialized and developing nations, a surprisingly large share takes place outside the framework of official government programs, and outside 'organized' private programs, such as those supported by private foundations. It appears, for example, that well over half of the students from developing nations who study at the universities of western Europe and North America do so on an individual basis, without official support or organized private sponsorship.[4] While available evidence suggests that

4. 'In fairness, it should be pointed out that the great majority of developing country nationals studying abroad are not financed in this way [i.e., with an official support]. . . .' OECD, *Technical Assistance to Developing Countries. Problems of Requirements and Supply* (Paris: Development Assistance Committee, Working Party on Assistance Requirements, 1968).

these nonsponsored foreign students, who are in the majority, are the more likely candidates for the 'brain drain,' exchange programs, sponsored by governments and major private organizations, have a comparatively good record of returning their exchange participants back to their home base.

The picture is very different with regard to teachers, professors, scientists, educational advisers, as well as capital funds for educational facilities and equipment, flowing *from* industrialized nations to developing countries. Here the external assistance programs of international agencies, individual governments, and major foundations account for a heavy portion of the total traffic. Unesco, for example, both through its own budget and in collaboration with the United Nations Development Program, the World Bank, and Unicef, has become a major positive force in the educational life of many of its member states in Africa, Asia, and Latin America. The major bilateral programs have likewise had a considerable impact upon education in many developing countries.

There are, unfortunately, no fully satisfactory figures to draw on in trying to sketch an over-all picture of the size, form, sources, and geographic distribution of educational assistance to developing countries. But the following rough approximations will suggest the general magnitude and shape of things.[5] Developing countries as a whole are spending around ten billion dollars annually on education. This is roughly 4 per cent of their aggregate GNP, or something like 250 billion dollars. Of the total educational expenditures, it appears that about one billion dollars, or 10 per cent, comes from external sources. In turn, somewhere between 10 and 20 per cent of this total external assistance to education comes through United Nations and other multilateral agencies, and the remaining 80 to 90 per cent through bilateral channels, private as well as governmental. Of the total external assistance to education, private sources probably account for 10 to 20 per cent, the rest being financed directly and indirectly by governments.

How is this total external assistance to education distributed as among different forms and objectives? Apparently 10 to 20 per cent goes into scholarships and fellowships, mostly for study abroad; another 20 to 30 per cent goes for 'hardware' such as buildings and equipment. The remaining 60 to 70 per cent is accounted for by personnel—mostly teachers, educational experts, and advisers sent to assist developing countries.

5. See Appendix 34.

In 1965, over 35,000 'technical assistance' teachers and another 8000 volunteer teachers were serving in developing countries.[6]

The picture showing the geographical distribution of the educational assistance is an uneven one, with great variations between regions and between countries within them. The over-all average of external assistance to the developing countries—amounting to 10 per cent of the total educational outlays of those countries—breaks down into a wide range, running from as little as 1 per cent for some countries to 30 per cent or more for others. Asian and Latin American nations seem to fall generally into a range of 1 to 5 per cent, English-speaking African countries into a range of 12 to 15 per cent, and a number of French-speaking African nations reach as high as 30 per cent.[7]

Three other important points stand out in a perspective view of the *quantitative* dimensions of external assistance to education. First, educational assistance accounts for a relatively small part—in the order of one-tenth—of total development assistance of all sorts, including loans, but for a somewhat higher proportion of total 'technical assistance.' With two or three important exceptions such as France, few 'donor' nations and few international agencies other than Unesco appear to be giving a high priority to educational development, though some are giving it greater attention than was the case several years ago. Second, the over-all amount of educational assistance, like development assistance generally, has leveled off in recent years and, allowing for inflationary factors, has probably declined since 1961. In any event, the developing countries are supporting the overwhelming proportion of their total educational development burden with their own resources. Finally, most developing countries are concentrating half or more of their own educational effort at the primary level, where outside help is minimal; hence external assistance has its greatest significance at the secondary and university levels and in teacher training. Within these educational sectors, the largest effort has gone into new institutions and programs such as intermediate and higher technical institutes, science education, new types of secondary schools, teacher training, and work-oriented literacy.

Even more important than the quantitative dimensions of external assistance are the *qualitative* dimensions. There is undoubtedly a rough

6. See Appendix 34.
7. See, for example, L. Cerych, *L'Aide extérieure et la planification de l'éducation en Côte-d'Ivoire*, Monographies africaines, no. 12 (Paris: Unesco/IIEP, 1967), and *The Integration of External Assistance . . . , op. cit.*

sort of correlation between the size of the assistance effort and its effectiveness. But even small specific efforts can at times have a beneficial impact out of all proportion to their cost if the right man is in the right
place at the right time, with the right assignment. The able and creative
planning adviser, for example, makes an immeasurably important contribution if he succeeds in helping the host country to plan its educational development better and thus use its own resources more productively. This is true also of the foreign expert who helps a country
revise its curriculum and create more relevant and effective teaching
materials to go with it, or who helps design cheaper yet better school
buildings, or who helps set up a viable work-oriented literacy program
or farmer training program. It is again true of the visiting professor who
stays around long enough to train twenty first-rate school administrators
or fifty good teachers. Any one of these different kinds of visitor may
help a developing country to negotiate an historically important educational turn, at modest investment in external assistance.

This is not to say that external assistance is a bargain basement. It is
not. It is only to say that quality counts even more than quantity, and
that more of both is needed. Not every foreign expert or teacher, of
course, turns out to be a 'winner.' Being human, and not always well
chosen or well trained for what is one of the most exacting, delicate,
and challenging assignments in the world, some turn out to be mediocre
and contribute little. Nor do all the new educational institutions and
programs which foreign experts and money help to create, turn out to
be 'winners.' In extreme cases, some never get off the ground. Others
that manage to do so, do not fit the local situation, but may linger on to
become a problem to the host country.

But what can be said on balance about the efficacy of educational assistance taken as a whole? If one must prove one's conclusions with
scientifically established facts, very little can be said in answer to the
question. Unfortunately, after many years of experience, and after many
millions of dollars have been devoted to educational assistance, there
still is little solid and systematic evidence for judging the efficacy even
of individual projects, much less the net benefits of the over-all effort.

Still, this is not surprising to anyone who has seen the effort in action.
Everyone involved in it has been too busy trying to move ahead to find
time for retrospective reflections. Moreover, there is a high rotation of
the people and the posts concerned. Many individual experts who move
from post to post and country to country do in fact accumulate a good

deal of experience and wisdom in the process. But their agencies have not taken full advantage of this fact and, having failed to learn the lessons of experience, have often repeated old mistakes. This is not the universal case, but it is a common enough phenomenon to warrant comment.

Repeated proclamations about the need to evaluate projects and programs are usually sounded in the midst of a budget battle, or just after one has been lost. But these have been rarely followed up with the funds and talent necessary for such evaluations. Even if they were, however, any such evaluations would be at best extremely difficult, and their conclusions would be tenuous. A specific project has to be conspicuously successful, or close to disastrous, before a sober man will stand firm by unqualified findings, for he knows that his assessment may prove to be incomplete and premature. Side effects, not intended or anticipated, but emerging years later, may prove far more important than success or collapse of the original objective.

Still, in the face of all grounds for doubt, a positive note must be struck: anyone who has traveled in this realm of development is forced to the general conclusion that despite many failures, the years of external assistance to educational development have had a very sizable and salutary impact on the recipient countries. John Hilliard of the Ford Foundation—himself a veteran worker in overseas development—explored the claims and counterclaims made in the over-all field of development assistance, and his conclusions apply to the specific field of education. He found both types of claims defective, and this led him to say:

> Perhaps a more valid appraisal is found in the fact that many of the underdeveloped countries have made real and visible progress . . . there is undeniably a change in the climate of development, a perceivable connection with the future, better trained people, purposeful instructions, physical infrastructure, that were not there ten years ago . . . There also remain massive and enduring problems in all these areas, plus increasingly evident problems in population growth, urbanization, political maturity, and systems of communication essential to nationhood and international cooperation.[8]

To speak specifically of the educational crisis: it must be conceded that external assistance programs, despite their evident benefits, may well have contributed to the crisis in two substantial ways. For one thing, they may have heightened and accelerated the already strong popular

8. John F. Hilliard, *A Perspective on International Development* (Washington, D.C.: American Council on Education, 1967), a Ford Foundation reprint.

demand for education and stimulated bolder promises by local leaders than were warranted that this demand would be met. The very fact that outsiders shared their enthusiasm for education, and seemed to proffer sizable help in that direction, may have encouraged many insiders to inflate their own hopes and promises beyond the bounds of feasibility. But even if this is so—and no one can prove it absolutely true or false—the result can hardly be viewed as a case of willful wrongdoing. A cardinal wrong would have occurred if the peoples and leaders of developing countries had remained indifferent to the importance of education as a crucial lever for developing themselves and their nation.

In a second respect, referred to previously, one can more reasonably criticize the effects produced by outside helpers. Often, in good faith, developing countries have been encouraged and enticed to emulate the 'donor' countries' own educational models and practices—even when they were conspicuously ill-suited to the needs and circumstances of the imitating countries. This practice and its consequences are too well known to require elaboration here. It is perhaps enough to stress one point: to the degree that the educational crisis of developing countries stems from the unsuitability of their educational systems to their circumstances, the problem is not entirely of their own making. They have had plenty of 'expert help' from the outside.

The immediate question, however, is not what has been accomplished or not accomplished by educational assistance thus far, but what has been *learned* from past experiences that can now be put to good use in the task of shaping a better future. Certainly a good deal has been learned; a good many improvements have been made; and there is a greater awareness of the many practical difficulties that remain to be attacked in order to make the whole foreign assistance effort more efficient and effective. Because there have already been numerous candid and useful discussions among the parties interested—along with many serious inquiries, and outpourings of memos, reports, and articles on the matter —we need not dwell on the specific details of corrective action.[9] But for

9. Unesco, *Appraisal of Unesco's Programmes for the Economic and Social Council* (Paris: Unesco, 1960); John W. Gardner, *AID and the Universities: A Report to the Administrator of the Agency for International Development* (Washington, D.C.: AID, 1964); Ministère d'Etat chargé de la réforme administrative, 'La Politique de coopération avec les pays en voie de développement,' Paris, Report of the Study Commission set up on 12 March 1963 submitted to the government, 18 July 1963; W. L. Thorp, 'Development Assistance Efforts and Policies,' *1966 Review* (Paris: OECD, 1966); P. H. Coombs, 'Ways to Improve United States Foreign Educational Aid,' in *Education and Foreign Aid* (Cambridge: Harvard University Press, 1965); L. Cerych,

their bearing on the broad outlines of future strategy, two general observations may be worth setting down here.

The first is that there should be a strategy, devised and shared by all the parties and based on a long-term view. Its object should be to get the maximum effect from external assistance by concentrating that assistance on the most critical needs—as they appear in the context of rationally drawn educational development plans—which recipient countries are least likely to be able to meet with their own resources.

To some people, this may sound like a statement of the obvious, to others, it may sound like a counsel of perfection. It is intended to be neither, but rather reflects an old proposition that needs a more extensive application in actual practice. Specifically, just because the educational systems of developing nations are short of virtually everything, it does not follow that a hit-or-miss, piecemeal approach to helping them is justified. There will always be room for differences of opinion as to *what* the priorities should be, but there can never be reasonable doubt that there *should be* priorities. A rifle's aim ensures far better results than that of a spray gun in such circumstances. The difficulties of shaping such a strategy must not, however, be underestimated. The criteria and methodologies for doing so have yet to be better clarified, though encouraging progress is being made.

A second observation concerns the quantity of external assistance, and its duration. If there is anything which by now is clear, it is that the nations and educational systems of the world had better plan to help each other, on a substantial scale, for a long time to come. Educational assistance programs, whatever future labels they may wear, must become an accepted fact of life for at least the balance of this century. And they must acquire much larger dimensions—of size, quality, creativity, and sophistication—than anything seen to date. This is in no sense to disparage any of the valiant efforts thus far made. On the contrary, it is to commend them, and then to state bluntly what the future urgently requires.

We have observed that the efforts to date have unquestionably helped many developing countries make a good start toward the development of the modern educational systems they must have if they are to become strong and modern nations. But educational systems, unlike a new fer-

---

*Problems of Aid to Education in Developing Countries* (New York: Praeger Special Studies in International Economics and Development, 1965); and *Aid to Education, An Anglo-American Appraisal* (London: Overseas Development Institute, 1965).

tilizer industry or a new steel industry, cannot be created in a few years. None of the 'leading' educational systems of the world today were built in less than several generations. Today's developing countries do not have that much time at their disposal, yet even with the stoutest of hearts and the best will in the world they cannot work a miracle in the race against the absolutes of time itself.

Right now the developing nations are running behind in that race. An economic and educational gap is widening ominously—not simply between them and the industrialized world but, perhaps even worse, between the urban and rural areas of the developing countries themselves, between their modern and traditional sectors, and between their new elites and their masses. The educational crisis that already grips them is not theirs alone. It is the crisis of all nations who live together with them on this shrunken planet—and who would like to keep living together.

*Special Tasks for Universities*

UNIQUE ROLE AND POTENTIAL OF UNIVERSITIES · THEIR SPOTTY
RECORD · OLDER UNIVERSITIES NOT DESIGNED FOR PRESENT CHALLENGES
· FAILURE OF MANY UNIVERSITIES TO HELP POORER NATIONS · URGENT
NEED FOR UNIVERSITIES TO HELP PRIMARY AND SECONDARY SCHOOLS ·
OPPORTUNITIES TO COLLABORATE ON COMMON NATIONAL PROBLEMS
· EIGHT SPECIFIC TASKS.

Within the boundaries of external assistance programs, and extending well beyond them, there are many opportunities to strengthen educational intercourse among nations, thereby easing the educational crisis for all and helping to make the world a better place for all to dwell in. But whose responsibility is it to seize these opportunities?

There is obviously no single answer to the question. The brokerage role in international educational commerce is spread among a host of agencies —Unesco, regional organizations, national governments, professional societies, foundations, other private organizations, and many individuals. To a marked degree, however, the fruitfulness of their efforts will depend on the extent to which education's own capstone agency—the university—

plays in each country a direct role of leadership in the international affairs of education. In this respect, the record of the world's universities to date is spotty. Some brilliantly encouraging examples are offset by some dismal ones. There would seem to be much room for improvement.

The universities, being at the apex of the educational system, are expected by tradition and common consent to provide the system with its leadership. In addition, they are intended to be the guardians of truth, the seekers of new truths, and the upsetters of old dogmas, the conservators of society's heritage, the moulders of its youth, and the pathfinders of its future. To accomplish these heavy tasks, the university is allowed a privileged sanctuary. It stands at one remove from the hurly-burly of society's day-to-day commitments, quarrels, and passions, the better to see them more clearly.

Of late, however, a good many critics—and the chief among them are members of the university community—have been asking with growing insistence whether in fact the universities are living up to their part of the social bargain. Some of these critics, having in mind especially the older and more traditional universities of Europe and Latin America, have framed a harsh indictment. They charge that the universities have in fact perverted and forsaken their social trust. Instead of seeking new truths, they have busied themselves building academic ramparts to protect old beliefs. Instead of keeping merely at arm's length from society's untidy confusion, they have removed themselves astronomical distances from the urgent problems of society on which their help is needed. Instead of guarding their autonomy as a prerequisite for honest and productive intellectual effort, they have fiercely defended that autonomy as a privilege and an end in itself. Instead of moulding today's youth to be tomorrow's solvers of society's problems, they have trained and encouraged youth to escape from these self-same problems.

These criticisms are clearly overstated and certainly do not apply with equal force to all universities and all nations. Nonetheless, there is enough truth in them to warrant honest concern.

The reality is that the universities, and especially the older ones, were never designed for the kind of world they now inhabit, and they have found it even harder than the lower levels of education to adapt themselves to the vastly changed conditions of their environment. It would seem to be the case also that, in country after country, the university's abandonment of its leadership role for the educational system as a whole occurs at that point where the system begins its transition from mainly serving a selected elite to trying to serve the masses. Yet it is precisely at that point that the primary and secondary schools, the teacher training institutions, and the managers of education, being overwhelmed by a torrent of unfamiliar and sticky problems, are in greatest need of help from their senior colleagues in the universities. In some places, as in North America and the Soviet Union, they are beginning to get more help of this kind, but it has taken a long time. In other places, the universities continue not only to react with indifference to the plea for help but then to complain bitterly that the schools are not adequately preparing the human inputs of the university.

This same slow response to the need for adaptation can be seen in connection with the international role of universities, again with marked differences among countries and among individual institutions within them. In their ancient and honorable tradition, universities almost everywhere have continued to welcome foreign students and scholars in ever increasing numbers. If they have failed in any respect here, it is in what they have offered to teach these visitors. All too often they teach what is relevant to their own country but irrelevant to the visitor's needs and the development needs of his own country. This conditions the visitor to join the 'brain drain.'

But where the universities have failed most singularly—to the extent that they have failed—has been in the matter of taking the initiative in stretching their own institutional arms across the seas to help struggling new sister institutions, educational systems, and societies to get firmly rooted and to grow in directions best suited to their own conditions and aspirations. (American universities, on the whole, are a notable exception.) We have observed that an endless stream of individual university teachers, advisers, and scholars have crossed the oceans to lend a helping hand to peoples elsewhere. But all too often they have gone as academic truants, without the support and sponsorship of their universities, and frequently at considerable risk to their own academic careers at home.

In the same way, universities in industrialized countries, as living institutions and not merely boardinghouses for assorted individual scholars, have been slow to take initiatives in building sturdy bridges to academic communities in other industrialized countries. The bridges in fact exist; they have been fashioned from reeds and have been heavily traveled by numerous individual scholars and students. But they are not as broad and sturdy as the bridges now need to be. To make them so, the universities themselves, as creative institutions, must enter more heavily into the bridge-building business.

Why they have been slow to do so is understandable enough. It is fundamentally contrary to their nature. The medieval university and its offshoots saw themselves as homes for itinerant scholars, not as itinerants themselves. The typical European-style university, as an organization, was designed to play a passive role, not to take initiatives. Indeed, as we noted earlier, most such universities, including their Latin American cousins, virtually lack the organizational means and discipline to make institutional decisions, to set policies, to undertake commitments, to make plans for their own future and implement them. In earlier times this was no problem. The institution fitted the circumstances. But now the circumstances have vastly changed, and hence the institution itself must change if it is to honor its contract with society.

These internal changes in the university, which may be essential to their very survival, and which are certainly essential to the perpetuation of their great social role and influence, will not come about easily. Such changes have occurred more rapidly and less painfully in North America because universities there, starting later in history and in a frontier society, acquired very early in their career a tradition of public service and of adaptation to society's needs. In the past twenty years, many of them have extended their campus borders to the far corners of the earth. And having the kind of institutional machinery to make decisions and commitments, a number have committed themselves *as institutions* to assist in establishing and strengthening new educational institutions in developing countries. They have, in short, become agencies of educational development.

But lest the picture seem too rosy, it should be observed that the North American universities, too, have failed to make an easy transition into an international community; and the transition even now is only partial. In the last ten years, an extensive literature of criticism, diagnosis, and recommendation has proliferated around the subject of 'the university's role in world affairs.' One consequence is that the major United States private foundations joined together in 1963 to create a new independent institution—called Education and World Affairs—to help universities chart their course and facilitate their work in the world arena. Further encouragement was given to American education—to universities and schools alike—to 'join the world,' by the passage in 1966 of the International Edu-

cation Act. It is an excellent and farsighted piece of legislation, but unhappily Congress long delayed the appropriation of funds with which to
implement it.[10]

Internal reforms in university structure and behavior come most readily
when there is a specific challenge, a definable job to be done, and a wide
consensus within the university that it should be done. With this in mind,
it is to the point here to indicate examples of the kinds of tasks that
urgently need to be done, and which are appropriate for the universities
to do. They can:

*Help establish or spur the growth of new higher educational institu-
tions in developing countries,* along lines which suit their needs and
circumstances and are not simply carbon copies of the assisting universities;

*Help the design and development planning (and implementation) of
educational systems in developing countries*—including provisions for
serving people outside the formal schools, and the creation of new
educational methods, content, and structures fitting each particular
society's needs and resources;

*Help develop research capabilities in developing regions*—sometimes
on a regional basis—especially in fields and on problems of priority concern and relevance to these developing areas, where research scholars
from industrialized nations will be anxious to go to work in collaboration with research scholars in the area, because of the unique opportunities and facilities for research that are offered;

*Help strengthen the dialogue among universities within developing
regions,* and between them and universities in industrialized countries,
so that knowledge, experience, and ideas for educational improvement
may circulate more fully and swiftly throughout the world;

*Take the leadership in educational innovation,* at all levels, with the
object of solving urgent problems that defy solution by conventional
means, and of helping in the rapid circulation and exchange of reliable

10. R. A. Humphrey (ed.), *Universities . . . and Development Assistance Abroad*
(Washington, D.C.: American Council on Education, 1966); 'The Role of Universities in Development Assistance, Report of the meeting held at Maarn, the Netherlands, September 1964,' The Hague, Netherlands Universities Foundation for International Co-operation (NUFFIC), 1965; 'The University Looks Abroad: Approaches
to World Affairs at Six American Universities' New York, Report from EWA, 1965;
'The University and World Affairs,' New York, a Report of the Committee on the
University and World Affairs, 1960; and 'Education and World Affairs,' Report on
the 1963-64 program, New York, 1965.

evaluation and research results pertaining to educational experimentation, whenever it may occur;

*Encourage and assist small neighboring countries in developing regions to collaborate* in the establishment and successful operation of *co-operative* higher educational facilities, providing specialized training and research on a scale sufficient to be economically feasible and compatible with the highest norms of excellence;

*Take such actions as are within their power to reduce the drainage of needed talent from developing regions*—for example, by adapting their own training programs to fit the priority needs of foreign students from particular nations and regions; by refraining from undue encouragement to the best of these foreign students to overstay their leave; and by pursuing hiring policies with regard to foreign talent which give conscientious weight to the urgent manpower needs of the developing countries;

*Establish institutional arrangements that will facilitate and encourage collaboration among scholars in various industrialized countries,* whatever their form of social and political organization, in attacking jointly and more thoroughly some of the major common problems that beset their respective societies—such as urban renewal, preservation of natural resources (including clean air and water), help to the culturally handicapped and the disenfranchised, orientation of youth in a confusing world, adaptation of educational systems to changing conditions.

The universities of the world have their work cut out for them. No one else can do this work as well as they, if only they arrange themselves to carry new responsibilities. If they refuse the responsibility, they and all civilization will be the losers. But if they accept it and rise to meet it, the productive search for truth and knowledge, human development and progress toward peace itself will unquestionably move ahead in future years at a pace even now undreamed of.

# VII

## Conclusions for Strategy

---

The primary purpose of this book has been diagnostic, not prescriptive. Still, having explored the salient traits and causes of the world educational crisis, we can hardly now avoid a concern for the operative question: What can be done about the crisis?

In the process of diagnosing the question, some of the logical directions in which solutions lie have become evident. At the same time, the *illogic* of certain familiar 'panaceas' has also become evident, as in the case of those expressed in statements like 'all it takes is more money,' or 'simply get a new head man,' or 'just make the students and teachers work harder.'

We are convinced that simple solutions do not exist. Yet we are also convinced that there are multiple solutions. They are difficult, and, if applied, will require the passage of time before they show their full effects.

The main hope for coping with this crisis lies, we believe, in the formulation of balanced national and international strategies, carefully geared to match all the large components of the crisis. Further, they must be pressed steadily and vigorously over a time-span extending from immediate tactical needs to the prospective shape of things five, ten, and twenty years hence. The alternative to such strategies is to stumble into what is clearly a perilous educational future with no road map whatsoever, rising each morning to go wherever the wind blows—even perhaps turning in a circle or going nowhere at all.

162

## Nature of an Educational Strategy

An educational development strategy, as the term is used here, is a framework for specific educational policies, intended to keep these policies reasonably balanced and integrated, well timed, properly weighted, and headed in the right direction. Like the policies themselves, the strategic framework must be flexible. It must be constantly subject to review, and modified in the light of progress, surprises, new knowledge, and fresh insights. Yet it cannot be so flexible that it is blithely dismantled and reassembled in a quite different form each time a new minister or a new party takes office. Without reasonable continuity and durability, and without the cumulative momentum that only continuity and consistency can bring, a strategy is little more than a stage set—all front and no back. Press hard against it, and it topples.

A real strategy must be firmly founded in a broad consensus, which embraces diverse political, social, and educational interests and enjoys especially the authentic enthusiasm and loyalty of numerous leaders of these diverse groups. Some nations, unhappily, may not yet be ready for such a strategy. They may not yet have attained the political, social, economic, and administrative preconditions which are essential for building and pursuing a strategy of educational development—or of economic and social development generally. Nonetheless, an effort to mount a strategy must be made even in such cases, because nothing at all can be gained by doing nothing, while the effort, itself, may help create the very preconditions for success that have been missing.

An educational development strategy is not something that exists in a vacuum, or that can be put together in the back room of a ministry by an expert, a statistician, and a calculating machine. It must be built of widely shared aims, of rational perception and will power rising directly from the economic, social, and cultural milieu to which it is to make its contribution. As such, strategy has a tangible shape, existing at several levels, and fashioned to fit the peculiar circumstances and responsibilities of each level and place. There can be international, regional, national, state, and local strategies, formed in each instance by appropriate hands. But if strategies at different levels and in different places are to be mutually reinforcing, they must share a common approach to diagnostic acts, must proceed along basic lines of direction and priorities that are generally agreed to, and must be supported from several directions.

In our diagnosis, we have reached certain general conclusions concerning the nature of the world educational crisis, how it arose, where it stands, and where it seems to be trending. For its bearing on the work of strategy building, we can now recapitulate these conclusions in capsule form, at the inevitable risk of oversimplification.

## Recapitulation of the Book's Findings

Seen through the wide-angle lens of a systems analysis, the crisis was clearly born of the historic conjunction of five factors, each finding its origin in the rampaging forces of change that have swept all civilization in our time. We can give names to these five forces:

*The student flood*—There has been an inexorable and almost overpowering rise in demand for more education, of every sort and at every level, covering almost every village and hamlet. The flood of aspiring students, released in the first place by an explosion of human expectations, then enlarged by a population explosion, has inundated every educational system. The managers of these systems have been so thoroughly occupied merely with staggering problems of rescue and logistics that they have had little time even to think of other things, such as the quality and efficiency of the whole operation. The flood of numbers will not subside; on the contrary, it promises in many places to keep rising, even faster than presently, for a long time to come.

*Acute resource scarcities*—To cope with the flood of students, and paradoxically to swell it, the resources devoted to education have multiplied in an unprecedented manner since the early 1950's. And yet the supply of teachers and buildings, equipment and textbooks, scholarships and fellowships, and the money required for each of these, has lagged well behind the rising educational demand, thereby imposing severe restraints upon the ability of educational systems to respond satisfactorily to the demand. The outlook here is similar to that for the supply of students: resource scarcities relative to need will certainly persist and may well get worse. The outlook is agonizingly troublesome in the case of many developing nations, who are even now straining their financial limits to near the breaking point, with no relief in sight.

*Rising costs*—Increasingly stringent resource limitations will add even more to the afflictions of educational systems because of the inexorable upward trend of their real costs per student. Apart from the familiar havoc which inflation plays with educational budgets and teacher incomes, this upward trend of unit costs centers mainly in the fact that education remains a labor-intensive industry, still close to the handicraft stage. Indeed it becomes even more so with each effort to raise its quality through its conventional means.

*Unsuitability of output*—In these already harrowing circumstances, educational systems are further beset by evidence that what they are teaching and what they are turning out—in the way of individual students and in their 'product mix'—seems in important respects not to be right for the times and the occasion. The outputs of educational systems are evidently ill-fitted, on the one hand, to the rapidly altering needs of national development, and to the similarly changing needs of individuals in changing societies. But on the other hand, the attitudes, job preferences, and status patterns given to students by their environment work against a proper use of the outputs of a modern educational system and against the promotion of an authentic development process bent toward social change and economic modernization. A kind of three-way deadlock results—among old attitudes and employment arrangements coupled with new aspirations, the real needs of development, and education itself. A major consequence of this deadlock is the growing inability of the economies of developing countries to absorb the human output of the educational systems, thereby exacerbating the lethal problem of 'educated unemployed.'

*Inertia and inefficiency*—Caught in this desperate squeeze, educational systems have responded mainly with 'business-as-usual' methods. But this has not worked. The old arrangements that had served them well before —the system of administration, the syllabus and curriculum and teaching methods, the self-contained classroom, the means of teacher training and recruitment, these and all those other things that have characterized traditional educational processes—have proved no match for the new situation. What seemed like 'business-as-usual' actually became 'business-worse-than-usual,' as attested by echoing protests against quality deterioration.' This business-as-usual approach—another name for the inherent inertia of educational systems—has deterred them in the work of adapting their internal affairs with sufficient speed to meet a fast changing set of circumstances.

And so, for these combined reasons, educational systems throughout the world find themselves today in crisis. The crisis, to be sure, differs in timing and intensity and from place to place. Its most severe manifestations are to be found in the poorer countries. They are in deep trouble at a time when they have barely begun to build balanced, well-integrated, popular educational systems. Moreover, quite apart from their resource scarcities, they have an inherently more difficult pedagogical challenge to meet: they must lift most of a whole generation out of a tradition-bound world of illiteracy into the mobile, modern world of science.

But the crisis in the industrialized nations should not be taken lightly, just because it is relatively less conspicuous. Academic arteriosclerosis comes more readily to older educational systems and is harder to cure. Their inputs may be richer, but their internal efficiency can be just as low and their outputs just as ill-matched to real needs as in the poorer countries.

According to one's disposition, it is possible to view this pattern of forces in one of two ways. One way would be to see in it a kind of *Götterdämmerung*—the final cataclysmic confrontation between science's ability to create revolutionary technologies, and man's inability to assimilate and master them. The second way is to see in it one of those great moments of history when germinating forces leap to life, challenge man's ingenuity, and evoke from him a stirring response which makes civilization jump upward. Those who would build strategies of educational development must, perforce, be imbued with the latter view.

### Suggested Elements of a Positive Strategy

But what could the strategy be? Without attempting a full answer, we can suggest straightaway that there are two indispensable features which it must have. First, it must focus on the *relationships* of things. It must seek to improve a whole series of relationships—including those within the educational system, between its various levels and internal working parts, and between the educational system and its environment, on both the input and the output sides. These relationships, now badly out of line vis-à-vis each other, must somehow be restored to a better balance and to mutually compatible rates of movement. This need to focus on relationships and to see the matter as a whole is precisely why a system approach is so essential to strategy building.

The second feature of strategy must be a heavy stress on *innovation*—innovation in virtually every aspect of every educational system; not change for its own sake, but changes carefully calculated to achieve needed improvements and adjustments. Society and the economy will not adjust unilaterally to the educational system. If there is to be an accommodation, the educational system must take the first initiative toward adjustment, not by being its 'old self' but by making a stronger effort to adapt itself to new circumstances. Thus, the heart of the matter is how to get sluggish educational systems to take such an initiative and to start changing themselves more rapidly and in the right direction.

Educational innovations, however, will not come about automatically. Even if they did, they would not be quickly assimilated. If proposed innovations come into the systems primarily from outside sources, they may be politely received, but then quietly shelved. If the strategy is to succeed, innovation must become what it has not been before. It must become a way of life for education.

This obviously requires two main things. The people most directly involved in education must be convinced that there is no other way out of the crisis—that, indeed, the way of innovation can bring a new excitement and sense of adventure to education. There must be, in other words, a new attitude toward change both within the educational fraternity and, no less, on the part of its most immediate clients—parents and students. Nobel prizes are won in science for challenging and upsetting old truths and discovering new ones. The same wholesome irreverence for 'time-honored truths' must somehow be instilled into the enterprise that is supposed to breed Nobel prize winners. This itself is a major educational undertaking, and there is no time to lose in launching it.

The other precondition for widespread innovation is that educational systems must themselves become equipped with the means for innovation. At the outset we observed that agriculture did not make the great transition from a traditional to a modern state until the mechanisms and approach of scientific research and development were placed at the farmer's disposal. Thereafter, the *process* of innovation, once institutionalized, became a habit of the farmer. Modern agriculture was thus born, and things have not been the same since. Yet, a half-century earlier, who would have believed that it ever could have happened? Education does not need an agricultural experiment station. But it needs its equivalent—and an effective extension service to go with it, that will spread the useful results of research and experimentation far and wide and quickly.

If there is to be a major effort toward educational innovation, there must also be an order of priorities. Everything cannot be done at once, and some things must happen first before other things can be done. Our analysis of the educational crisis leads us to suggest the following priority targets:

*Modernization of educational management*—Unless educational systems are well equipped with appropriately trained modern managers—who in turn are well equipped with good information flows, modern tools of analysis, research and evaluation, and are supported by well-trained teams of specialists—the transition of education from its semihandicraft state to a modern condition is not likely to happen. Instead, the educational crisis will grow steadily worse. In seeking to modernize its management system, education can find many useful clues in the practices—including the concepts and methodologies of systems analysis and of integrated long-range planning—of other sectors of society which have already made great strides in this direction.

*Modernization of teachers*—Today's teacher does not have a chance to be modern—to raise his productivity, to keep up with new knowledge and with new teaching techniques. He never did have. More likely than not, he is trained for yesterday's schooling, not for tomorrow's, or if by chance he is trained for tomorrow's, he is soon restrained from utilizing his training by the realities of his first teaching assignment. His professional growth from there on is problematical at best, especially if he heads off into the lonely isolation of a village school. It is really nobody's business to keep him growing professionally on the job. If he is lucky, he gets an occasional boost from the visiting inspector—if he is that kind of inspector—and from the infrequent rubbing of elbows and ideas with other isolated colleagues who attend the same 'in-service training course.' But that is about all, and perhaps by then he has given up and settled back into the security—and boredom—of teaching in the way his own teachers taught him.

Clearly, educational systems will not be modernized until the whole system of teacher training is drastically overhauled, stimulated by pedagogical research, made intellectually richer and more challenging, and extended far beyond preservice training into a system for continuous professional renewal and career development for *all* teachers.

A reform along such lines carries with it exciting possibilities for attracting more of society's best talent into educational systems, and for developing new 'divisions of labor' that will open opportunities for such talent to rise and be more efficiently used for teaching. When that day arrives, teachers and their organizations can happily bid farewell to the old monolithic salary structure and the monolithic job description which it rests on—both of which have too long smothered good teaching talent or driven it away.

*Modernization of the learning process*—But it is the students, after all, and not the teachers, who are the prime victims of archaic educational arrangements. When most of them enter school the first day, they are consumed with native curiosity about what makes everything tick. The questions they want answered could outstrip the reliable knowledge of the best teachers and the best educated parents, or the wisdom of a Socrates. The individual child soon discovers, however, that school is not the place to get answers to his questions. If he gets his answers anywhere, it will be in the playground at recess, or behind the barn, from his real teacher, who is one year older. The school, he discovers, has its own questions, and it is for him to give the right answers, if he is to be a 'good student.' If he learns these answers faster than the group at large, he soon becomes bored. If he learns them more slowly, he soon is defeated. There certainly must be better ways to capitalize on the natural curiosity of children, on their individual differences, and on the power of every child, whatever his level or type of intelligence, to learn things on his own. Indeed, it is difficult to conceive of a set of arrangements less likely to capitalize on these awe-inspiring human traits than those widely in vogue in traditional schools.

It is doubtful in the extreme, however, that there is any one way, one technique, one gadget, which all by itself could achieve better results than the generally unsatisfactory ones of the traditional teaching-learning process. It is a new *combination* of things, new 'systems' of teaching and learning, that must be evolved, to do a significantly better job than now, but without commensurately higher costs. African villages cannot have computerized teaching machines, regardless of how well they work. Neither, for that matter, can American schools, except for an occasional experiment. But even old bottle caps, buttons, and pieces of string have sometimes proved effective learning aids in the right context. Surely an educational system does not have to be affluent to improve the pedagogical and economic efficiency of its learning process, not does it have to have the world's finest teachers. Sometimes even a modestly larger investment in the original teaching machine—the textbook—can make a world of difference. But it need not stop there, and cannot. Therefore, along with new kinds of centers for teacher training and career development, it might pay great dividends to have places for the generation of *new systems of learning,* and for the creation and production of the instructional materials and other accessories required to implement these improved systems.[1]

*The strengthening of educational finance*—Our suggestions thus far— it will no doubt have been noticed—have all involved spending money, though it is to be hoped more productively than at present. Nevertheless, we cannot dodge the fact that educational systems, however more efficient and effective they may become, will require a good deal more money than, as things are going, they are likely to receive. Costly education can be poor, but good education is never cheap. And the world needs a great deal more good education.

The fact that more and more educational systems seem to be running up against hard financial limits does not mean that they cannot do better. Their present problems are in relation to their present methods and sources of finance. But, like educational methods, there is usually a fairly wide flexibility and range of options for tapping the national income flow on behalf of more funds for more and better education. One further element of strategy we would suggest, therefore, is that there should be a concerted effort to examine alternative and supplemenal sources of educational finance. A good way to begin would be to examine the existing diversity of financial practices and the ingenious devices that some systems have discovered, but which others may not have heard of. Inevitably, of course, it will be discovered that to tap the most promising supplemental financial sources will require the casting aside of certain taboos, including some socially laudable ones. But this may well prove to be the price that must be paid, at least for the time being, if education is to be kept from strangling financially in a tangle of high principles.

*Greater emphasis on nonformal education*—It has always seemed to us strangely artificial to say that a person who went to school was 'educated,' and that one who did not, was not. The facts belie this distinction. It seems equally strange to accept the assumption that if a nation can only get half of its children into little red schoolhouses, or little brown ones, the other half must be condemned to a life of illiteracy and thwarted opportunity. Can someone who really wants to learn, *only* do so in a conventional classroom, before a teacher and blackboard? Our common sense and our own experiences tell us that this is an absurd proposition.

1. For a discussion of what is meant by 'new systems of learning,' see Schramm *et al., op. cit.* On proposed centers for creating new learning systems, see also Wilbur Schramm, 'The Newer Educational Media in the United States,' a paper prepared for the Meeting of Experts on the Development and Use of New Methods and Techniques of Education, Paris, Unesco, March 1962.

Yet it is the proposition upon which educational policy and practices almost everywhere seem to be based.

Our suggestion is that serious reconsideration be given to the whole division between 'formal' and 'nonformal' schooling, as part of the strategy for overcoming the educational crisis. It would clearly be beneficial in many countries to deploy resources more heavily into various familiar types of adult education—to those, that is, which are linked both to the growth of individuals and to that of the economy. But we wonder whether this is enough, and whether there are not much more radical innovations awaiting discovery which could, within the limits of available resources, strike much bolder and quicker blows against ignorance.

Learning takes time and it takes motivation, and millions of youngsters and adults who cannot get to school have plenty of both. What they need beyond this, however, is access to the 'stuff' of learning. Surely, with all the modern miracles of communication, and of documents reproduction, some systems could be devised to feed the appetites of these learning-hungry people. Not everyone would be interested. Perhaps only a minority would muster the motivation and sustained energy required for effective self-instruction. But a number of the great leaders of the past— well before the dawn of modern communications—achieved surprising self-development by lonely candlelight study. In the developing countries, the lost leaders of tomorrow are the bright and ambitious youngsters of today who, by accident of birth and place, are deprived of access to the stuff of learning in any digestible form. Here would seem to be another challenging opportunity for educational innovation, possibly more far-reaching in its consequences than anything done to formal schools.

In the past few pages, we have touched only lightly upon several central themes and targets which, in our view, strategy must embrace if it is to be commensurate with the crisis it is meant to solve. Others can certainly add to these thoughts, usefully modify them, or show why some of these suggestions are impractical. We would be the first to agree that they will not be easy. But if we declare them to be impossible, where then do we go?

In closing, we stress one further feature of strategy—namely, *international co-operation*. We agree that every nation must be the master of its own educational destiny, and that it must largely support its own educational system, however poor the nation may be. But on the grounds laid out earlier, we assert that no nation—given the crisis conditions affecting all—can successfully 'go it alone.' International educational co-operation on a vastly extended scale must, therefore, be a cardinal feature of our educational strategy for rich and poor nations alike.

What this implies is something far more than a greater diffusion of good will and mutual understanding among educators of the world, through periodic meetings in Paris or Geneva, New Delhi or Santiago, where old friends take in new ones and usefully exchange experiences. We do not underestimate the value of such contacts and interchanges. But co-operation must go well beyond the talk stage and the passing of resolutions. We have in mind very practical, concrete things which will place educators of many nations, and those collaborating with them, in direct working contact, jointly pursuing solutions to common problems and discoveries which can yield benefits to all. We mean also the strengthening of the practical mechanisms for monitoring new developments, wherever they may occur, and for spreading the news widely, reliably, and quickly—a task for which international agencies are peculiarly well fitted. We mean, finally, a new sort of partnership between the educational systems of rich and poor countries.

Such a partnership must be based on a due recognition given to three key propositions:

In the present and for a long time to come, the industrialized countries must give substantially more help to the developing nations than they have done to date.

Such support should not be a conveyor belt for conventional educational forms from 'donor' countries to 'recipient' ones, but rather a common act of exploration to find patterns that really fit the needs and pocketbooks of the developing nations.

Even though in economic terms the support for educational development must flow largely in one direction, it does not follow that the developing nations cannot contribute equally to the advancement of education in the industrially developed countries. Indeed they can, if for no other reason than because they are writing on a relatively cleaner educational slate, and because their problems and their version of the world educational crisis are so much more visible and instructive. For these very reasons, the educational leaders and teachers in developing countries are likely to grasp more quickly and clearly the need to drop their folklore and their inhibitions and to strike out in new educational directions. The day may not be far off, therefore, when, in terms of educational innovations, the major flows of technical assistance across the world will be from the poorer to the richer nations.

In this enlarged and mutually beneficial educational interchange among nations, there will be plenty of work and responsibilities to go round for all sorts of organizations—public and private, international, regional, and national. The problem is how to harmonize their efforts and exploit the unique capabilities of each. Here again there is a great untapped potential—not merely for boosting the volume of external assistance and other forms of interchange, but even more for boosting their quality and effectiveness.

We end by returning full circle to where we began this analysis—by stressing the uniquely *world-wide* character of the educational crisis. To the reader who may accept this thesis as it applies to other countries, but denies it for his own, we say: You may well be right. But we would urge you, nonetheless, to look freshly and critically into your educational situation, for the hour may be later than you think. Finally, we would say to one and all: Whatever shape your educational system may be in, if others which must serve the vast majority of this planet's citizens are in a serious state of crisis, then no nation, however rich, can be exempt from the consequences. The educational crisis is everybody's business.

# Epilogue: How World Educational
# Leaders View the Crisis

---

What do forward-looking educational leaders around the world think about the crisis depicted in the previous pages? Do they concur that there *is* a crisis? If so, what do they propose should be done about it?

Ordinarily such questions could be answered only by surmise and speculation. In this case, happily, there is concrete evidence to go on. No one, of course, can speak for all such leaders. But a sizable and distinguished cross section of them did in fact examine a reasonable facsimile of this book, discussed its content for some days at Williamsburg, Virginia, and reached certain conclusions. These are set forth below, in the words of the conference's chairman. Judging from the acclaim with which Dr. James Perkins's Summary Report was greeted on the final day, he had succeeded in voicing a clear and strong consensus.

*Summary Report of the Conference Chairman*
9 October 1967

The International Conference on the World Crisis in Education was a gathering of 150 educational leaders from 52 countries, held in Williamsburg, Virginia, in October 1967. It was conceived by President Lyndon B. Johnson because he felt, and educators agreed, that the times required reassessment of the capabilities of education to meet the rising aspirations of people everywhere for a better and freer life.

The conference subscribed to the following proposition as the basis for constructive action:

1. That education is now a central preoccupation of every nation in the world and, further, that educational plans can be carried out with maximum success only if they are made in relation to educational systems and plans in other countries.

2. That within each country education can no longer be regarded as a series of unconnected enterprises, conducted at different levels with purposes independent of each other. Education within any society must be

considered as a unified whole, its parts in balance and the balance in turn reflecting society's requirements and the resources available to meet them.

3. That there is indeed a crisis in education's ability to match performance with expectations. The crisis takes two forms. The first is the world-wide disparity between the hopes of individuals and needs of society, on the one hand, and, on the other, the capabilities of the educational system. The second is an even greater disparity between the developing countries, faced with the cruel restraints of grossly inadequate resources, and the developed countries, which are increasingly preoccupied with their own internal needs.

4. That in all countries, rich and poor alike, educational programs, structures, management, and the learning process itself require the most immediate attention to ways and means of replacing inflexibility with innovation, traditional or outmoded ideas with fresh approaches and new ventures.

The conference believed that these postulates must be accepted both by educators and by the society that supports them if education is to rise above an attitude of business-as-usual and perform the tasks that the very future of mankind requires.

With these postulates securely in mind, the conference turned to the actions required to improve the performance of education in six areas: information about education, management and structure, teachers and students, curriculum content and teaching methods, resources, and international co-operation.

A. *Information about education*

To improve itself, an educational system must know what it is doing and how well it is doing. Further, if a society is to strengthen its educational system, many people besides educators must have access to the essential facts.

The following recommendations are therefore in order:

1. Every educational system should regularly gather, analyze, and disseminate accurate and up-to-date information about teachers, students, income, and expenditures. Trained statisticians are imperative. When they are not available, they must be borrowed from other countries, and when borrowed, native statisticians must be trained to take their place.

2. Every educational system should establish effective machinery to

evaluate its own performance on a continuing basis, to see specific ways for increasing the quantity and quality of educational services within the limits of available resources, and to point the way to needed and promising innovations of every kind. Such evaluations should begin with a questioning look at the whole framework of education, from the curriculum to procedures in the classroom. (For example: Must students sit still facing the teacher for six hours a day? Do the traditional classifications of subject matter still make sense? Are current style textbooks useful?) Furthermore, in the design of new educational programs and projects, evaluation of their success should be built into the programs themselves.

3. Besides continuing self-evaluation, educational systems should periodically subject themselves to friendly but critical external scrutiny by their peers. The feasibility and value of such 'confrontations' have been clearly shown in the country studies arranged by the Organization for Economic Co-operation and Development. For the developing regions of the world, a comparable process of mutual examination by neighbors might be arranged through Unesco or an appropriate regional organization.

4. A concern for proper information must also be directed toward society itself and particularly those parts that have the deepest interest in education's performance. This concern requires two measures. The first is improved methods by which relevant information is made available. This is the responsibility of education. The second is improved understanding on the part of the media—the press, television, and radio—that are the main communication channels between education and the public. It is important that these media employ and support highly competent education reporters, trained and continually refreshed by contact with the educational world. Such reporters should have a status in their media reflecting the importance of education, and the subject should receive the same level of attention given to sports and financial news.

B.  *Management and structures*

The precondition for attaining any kind of innovation in an educational system is improved management at every level.

To modernize management, these steps should be taken:

1. Recruitment of managers and specialists should be concentrated mainly in the ranks of teachers and professors. Educational management is best served by those who have had teaching experience and who show

talent for administrative tasks. Good managers can sometimes be found in other professions, but they must be carefully retrained for educational tasks.

2. For the training of managerial talent, each country should have an administrative staff college or its equivalent, able to offer both pre-service and in-service programs. Universities in the developing as well as the industrialized countries should examine ways in which they can help to nurture this precious managerial talent.

3. A central task of management is planning. Unesco has attached a high priority to this activity, and even wider use of the International Institute for Educational Planning should be made.

4. Management and planning take place through educational structures. Good management must go hand in hand with structures designed to perform the specialized tasks that education now faces. Structures must always respond to functions; as the functions of education diversify in response to changing needs, structures must be kept flexible to receive new curricular changes, new levels of education, and pressing specialized tasks in agriculture, science, or technology.

It is important to note here the need to provide education for those who do not fit into formal programs. In the industrialized nations, formal education does not now sufficiently reflect the need for lifelong learning. The formal educational structures must make it easier for students to use the system by establishing more acceptable entry and exit points—through such devices as junior colleges, vocational programs for dropouts, and preschool education for the culturally handicapped.

In the developing nations, nonformal programs of work training, second-chance schools for those who have left school long before they are ready for jobs, rural extension programs, all must be planned and organized as a supplement to formal education.

In all countries, there must be considerably more research on the way different people learn at all stages in their lives. Teachers should be given special training for working with adults and other students who have special needs. And education outside the formal structure must be given more attention by researchers and planners and by society itself. Education by television and other forms of mass communication must be explored to help overcome the frustrations of those for whom formal systems fail to provide.

5. The university, as the capstone of the educational system, must be particularly responsive to the needs of the whole system. But it cannot

innovate if it is too closely controlled by the central ministry; it cannot
be useful if it is not prepared to turn out the highly trained manpower
that the society so badly needs; and it cannot modernize itself without
strong administrative direction.

### c. *Teachers and students*

The teacher and student are the center of the educational process. In a
real sense, everything else must serve to improve them as individuals and
to enhance the prospect of their constructive relationship.

1. The recruitment of good teachers is a top priority on the education
lists of all countries. All too often men and women who would be good
teachers are attracted to other professions, both because the rewards and
incentives of teaching are relatively weak and because the conditions of
work are not conducive to high performance. The best teachers should
receive salaries equal to those of the best paid professionals in the country.

But to justify these salaries, good teachers must operate at the highest
level of productivity. This means that for a good teacher old notions of a
fixed student-teacher ratio must be changed and that new criteria for
salary levels will have to be established, based on performance and productivity rather than tenure.

Good teachers should be expected to play an important role outside the
classroom. They must become a major force for social development, participating in important efforts to improve the communities in which they
work. Both the teachers and the classroom must become an integral part
of the social process that is transforming their society. This mission cannot be ignored in either the industrialized or the developing nations.

2. The proper preparation of teachers who are operating at new professional levels will require a new definition of institutions for teacher
training. These institutions must be deeply involved in research and
experimentation and be themselves influential centers of innovation. They
must be prepared to disseminate the tested results of research and to
encourage their practical application.

These institutions should be in close touch with society, making sure
that their work is relevant. At the same time they must maintain equally
close ties with schools and classroom teachers so that neither the schools
nor the training institutes will be isolated from new ideas on curriculum
or from educational inquiry. However they choose to fill their role, teacher

training institutes must be an aggressive force for change in education, not a reflection of the status quo.

3. Obviously, this new style of teacher is one whose high level of productivity will in most cases require the use of new technology. Programmed instruction, team teaching, film, radio, and television will be increasingly the tools of the trade. Technology must never become the master of the teacher, but this can only be assured if the teacher takes a positive attitude toward using technology for his own needs. Properly employed, technology may be one of our main hopes for bringing the good teacher into contact with an increasing number of students.

4. Students themselves must become a more active part of the educational process. Not only do students have much to contribute toward keeping an institution on its toes, but their attitude toward their own personal development will be the decisive factor in their education. Because change is the order of the day, students will need to come into the system more highly motivated for independent work, equipped to handle the variety of self-teaching devices that are available, satisfied and indeed anxious to work on their own, and prepared to use the institution for their own developing needs.

D. *Content and methods*

The forces of change that bear so heavily on manager, teacher, and student naturally have their impact on the content and methods of education as well. Here, too, change and innovation call for specific relevant proposals.

1. The curriculum must contain subject matter that can be used by the student in the life he faces when he graduates. In a predominantly agricultural economy, it is obviously important that the student be exposed to a curriculum that will prepare him for his most probable future vocation. If the educational system is content to give him a traditional classical education, it will only prepare him for the ranks of the unemployed. In an urban society it is equally important that the student have some exposure to problems of the industrial world, because he will be immersed in it soon enough. In all societies as they mature, the needs for special training increase, and the standard classical curriculum has to be modified to include more specialized programs.

It is well, however, to state a caution against orienting education too far toward a vocational purpose. There are certain basic intellectual tools to which the student must be exposed and certain basic information that he must acquire in order to be an educated man in the modern world and to form an accurate image of himself and his society. As with all things, it is a matter of balance, but part of that balance surely involves a close attention to the relevance of the curriculum both to the needs of the student and to the needs of the society.

2. Content and technique are two closely related matters; each affects the other. New techniques are bound to be introduced as the new tools of technology become available to the educational process. Demonstration schools should be considered a means of making visible the ways in which the new technology can be applied in a complete school system. Special training programs for those who will operate at the interface between curriculum and technology will be needed. And as the communications satellite opens up new vistas for bringing good teaching to students all over the world, curriculum and methods of teaching will have to adapt themselves to these new sources of instruction.

3. These developments highlight the importance of research in the whole spectrum of requirements. M. René Maheu, Director-General of Unesco, has suggested that 2 per cent of the educational budget could appropriately be applied to the research process. Education can no longer afford the luxury of being one of the last of the handicraft industries. But the price of successful innovation will be increased research. It has been said that education is the only enterprise that throws away its own experience. This experience must be examined and made available on an international basis so that those successful in breaking open old bottlenecks can put their experience to the use of others.

E. *Educational resources*

Certainly the improvements that have been suggested here cannot be accomplished without additional funds allocated to education. Several sources of supply must be explored.

1. It has been pointed out many times that the allocation of resources is basically a politicial decision made against many competing claims on national budgets. Resources currently allocated to defense measures, for example, absorb about $150 billion of the world's national budgets. Clearly, a large increase in resources for education would be possible if countries were prepared to allocate to education a part of the funds currently going to security programs. Even a 10 per cent reallocation of funds

from defense to education would make possible a great many of the specific measures that have been recommended here. It is a dismal commentary on the world's priorities that such reallocations have not already been made. Indeed, it may be one of the most important tasks of the educational establishment to make learning so exciting and interesting that it will displace the fear, tension, and misunderstanding that lie at the base of much international conflict.

The largest expenditures on armaments, of course, are to be found in the most highly developed countries. A reallocation of internal priorities would require immediate attention to the increased resources needed by the developing countries. In the meantime, René Maheu has recommended that the one billion dollars which currently flow from developed to developing countries for educational purposes be doubled. This is surely something that is possible to accomplish now.

2. In addition, private sources of funds for the direct support of education have been largely untapped. A careful review of these sources should be made by every country. Tax laws must be re-examined to encourage the flow of private funds for educational purposes. Gifts from industry and alumni, for example, have not even been considered in most countries. Employer taxes might be levied to support technical training and youth programs; educational fees might be used as a transitional measure, coupled with scholarships for the needy. Such sources are important not only for the additional funds but for the balance that private support can provide to offset too much control by the state.

3. Resources that are already available must be used wisely and effectively. Much can be done with limited funds and unlimited imagination. Starter funds from central governments can provide incentives to produce new schools. Energy and expertise now locked up in homes, factories, and perhaps even jails could be applied to educational needs at relatively little cost. A multiplicity of small institutions might be consolidated into a few good institutions at substantial savings. Technology must be made available that can alleviate the necessity of reproducing expensive libraries and perhaps even laboratories.

No matter how much resources are increased, there will still not be enough money to satisfy the ambitions of those who would expand and improve our educational systems. Expectations may bear so heavily on inadequate resources that unless they are brought into balance, they may in time give rise to disillusion and set the stage for the demagogue to make public sale of measures that promise a quick fix and that could destroy the very educational systems we are trying to build. Politicians will have a special responsibility to exercise restraint and realism in making campaign promises on behalf of education.

F. *International co-operation*

Although external financial aid is but a fraction of the total traffic in international educational co-operation, it is a highly strategic fraction. Yet at the very time when developing nations are most in need of it, external financial aid shows signs of an eclipse. It is urgent that the world-wide volume of such aid be increased from its present level of approximately one billion dollars per year to double this amount within the next three to five years. Such an increase should be entirely manageable if it is spread among donor nations and if they have the will to sustain the costs.

But it is not enough merely to increase the level of external assistance. It is equally important to make such aid more efficient and effective. This can be done on four conditions:

1. The parties rendering and receiving such assistance must jointly formulate a careful strategy and set of priorities for the use of such assistance.

2. There must be a system for regular evaluation of the various projects that entail the use of external aid in order to arrive at guidelines for the future.

3. Assistance from numerous sources must be better harmonized.

4. The recipient country must have a well-conceived plan of educational development.

Priorities for external aid in support of education will of course differ from country to country. But the factors discussed here must be considered—educational planning, innovation, curriculum revision, strengthening and modernizing management, reform of teacher training, teaching materials and libraries, rural transformation and increased agricultural productivity, and education for international understanding.

The major international programs—Unesco, the World Bank's International Development Association, and the United Nations Development Programme—are clearly identifiable and at least potentially adaptable to a clear strategy. In a number of bilateral programs, on the other hand—and these account for some 90 per cent of the total volume—educational aid is entangled beyond easy recognition in a web of other forms of aid—social, economic, and military. Only if educational assistance is given a clear identity and visibility will it be possible to apply a rational strategy and to secure maximum public support in donor nations.

Bilateral and multilateral channels of aid each has its special advantages and limitations. There is, however, a third and untried middle position which should be seriously explored in the case of education.

It would entail the use of consortia, or consultative groups, of international and bilateral agencies which would harmonize their efforts toward meeting the needs of large individual developing countries, or of clusters of smaller ones.

We end where we began, by stressing the fact that education has become a global enterprise—a matter of mutual concern and mutual dependence involving literally all nations. United, the nations of the world can bring under control the educational crisis which affects them all. Divided, it is most unlikely that they can do so.

In this conviction we close with a final proposal. As the modern world enters upon the final third of the twentieth century, it would be fitting to declare, under appropriate auspices, an International Education Year. It is not that concerted world attention in a single year would solve the crisis in education, for this crisis will endure at best for years to come, but a common effort could mobilize energies and inspire world-wide initiatives that would give this subject the priority it deserves.

# Appendixes

*Enrollment trends in different areas of the world* (1950 = 100)

| | PRIMARY EDUCATION | | SECONDARY EDUCATION | | HIGHER EDUCATION | |
|---|---|---|---|---|---|---|
| | 1960 | 1963 | 1960 | 1963 | 1960 | 1963 |
| *World* | *140* | *157* | *172* | *210* | *179* | *230* |
| Europe | 114 | 119 | 160 | 186 | 161 | 211 |
| North America | 142 | 153 | 161 | 192 | 157 | 197 |
| Africa | 223 | 273 | 271 | 364 | 267 | 345 |
| Western | 298 | 356 | 388 | 600 | 722 | 1 622 |
| Eastern | 210 | 259 | 306 | 449 | 700 | 1 083 |
| Middle | 203 | 268 | 366 | 641 | — | — |
| Northern | 230 | 291 | 332 | 407 | 302 | 400 |
| Latin America | 175 | 203 | 227 | 325 | 203 | 262 |
| Tropical | 193 | 229 | 255 | 369 | 205 | 280 |
| Middle | 186 | 230 | 255 | 401 | 220 | 311 |
| Temperate | 134 | 144 | 184 | 231 | 213 | 255 |
| Caribbean | 166 | 174 | 199 | 311 | 151 | 180 |
| South Asia | 175 | 204 | 213 | 267 | 240 | 273 |
| Middle South | 181 | 214 | 199 | 250 | 266 | 278 |
| South East | 160 | 181 | 271 | 332 | 179 | 237 |
| South West | 201 | 249 | 341 | 449 | 287 | 420 |

*Source:* Computed from data given in Unesco, *Statistical Yearbook, 1965, op. cit.*, pp. 105-107.

*United States enrollment trends* (*in thousands*)

| YEAR | GRADES 1-8 AND KINDERGARTEN | GRADES 9-12 | HIGHER EDUCATION | TOTAL |
|---|---|---|---|---|
| 1899/1900 | 16 261 | 699 | 238 | 17 199 |
| 1909/10 | 18 529 | 1 115 | 355 | 19 999 |
| 1919/20 | 20 964 | 2 500 | 598 | 24 062 |
| 1929/30 | 23 740 | 4 812 | 1 101 | 29 653 |
| 1939/40 | 21 127 | 7 130 | 1 494 | 29 751 |
| 1949/50 | 22 207 | 6 453 | 2 659 | 31 319 |
| 1959/60 | 32 412 | 9 600 | 3 216 | 45 228 |
| 1965/66 | 36 000 | 13 000 | 5 500 | 54 500 |

*Source:* U.S. Dept. of Health, Education, and Welfare, *Digest of Educational Statistics,* 1966 edition (Washington, D.C., 1966).

APPENDIX 3

*U.S.S.R. enrollment trends ( in thousands )*

| LEVEL OF EDUCATION | ENROLLMENT | | | NUMBER OF PUPILS PER 10,000 INHABITANTS | | |
|---|---|---|---|---|---|---|
| | 1914 | 1940 | 1966 | 1914 | 1940 | 1966 |
| General | 9 656 | 35 552 | 48 170 | 607 | 1 864 | 2 040 |
| Vocational | 106 | 717 | 1 961 | 7 | 38 | 83 |
| Secondary specialized | 54 | 975 | 3 994 | 3 | 51 | 170 |
| Higher | 127 | 812 | 4 123 | 8 | 42 | 175 |
| *Total* | 9 943 | 38 056 | 58 248 | 625 | 1 995 | 2 468 |

Source: Nozhko, *et al., op. cit.*

APPENDIX 4

*Percentage of qualified entrants refused admission to secondary technical and trade schools*

| | 1955/56 | 1956/57 | 1957/58 | 1958/59 | 1959/60 |
|---|---|---|---|---|---|
| All Austria | 15.4 | 7.7 | 2.7 | 22.2 | 6.6 |
| Vienna | 29.1 | 16.4 | 15.9 | 32.3 | 3.6 |

| | 1960/61 | 1961/62 | 1962/63 | 1963/64 | 1964/65 |
|---|---|---|---|---|---|
| All Austria | 6.4 | 8.4 | 9.7 | 3.7 | 4.6 |
| Vienna | 8.0 | 11.0 | 12.7 | 3.7 | 1.9 |

'One of the most obvious examples of the shortfalls between supply of places and actual demand is the number of qualified entrants who were not admitted to school. Entry to secondary technical and trade schools in Austria is at the age of fifteen, and the following table shows the percentage of qualified entrants refused entry to their schools in Austria and in Vienna.

'In Austria, a proportion varying between 2.7 per cent and 22.2 per cent were turned away because of lack of places between 1955/56 and 1964/65.'

Source: OECD, *Educational Planning and Economic Growth in Austria 1965-1975, op. cit.*

APPENDIX 5

*Growth of school-age population (5-14 years) in different areas of the world*
(1960 = 100)

|  | 1965 | 1970 | 1975 | 1980 |
|---|---|---|---|---|
| *World* | *105.9* | *122.3* | *131.7* | *142.2* |
| North America | 110.3 | 115.3 | 116.7 | 125.7 |
| Europe | 102.2 | 103.7 | 102.3 | 101.8 |
| U.S.S.R. | 116.0 | 118.5 | 112.7 | 112.2 |
| Africa | 112.7 | 127.0 | 144.7 | 166.7 |
| Northern | 114.5 | 131.9 | 154.3 | 181.0 |
| Western | 114.5 | 132.5 | 153.1 | 180.1 |
| Southern | 113.1 | 129.1 | 148.2 | 170.1 |
| Middle | 107.7 | 117.9 | 131.9 | 149.1 |
| Eastern | 110.6 | 118.4 | 129.0 | 147.4 |
| Latin America | 117.7 | 136.3 | 157.1 | 179.5 |
| Middle | 122.2 | 143.8 | 167.7 | 198.9 |
| Tropical South | 118.9 | 139.4 | 162.4 | 185.9 |
| Caribbean | 112.2 | 126.3 | 142.4 | 158.3 |
| Temperate South | 107.9 | 116.4 | 125.2 | 132.1 |
| East Asia | 107.7 | 111.7 | 115.1 | 119.8 |
| Mainland | 109.9 | 114.7 | 118.1 | 122.4 |
| Japan | 84.0 | 77.0 | 76.0 | 79.7 |
| Other countries | 123.4 | 139.6 | 153.3 | 165.5 |
| South Asia | 117.4 | 134.8 | 151.7 | 166.4 |
| South East | 122.4 | 142.6 | 159.2 | 175.1 |
| South West | 115.0 | 128.6 | 146.3 | 172.4 |
| Middle South | 115.5 | 132.5 | 149.3 | 162.4 |
| Oceania | 109.6 | 117.7 | 124.8 | 134.1 |

*Source:* Computed from data given in Unesco, *Statistical Yearbook, 1965, op. cit.*, pp. 24-27.

In the case of the U.S.S.R. it is more relevant to choose the age group 7-15 years, although it is more difficult in that case to make international comparisons. The following figures are estimates made by the IIEP from official sources:

|  | 1960 | 1965 | 1970 | 1975 | 1980 |
|---|---|---|---|---|---|
| Age group 7-15 (in thousands) | 32 897 | 41 028 | 43 762 | 40 614 | 36 406 |
| Index | 100 | 125 | 133 | 123.5 | 110.5 |

APPENDIX 6

*Infant mortality rates in selected countries from 1950-64*
*( number of deaths under 1 year of age per 1 000 live births )*

|  | 1950-54 | 1960 | 1963 | 1964 |
|---|---|---|---|---|
| *Developing countries* | | | | |
| Burma | 240.3 | 148.6 | — | 128.1 |
| Colombia | 113.3 | 99.8 | 88.2 | — |
| Gambia | 104.9 | 66.9 | 68.1 | 79.4 |
| El Salvador | 81.8 | 76.3 | 67.7 | 65.5 |
| Honduras | 65.4 | 52.0 | 47.0 | — |
| Hongkong | 81.8 | 41.5 | 33.0 | 26.4 |
| Madagascar | 91.9 | 69.1 | — | 76.3 |
| Mauritius | 83.1 | 69.5 | 59.3 | 56.7 |
| Mexico | 91.8 | 74.2 | 67.7 | — |
| Nicaragua | 76.7 | 70.2 | 54.4 | 53.9 |
| Réunion | 138.9 | 83.3 | 70.3 | 74.2 |
| Singapore | 69.4 | 34.8 | 27.9 | 29.7 |
| Venezuela | 75.0 | 53.9 | 47.9 | — |
| *Industrialized countries* | | | | |
| France | 46.2 | 27.4 | 25.4 | 23.3 |
| Germany ( Federal Republic ) | 49.3 | 33.8 | 25.2 | 23.8 |
| Sweden | 20.0 | 16.6 | 15.4 | 14.2 |
| U.S.S.R. | 75.2 | 35.0 | 30.9 | 29.0 |
| United Kingdom | 29.0 | 22.5 | 21.8 | 20.6 |
| U.S.A. | 28.1 | 25.9 | 25.2 | 24.8 |

*Source:* United Nations, *Demographic Yearbook, op. cit.,* 1961, 1964, and 1965.

*Death rates by age of African, Asian, and European populations in South Africa,*
*1961 ( per thousand )*

| AGE GROUPS | AFRICAN | | ASIAN | | EUROPEAN | |
|---|---|---|---|---|---|---|
|  | Male | Female | Male | Female | Male | Female |
| 0- 4 | 50.5 | 46.0 | 18.8 | 14.0 | 7.8 | 6.1 |
| 5- 9 | 1.7 | 1.6 | 1.0 | 1.5 | 0.7 | 0.5 |
| 10-14 | 1.1 | 1.2 | 1.0 | 0.6 | 0.6 | 0.4 |
| 15-19 | 2.2 | 1.7 | 1.7 | 1.3 | 1.3 | 0.4 |
| 20-24 | 3.8 | 2.5 | 1.8 | 1.5 | 2.6 | 0.8 |
| 25-29 | 5.0 | 3.1 | 2.4 | 2.3 | 2.1 | 1.2 |
| 30-34 | 6.4 | 4.6 | 3.1 | 2.7 | 2.8 | 1.4 |
| 35-39 | 8.0 | 6.8 | 3.7 | 3.9 | 3.5 | 1.9 |
| 40-44 | 10.7 | 6.6 | 6.5 | 5.7 | 5.6 | 3.2 |
| 45-49 | 15.2 | 9.1 | 14.2 | 9.4 | 8.0 | 4.3 |
| 50-54 | 22.5 | 14.0 | 18.7 | 13.7 | 13.1 | 7.3 |
| 55-59 | 26.2 | 16.2 | 26.6 | 20.0 | 20.6 | 10.8 |
| 60-64 | 42.4 | 34.6 | 37.4 | 37.6 | 30.7 | 17.0 |
| 65-69 | 54.6 | 40.8 | 64.2 | 75.4 | 46.3 | 25.2 |
| 70 | 107.5 | 94.0 | 135.6 | 125.6 | 105.6 | 76.7 |
| *All groups* | *16.7* | *14.2* | *8.6* | *6.1* | *9.9* | *7.3* |

APPENDIX 6 (*continued*)

*Comparison of death rates by Age of African, Asian, and European*
*populations of South Africa, 1961*

| | MALE | | | FEMALE | | |
|---|---|---|---|---|---|---|
| AGE GROUPS | European | Asian | African | European | Asian | African |
| 0- 4 | 1 | 2.4 | 6.5 | 1 | 2.2 | 7.5 |
| 5- 9 | 1 | 1.4 | 2.4 | 1 | 3.0 | 3.2 |
| 10-14 | 1 | 1.7 | 1.8 | 1 | 1.5 | 3.0 |
| 15-19 | 1 | 1.3 | 1.7 | 1 | 3.2 | 4.2 |
| 20-24 | 1 | 0.6 | 1.5 | 1 | 1.9 | 3.1 |
| 25-29 | 1 | 1.1 | 2.4 | 1 | 1.9 | 2.6 |
| 30-34 | 1 | 1.1 | 2.3 | 1 | 1.9 | 3.3 |
| 35-39 | 1 | 1.0 | 2.3 | 1 | 2.1 | 3.6 |
| 40-44 | 1 | 1.1 | 1.9 | 1 | 1.8 | 2.1 |
| 45-49 | 1 | 1.7 | 1.9 | 1 | 2.2 | 2.1 |
| 50-54 | 1 | 1.4 | 1.7 | 1 | 1.9 | 1.9 |
| 55-59 | 1 | 1.3 | 1.3 | 1 | 1.9 | 1.5 |
| 60-64 | 1 | 1.2 | 1.4 | 1 | 2.2 | 2.0 |
| 65-69 | 1 | 1.4 | 1.2 | 1 | 3.0 | 1.6 |
| 70 | 1 | 1.2 | 1.0 | 1 | 1.6 | 1.2 |

*Source:* Figures computed from data given in United Nations, *Demographic Yearbook, op. cit.,* 1964.

*Comparative structure of population by age, in developed and developing countries*

| CUMULATIVE AGE GROUPS | INDUSTRIALIZED COUNTRIES | | | AFRICA | | | ASIA | | | LATIN AMERICA | | |
|---|---|---|---|---|---|---|---|---|---|---|---|---|
| | Germany (Fed. Rep.) | France | United States | Ghana | Niger | Morocco | (Rep. of) China | Korea (Rep. of) | India | Costa Rica | Honduras | Nicaragua |
| 0-4 | 835 | 868 | 1 076 | 1 927 | 1 734 | 1 887 | 1 690 | 1 611 | 1 506 | 1 836 | 1 812 | 1 823 |
| 0-9 | 1 553 | 1 729 | 2 131 | 3 442 | 3 573 | 3 497 | 3 264 | 3 140 | 2 979 | 3 489 | 3 369 | 3 558 |
| 0-14 | 2 241 | 2 621 | 3 089 | 4 454 | 4 549 | 4 429 | 4 605 | 4 234 | 4 102 | 4 764 | 4 561 | 4 836 |
| 0-19 | 2 860 | 3 328 | 3 937 | 5 259[a] | 5 304[a] | 5 050[a] | 5 416[a] | 5 179[a] | 4 919 | 5 737[a] | 5 493[a] | 5 805[a] |
| 0-24 | 3 696 | 3 921 | 4 621 | 6 137 | 6 192 | 5 828 | 6 088 | 6 013 | 5 770[a] | 6 511 | 6 292 | 6 582 |
| 0-29 | 4 448 | 4 584 | 5 204[a] | 7 007 | 7 094 | 6 652 | 6 818 | 6 777 | 6 604 | 7 145 | 6 952 | 7 290 |
| 0-34 | 5 128[a] | 5 292[a] | 5 786 | 7 733 | 7 778 | 7 375 | 7 490 | 7 395 | 7 306 | 7 722 | 7 510 | 7 832 |
| 0-39 | 5 795 | 5 994 | 6 421 | 8 294 | 8 315 | 7 926 | 8 083 | 7 944 | 7 886 | 8 228 | 7 996 | 8 389 |
| 0-44 | 6 408 | 6 563 | 7 067 | 8 757 | 8 754 | 8 441 | 8 575 | 8 412 | 8 407 | 8 629 | 8 373 | 8 764 |
| 0-49 | 6 941 | 7 065 | 7 657 | 9 081 | 9 093 | 8 740 | 8 976 | 8 821 | 8 819 | 8 968 | 8 684 | 9 075 |
| 0-54 | 7 643 | 7 688 | 8 201 | 9 347 | 9 373 | 9 103 | 9 322 | 9 152 | 9 208 | 9 277 | 8 942 | 9 342 |
| 0-59 | 8 314 | 8 287 | 8 670 | 9 507 | 9 575 | 9 259 | 9 570 | 9 427 | 9 432 | 9 477 | 9 125 | 9 514 |
| 0-64 | 8 894 | 8 820 | 9 070 | 9 682 | 9 728 | 9 572 | 9 746 | — | 9 688 | 9 668 | 9 304 | 9 715 |
| 0-69 | 9 326 | 9 235 | 9 395 | 9 773 | 9 848 | 9 675 | 9 860 | — | 9 798 | 9 782 | 9 400 | — |
| *Total Population* | *10 000* | *10 000* | *10 000* | *10 000* | *10 000* | *10 000* | *10 000* | *10 000* | *10 000* | *10 000* | *10 000* | *10 000* |

*Source:* Computed from data given in Table 5, 'Population by age and sex,' United Nations, *Demographic Yearbook, op. cit.,* 1964, pp. 130-155.
a Median age of population.

APPENDIX 7

*India: The impact of rising population and rising participation rates on enrollments*
(1950 = 100)

| EDUCATION LEVEL | 1965 | 1975 | 1980 | 1985 |
|---|---|---|---|---|
| Lower primary | | | | |
| Population of the age group | 148 | — | 199 | — |
| Enrollment ratio | 183 | — | 293 | — |
| Enrollment | 272 | — | 584 | — |
| Higher primary | | | | |
| Population of the age group | 151 | — | 220 | — |
| Enrollment ratio | 258 | — | 596 | — |
| Enrollment | 389 | — | 1 311 | — |
| Secondary | | | | |
| Population of the age group | 137 | — | 207 | — |
| Enrollment ratio | 309 | — | 594 | — |
| Enrollment | 420 | — | 1 232 | — |
| Higher | | | | |
| Population of the age group | 138 | — | — | — |
| Enrollment ratio | 300 | — | — | — |
| Enrollment | 416 | 837 | — | 1 582 |

*Source:* India, *Report of the Education Commission (1964-66)* . . . , *op. cit.*

APPENDIX 8

*Sweden: Parental background of newly registered university students*

| FATHER'S OCCUPATION OR EDUCATION | 1947 | 1953 | 1960 |
|---|---|---|---|
| | per cent | per cent | per cent |
| Teachers, university graduates, military officers, managers[a] | 38 | 35 | 35 |
| Workers[b] | 8 | 11 | 14 |
| Others | 54 | 54 | 51 |

*Source:* OECD, *Educational Policy and Planning, Sweden, op. cit.,* p. 213.
a According to election statistics, no more than 5 per cent of the entire male population belonged to these categories.
b 55 per cent of the male population.

*United Kingdom: Student's highest educational attainment in relation to father's occupation*

| FATHER'S OCCUPATION | HIGHER EDUCATION Full time | | Part-time | A-LEVEL | OTHER POST-SCHOOL COURSE OR O-LEVEL | NO POST-SCHOOL COURSE OR O-LEVEL |
|---|---|---|---|---|---|---|
| | Degree level | Other | | | | |
| | per cent | per cent | per cent | per cent | per cent | per cent |
| Higher professional | 33 | 12 | 7 | 16 | 25 | 7 |
| Managerial | 11 | 8 | 6 | 7 | 48 | 20 |
| Clerical | 6 | 4 | 3 | 7 | 51 | 29 |
| Skilled manual | 2 | 2 | 3 | 2 | 42 | 49 |
| Semi- and unskilled | 1 | 1 | 2 | 1 | 30 | 65 |
| *All children* | *4* | *3* | *4* | *3* | *40* | *47* |

Source: United Kingdom, *Higher Education. The Demand for Places in Higher Education, op. cit.,* part IV, p. 40.
Note. Owing to rounding, the total percentage of 'All children' exceeds 100.

In a highly industrialized *non*-European country such as Japan a similar situation prevails:

*Japan: Distribution of university students by parental income level, 1962*

| LEVEL OF INCOME (in yen) | DAYTIME COURSE | EVENING COURSE | MASTER'S COURSE | DOCTOR'S COURSE |
|---|---|---|---|---|
| | per cent | per cent | per cent | per cent |
| Less than 300 000 | 11 | 16 | 14 | 19 |
| 300 000 to 660 000 | 40 | 46 | 47 | 42 |
| 660 000 to 900 000 | 17 | 19 | 14 | 15 |
| More than 900 000 | 32 | 19 | 25 | 24 |

Source: Ministry of Education, *Education in 1962, Japan,* Tokyo, 1963, p. 38.
Note. 1 yen = 0.278 U.S. cents.

APPENDIX 9

*French-speaking Africa: Enrollment of terminal primary year versus admission to initial secondary year*

| | ENROLLMENT OF PRIMARY TERMINAL (I) | PERMITTED TO SIT FOR SECONDARY ENTRANCE EXAM (II) | ADMITTED TO SECONDARY EDUCATION (III) | PER CENT OF (II) OVER (I) | PER CENT OF (III) OVER (I) |
|---|---|---|---|---|---|
| Ivory Coast[a] | 35 948 | 16 486 | 5 571 | 45.9 | 15.5 |
| Dahomey[b] | 15 913 | 6 021 | 2 557 | 37.8 | 16.0 |
| Madagascar[c] | 24 068 | 12 548 | 3 939 | 49.9 | 16.3 |
| Congo (Brazz.)[a] | 13 259 | 6 647 | 2 270 | 50.1 | 17.1 |
| Togo[a] | 12 812 | 5 550 | 2 219 | 43.3 | 17.3 |
| Chad[b] | 9 364 | 5 044 | 1 763 | 53.9 | 18.9 |
| Centr. Afr. Rep.[d] | 6 082 | 5 491 | 1 215 | 90.3 | 20.0 |
| Upper Volta[b] | 8 907 | 5 388 | 1 870 | 60.5 | 21.0 |
| Gabon[a] | 6 202 | 3 591 | 1 370 | 57.9 | 22.0 |
| Senegal[a] | 20 617 | 15 873 | 5 009 | 77.0 | 24.3 |
| Niger[b] | 3 912 | 2 360 | 960 | 60.3 | 24.5 |

a 1963/64.
b 1964/65.
c 1961/62.
d 1962/63.

*French-speaking Africa: Shrinkage of enrollment through primary grades and in admission to secondary education*

| | CLASS I YEAR 0 | II 1 | III 2 | IV 3 | V 4 | VI 5 | ADMITTED TO SECONDARY EDUCATION: 6 |
|---|---|---|---|---|---|---|---|
| Cameroon | 1 000 | 640 | 499 | 407 | 379 | 398 | 64 |
| Chad | 1 000 | 449 | 355 | 295 | 268 | 312 | 64 |
| Togo | 1 000 | 638 | 565 | 473 | 446 | 469 | 66 |
| Cent. Afr. Rep. | 1 000 | 567 | 475 | 398 | 348 | 335 | 67 |
| Dahomey | 1 000 | 772 | 701 | 617 | 592 | 627 | 77 |
| Congo (Brazz.) | 1 000 | 686 | 591 | 506 | 454 | 431 | 91 |
| Gabon | 1 000 | 480 | 432 | 360 | 386 | 418 | 92 |
| Ivory Coast | 1 000 | 668 | 577 | 490 | 474 | 510 | 95 |
| Madagascar | 1 000 | 660 | 515 | 417 | 231 | 227 | 96 |
| Upper Volta | 1 000 | 838 | 724 | 635 | 537 | 568 | 103 |
| Niger | 1 000 | 882 | 728 | 607 | 550 | 527 | 129 |
| Mauritania | 1 000 | 844 | 678 | 775 | 509 | 531 | 156 |
| Senegal | 1 000 | 987 | 881 | 808 | 766 | 843 | 217 |

*Sources:* IEDES, *Les Rendements de l'enseignement du premier degré en Afrique francophone,* op. cit.

APPENDIX 10

*Nigeria: Improvement in teacher qualifications*

|  | 1961 | | 1962 | | 1963 | | 1964 | |
|---|---|---|---|---|---|---|---|---|
|  |  | per cent |  | per cent |  | per cent |  | per cent |
| Western Nigeria |  |  |  |  |  |  |  |  |
| Untrained | 27 990 | 69 | 26 700 | 67 | 25 777 | 67 | 11 777 | 51.5 |
| Grade III | 9 502 | 24 | 9 977 | 25 | 9 082 | 23 | 7 634 | 33.5 |
| Grade II | 2 670 | 7 | 3 320 | 8 | 3 792 | 10 | 3 455 | 15 |
| Total | 40 162 | 100 | 39 997 | 100 | 38 651 | 100 | 22 866 | 100 |
| Eastern Nigeria |  |  |  |  |  |  |  |  |
| Untrained | 24 664 | 59 | 23 053 | 52 | 13 782 | 35 | 7 938 | 23.5 |
| Grade III | 11 102 | 26.5 | 13 770 | 31 | 15 438 | 40 | 16 997 | 50 |
| Grade II | 5 798 | 14 | 6 986 | 16 | 9 214 | 24 | 8 456 | 25 |
| Grade I | 360 | 0.5 | 516 | 1 | 520 | 1 | 392 | 1.5 |
| Total | 41 924 | 100 | 44 325 | 100 | 38 954 | 100 | 33 783 | 100 |

*Source:* Nigeria, Federal Ministry of Education, *Annual Digest of Education Statistics* (1961), p. 41; (1962), p. 51; and *Statistics of Education in Nigeria* (1963), p. 45; (1964), p. 42.

APPENDIX 11

*India: Trend of teachers' salaries, 1950-1965*

|  | AVERAGE ANNUAL SALARY (in rupees,[a] at current prices) | | | | SALARY IN 1965/66 ADJUSTED TO 1950/51 PRICES |
|---|---|---|---|---|---|
|  | 1950/51 | 1955/56 | 1960/61 | 1965/66 |  |
| *Higher education* |  |  |  |  |  |
| University depts. | 3 759 | 5 456(145) | 5 475(146) | 6 500(173) | 3 939(105) |
| Arts/science colleges | 2 696 | 3 070(114) | 3 659(136) | 4 000(148) | 2 424(90) |
| Professional colleges | 3 948 | 3 861(98) | 4 237(107) | 6 410(162) | 3 885(98) |
| *Schools* |  |  |  |  |  |
| Secondary | 1 258 | 1 427(113) | 1 681(134) | 1 959(156) | 1 187(94) |
| Higher primary | 682 | 809(119) | 1 058(155) | 1 228(180) | 741(109) |
| Lower primary | 545 | 652(120) | 873(160) | 1 046(192) | 634(116) |
| Pre-primary | 914 | 770(84) | 925(101) | 1 083(118) | 656(72) |
| Vocational | 1 705 | 1 569(92) | 2 041(120) | 2 887(169) | 1 750(103) |
| *All teachers* | 769 | 919(120) | 1 218(158) | 1 476(192) | 895(116) |
| *Cost of living index for working classes* | (100) | 95 | 123 | 165 |  |
| *National per capita income, current prices* | 267 | 255(96) | 326(122) | 424(159) |  |

*Note.* Figures in brackets show index of growth: 1950/51 = 100.
a One rupee = 0.21 U.S. dollars.

APPENDIX 11 (continued)

'The largest proportional increase has taken place in the salaries of teachers in primary schools. . . . The improvement in the salaries of teachers in the universities, vocational schools and colleges is also noticeable. But in the colleges of arts and science . . . there has been an actual decrease in remuneration in real terms. [The picture in the pre-primary stage might be explained by the fact that the salaries in pre-primary schools are governed, not so much by departmental regulations, as by market conditions.] This is because most of the pre-school institutions are unaided and located in urban areas where an over-abundant supply of women teachers is available. . . . On the whole, there was some improvement in the remuneration of teachers in real terms up to 1960-61. This has since been almost completely neutralized by the sharp increase in prices that has taken place in the last two or three years.'

Source: India, Report of the Education Commission (1964-66) . . . , op. cit., p. 47.

APPENDIX 12

Examples of the wide spread in teacher salary structure: Northern Nigeria and Uganda
(starting salary of typical untrained primary teacher = 100)

| | NORTHERN NIGERIA | | | | UGANDA | | | |
|---|---|---|---|---|---|---|---|---|
| | Starting salary £ p.a. | Index | Ending salary £ p.a. | Index | Starting salary £ p.a. | Index | Ending salary £ p.a. | Index |
| Standard un-trained primary teacher | 111 | 100 | 180 | 163 | 126 | 100 | 126 | 100 |
| Standard trained primary teacher | 247 | 222 | 468 | 421 | 189 | 150 | 354 | 281 |
| Trained teacher (subuniversity) in secondary school | 621 | 560 | 855 | 770 | 617 | 490 | 1 080 | 857 |
| University graduate in secondary school | 720 | 648 | 1 584 | 1 427 | 738 | 585 | 1 752 | 1 390 |

Sources: Northern Nigeria, Education Law of Northern Nigeria, Kaduna, Government Printer, 1964, Table 1, pp. 32-34; Uganda, Report of the Uganda Teachers' Salaries Commission, 1961, as amended by Uganda Ministry of Education Circular 1964, unpublished.

APPENDIX 13

Expatriates in the teaching staffs of four African countries:

*Ivory* The percentage of expatriates in teaching staff of secondary schools is 93.5
*Coast* per cent of the total ( 1965 ).

Source: L. Cerych, *L'Aide extérieure et la planification de l'éducation en Côte-d'Ivoire, op. cit.*

*Kenya* Estimated demand for new teachers for secondary schools from 1964 to
1970 is as follows: forms I to IV, total teachers 1573 (expatriates 1157);
forms V and VI, total teachers 254 (expatriates 219).

Source: Government of Kenya, *Development Plan 1964-1970*, Nairobi, Government Printer, 1964, p. 102.

*Nigeria* The percentages of expatriates in teaching staffs of secondary schools
1961-1964 were as follows:

| | YEAR | GRADUATES | TOTAL |
|---|---|---|---|
| All Nigeria | 1961 | 55.4 | 27.4 |
| | 1962 | 62.6 | 28.5 |
| | 1963 | 62.5 | 29.1 |
| | 1964 | 60.1 | 28.1 |
| Northern Nigeria alone | 1961 | 94.8 | 67.7 |
| | 1962 | 93.7 | 55.3 |
| | 1963 | 92.8 | 58.5 |
| | 1964 | 95.1 | 55.6 |

The percentages of expatriates in the teaching staffs of all Nigerian universities were as follows:

Junior academic staff
 1962/63 : 59 per cent 1963/64 : 52 per cent

Senior academic staff
 1962/63 : 86 per cent 1963/64 : 82 per cent

Source: L. Cerych, *The Integration of External Assistance with Educational Planning in Nigeria, op. cit.*

*Tanzania* Ratios of expatriates to Tanzanians in 1964 were as follows: in secondary
schools, 632 expatriates to 226 Tanzanians, i.e. 74 : 26; in technical secondary schools, 75 expatriates to 77 Tanzanians, i.e. 49 : 51; in secondary
teacher training colleges, 105 expatriates to 88 Tanzanians, i.e. 52 : 48.
The Tanzanian government is trying to solve this problem by the process
of tied bursaries, 50 per cent of those awarded to arts students and 30 per
cent of those awarded to science students being reserved for those who
agree to undertake the university education course, coupled with the fact
that all holders of government bursaries have to sign an undertaking either
to serve the government or to find employment approved by the government in the five years following graduation.

Source: A. Mwingira, S. Pratt, *The Process of Educational Planning in Tanzania*, African research monograph No. 10 ( Paris: Unesco/IIEP, 1967 ).

APPENDIX 14

*United States: median salaries (in dollars) of science staff in educational*
*institutions versus other sectors*

|  | SCIENCES | MATHS |  | SCIENCES | MATHS |
|---|---|---|---|---|---|
| National *Average*a | *11 000* | *11 000* | Nonprofit organizations | 12 000 | 14 000 |
| Educational institutions | 9 600 | 8 700 | Industry and business | 12 000 | 13 000 |
| Federal government | 11 000 | 12 100 | Self-employed | 15 000 | 20 000 |
| Other government | 9 000 | 9 500 | Others | 11 000 | 11 500 |

Source: United States, *Digest of Education Statistics, op. cit.,* 1966.
a Excludes 'military and public health.'

APPENDIX 15

*United Kingdom: structure of the teaching force by sex, 1964 and 1965*

|  | PRIMARY | | SECONDARY | | TOTAL | |
|---|---|---|---|---|---|---|
|  | 1964 per cent | 1965 per cent | 1964 per cent | 1965 per cent | 1964 per cent | 1965 per cent |
| Male | 26.0 | 25.9 | 58.7 | 59.5 | 42.0 | 42.3 |
| Female | 74.0 | 74.1 | 41.3 | 40.5 | 58.0 | 57.7 |

Source: United Kingdom, Department of Education and Science, *Statistics of Education, op. cit.,*
1965, part I, 1965, p. 23, table 4 (1964); p. 27, table 9 (1965). (See Appendix 4 of this book.)
    *Note.* The total includes sectors other than primary and secondary, and there is a comparatively
small proportion of presumably inseparable 'primary and secondary' which are not included in the
separate sectors in this table.

APPENDIX 16

*Costs or expenditures per pupil in six countries*

| | Canada, Ontario — Cost per pupil of average daily attendance | | | | France — Recurrent expenditure per pupil in public education (State budget, constant price 1963) | | | | | | | |
| --- | --- | --- | --- | --- | --- | --- | --- | --- | --- | --- | --- | --- |
| | PRIMARY | | SECONDARY | | PRIMARY | | SECONDARY | | TECHNICAL | | UNIVERSITIES | |
| | £ | ICTa | £ | ICTa | FF | Index | FF | Index | FF | Index | FF | Index |
| 1950 | — | | — | | — | | — | | — | | — | |
| 1951 | — | | — | | 305 | | | | | | 1 375 | |
| 1952 | 187.68 | 100 | | | | 100 | 1 578 | 100 | 1 735 | 100 | | 100 |
| 1954 | | | 405.22 | 100 | | | | | | | | |
| 1955 | — | | — | | — | | — | | — | | — | |
| 1956 | — | | — | | — | | — | | — | | — | |
| 1957 | — | | — | | — | | — | | — | | — | |
| 1958 | 241.95 | 120.5 | 524.22 | 121 | | | | | | | | |
| 1959 | | | | | 374 | 124.5 | 1 726 | 109 | 2 144 | 124 | 2 324 | 169.5 |
| 1960 | | | | | | | | | | | | |
| 1961 | 293.65 | 142 | 622.75 | 139.5 | | | | | | | | |
| 1962 | 309.04 | 148 | 631.61 | 140.5 | | | | | | | | |
| 1963 | 326.98 | 153.5 | 629.38 | 137 | | | | | 2 707 | 156 | 3 062 | 223 |
| 1964 | — | | — | | 578 | 189 | 2 588 | 164 | | | | |
| 1965 | — | | — | | — | | — | | — | | — | |

*Sources:* Ontario Department of Education, 'Report of the Minister, 1964'; R. Poignant, *Education and Economic and Social Planning in France, op. cit.*
a ICT = index at constant price, compiled by IIEP. The deflator is the consumer price index given in United Nations, *Monthly Bulletin of Statistics,* New York (May 1967).

APPENDIX 16  (continued)

| | Germany (Fed. Rep.) Expenditures per pupil in primary and secondary education combined (constant prices) | | Sweden Public expenditures per pupil, primary and secondary education combined (constant prices 1965) | | U. K. (England & Wales) Estimation of current expenditures of public authority per pupil | | | | United States Current expenditures per pupil in average daily attendance, primary and secondary combined | |
| | | | | | PRIMARY | | SECONDARY | | | |
| | DM | Index | Cr. | Index | £ | ICT[a] | £ | ICT[a] | $ | ICT[a] |
|---|---|---|---|---|---|---|---|---|---|---|
| 1950 | 290 | 100 | 2 091 | 100 | — | — | — | — | 210.34 | 100 |
| 1951 | — | — | — | — | — | — | — | — | — | — |
| 1952 | 320.5 | 110 | — | — | — | — | — | — | — | — |
| 1954 | 363 | 125 | — | — | — | — | — | — | — | — |
| 1955 | — | — | 2 283 | 109 | — | — | — | — | — | — |
| 1956 | 415 | 143 | — | — | 30.2 | 100 | 56 | 100 | 297.45 | 121.5 |
| 1957 | — | — | — | — | — | — | — | — | — | — |
| 1958 | — | — | — | — | — | — | — | — | — | — |
| 1959 | 442 | 153 | — | — | — | — | — | — | — | — |
| 1960 | — | — | — | — | 44.7 | 134.5 | 73.9 | 120 | 379.63 | 141.5 |
| 1961 | 464 | 160 | 2 559 | 122.5 | 47.4 | 137.5 | 78.9 | 123.5 | — | — |
| 1962 | 478 | 165 | — | — | 50.6 | 142 | 86.6 | 131 | 423.70 | 154.5 |
| 1963 | — | — | — | — | 56.1 | 155 | 99.4 | 148 | — | — |
| 1964 | — | — | — | — | 59.1 | 159 | 104.9 | 152 | — | — |
| 1965 | — | — | 3 662 | 175 | 60.1 | 155 | 110.4 | 153 | 484.00 | 168 |

Sources: (Federal Republic of Germany): IIEP estimation on the basis of data given by G. Palm, in *Die Kaufkraft der Bildungsausgaben. Ein Beitrag zur Analyse der öffentlichen Ausgaben für Schulen und Hochschulen in der Bundesrepublik Deutschland, 1950 bis 1962*, Olten und Freiburg im Breisgau, Walter-Verlag, 1966; (Sweden): OECD, *Educational Policy and Planning. Sweden, op. cit.*; (United Kingdom): IIEP estimation on the basis of data contained in *Statistics of Education, op. cit.*, 1965, pt. 1, tables 40, 26; and United Nations, *Monthly Bulletin of Statistics, op. cit.*, May 1967.; (United-States): *Digest of Educational Satistics, op. cit.*, 1965. The deflator is the G.D.P. price index given in United Nations, *Monthly Bulletin of Statistics* (May 1967.)

a ICT = index at constant price computed by IIEP.

APPENDIX 17

*Ceylon: Recurrent expenditures per pupil at current prices*

| | PRIMARY + SECONDARY (GOVERNMENT SCHOOLS) | | ALL UNIVERSITY EDUCATION | |
| | Rupees | Indices | Rupees | Indices |
|---|---|---|---|---|
| 1952 | 76.2 | 100 | 1 937 | 100 |
| 1956 | 82.2 | 113 | 2 680 | 139 |
| 1960 | 111.7 | 146.5 | 2 538 | 131 |
| 1962 | 126.5 | 166 | 2 075 | 107 |
| 1964 | 131.7 | 172.5 | 1 808 | 93.5 |

*Source:* Unesco, *Financing and Cost of Education in Ceylon. A Preliminary Analysis of Educational Cost and Finance in Ceylon, 1952-1964,* prepared by J. Alles, *et al.,* Paris, 1967 (SHC/WS/14).

*India: Recurrent expenditures per pupil at current prices*

| | LOWER PRIMARY | | HIGHER PRIMARY | | SECONDARY | |
| | Rupees | Indices | Rupees | Indices | Rupees | Indices |
|---|---|---|---|---|---|---|
| 1950 | 19.9 | 100 | 37.1 | 100 | 72.9 | 100 |
| 1952 | 22.6 | 113.5 | 41.7 | 112.5 | 76.9 | 105.5 |
| 1953 | 22.2 | 112.5 | 43.3 | 117 | 79.5 | 109.5 |
| 1954 | 22.9 | 115 | 44.2 | 119 | 79.3 | 109.5 |
| 1956 | 24.4 | 125 | 39.0 | 105.5 | 80.2 | 110 |
| 1957 | 26.9 | 135 | 41.0 | 110 | 83.6 | 115 |
| 1959 | 26.9 | 135 | 39.6 | 107 | 88.6 | 122 |
| 1960 | 27.6 | 139 | 40.5 | 109.5 | 91.7 | 126 |
| 1965 | 30 | 150 | 45 | 121.2 | 107 | 146.5 |

*Source:* India, *Report of the Education Commission (1964-66)* . . . , *op. cit.*

*Latin America: Recurrent expenditures per pupil at constant prices*
*(1960 = 100)*

| COUNTRIES | 1959 | 1960 | 1961 | 1962 | 1963 | 1964 | 1965 |
|---|---|---|---|---|---|---|---|
| *Primary* | | | | | | | |
| Argentina | 102.5 | 100 | 124 | 145 | 122 | 129 | 135 |
| Colombia | — | 100 | 109 | 136.5 | 115.5 | 171.5 | — |
| Costa Rica | — | 100 | 101.5 | 98.5 | 93 | 93 | 98 |
| El Salvador | — | 100 | 113 | 118.5 | 123 | 133 | — |
| *Secondary* | | | | | | | |
| Argentina | 107.5 | 100 | 119 | 152.5 | 127 | 133.5 | — |
| Colombia | — | 100 | 91 | 94.5 | 85.5 | 95 | — |
| Costa Rica | — | 100 | 110.5 | 97 | 94.5 | 92 | 100.5 |
| *Higher* | | | | | | | |
| Brazil | 119 | 100 | 107 | 96.5 | 90 | — | — |
| Colombia | — | 100 | 97 | 108.5 | 98.5 | 104 | — |
| Chile (1961 = 100) | — | — | 100 | 95 | 77.5 | 72.5 | 85 |
| Peru (1963 = 100) | — | — | — | — | 100 | 105 | 116.5 |

*Source:* A. Page, *L'Analyse des coûts unitaires et la politique de l'éducation en Amérique Latine,* Report of the Regional Technical Assistance Seminar on Investment in Education in Latin America, Santiago de Chile, 5-13 December 1966 (Paris: Unesco, 27 October 1966) (SS/Ed.INV/6.d).

APPENDIX 17 (*continued*)

*Nigeria: Recurrent expenditures per pupil for primary education by region*
*at current prices*

| | NORTH | | EAST | | WEST | | LAGOS | |
| | £ | Index | £ | Index | £ | Index | £ | Index |
|---|---|---|---|---|---|---|---|---|
| 1952 | 4.46 | 100 | 3.36 | 100 | 3.70 | 100 | — | — |
| 1955 | — | — | — | — | — | — | 5.80 | 100 |
| 1962 | 7.42 | 166 | 4.93 | 146.7 | 5.73 | 154.8 | 9.86 | 170 |

*Source:* A. Callaway, A. Musone, *Financing of Education in Nigeria,* African Research Monograph No. 15 (Paris: Unesco/IIEP, 1968).

*Senegal: Recurrent expenditures per pupil in public education* ( at current prices)

| | 1961 | | 1964 | |
| LEVEL | CFA francs | Indices | CFA francs | Indices |
|---|---|---|---|---|
| Primary | 18 216 | 100 | 17 638 | 96.8 |
| Secondary | 213 718 | 100 | 215 065 | 100.6 |
| Technical | 259 234 | 100 | 308 002 | 118.8 |
| Higher | 891 726 | 100 | 816 313 | 91.5 |

*Source:* Guillaumont, Garbe, Verdun, *op. cit.*

APPENDIX 18

*Trend of total educational expenditures (all levels) in industrialized regions*
( in millions of units of local currencies)

| | AUSTRIA | | FRANCE | | ITALY | | NETHERLANDS | |
| | A.Sch. | Index | FF | Index | 000's Lire | Index | Guilders | Index |
|---|---|---|---|---|---|---|---|---|
| 1955 | 2 862.8 | 100 | 4 760 | 100 | 435.5 | 100 | 1 080 | 100 |
| 1960 | 4 645.1 | 162 | 9 830 | 206 | 771.9 | 177.2 | 2 000 | 195 |
| 1961 | — | — | — | — | 854.7 | 196.3 | — | — |
| 1963 | 5 769.5 | 202 | — | — | — | — | — | — |
| 1964 | — | — | — | — | — | — | — | — |
| 1965 | — | — | 20 160 | 425 | — | — | 3 780 | 350 |
| 1970 | 1 081.8 | 378 | 33 600 | 705 | — | — | 5 065 | 470 |
| 1974 | — | — | — | — | — | — | — | — |
| 1975 | 1 486.2 | 519 | — | — | — | — | 7 000 | 650 |

| | SWEDEN | | U.K. | | U.S.A. | | U.S.S.R. | |
| | Crs. | Index | £ | Index | 000's $ | Index | Old roubles | Index |
|---|---|---|---|---|---|---|---|---|
| 1955 | 1 984[a] | 100 | 621.8 | 100 | 16.8 | 100 | 62 600 | 100 |
| 1960 | — | — | 1 044.1 | 166 | 26.8 | 160 | 84 400 | 135 |
| 1961 | 3 204 | 161.4 | — | — | — | — | — | — |
| 1963 | 4 162 | 209.8 | — | — | — | — | — | — |
| 1964 | — | — | 1 610.3 | 257 | — | — | 117 300 | 188 |
| 1965 | — | — | — | — | 39.0 | 232 | — | — |
| 1970 | — | — | — | — | 50.8 | 301 | — | — |
| 1974 | — | — | — | — | 57.1 | 340 | — | — |

*Trend of educational expenditures in industrialized regions as percentage of GNP*

|      | AUSTRIA | FRANCE | ITALY | NETHER-LANDS | SWEDEN | U.K. | U.S.A. | U.S.S.R. |
|------|---------|--------|-------|--------------|--------|------|--------|----------|
| 1955 | 2.4     | 2.79   | 3.15  | 3.6          | 4.1[a] | 3.20 | 4.2    | [b]      |
| 1960 | 2.88    | 3.31   | 3.85  | 4.7          | —      | —    | —      | 4.7      |
| 1961 | —       | —      | 3.88  | —            | 5.1    | 4.11 | —      | 4.94     |
| 1963 | 2.9     | —      | —     | —            | 5.3    | —    | —      | 5.38     |
| 1964 | —       | —      | —     | —            | —      | 5.03 | —      | —        |
| 1965 | —       | 4.36   | —     | 5.7          | —      | —    | 6.3    | —        |
| 1970 | 4.1     | 5.7    | —     | 6.3          | —      | —    | —      | —        |
| 1974 | —       | —      | —     | —            | —      | —    | 6.7    | —        |
| 1975 | 4.5     | —      | —     | —            | —      | —    | —      | —        |

a 1955/1956.
b Soviet GNP officially published is not quite comparable with GNP estimated according to the norms in the other industrialized countries; it is diminished by about 20 per cent. Figures in this column have been estimated so that percentages could be compared with those for other countries.

*Trend of educational expenditures in industrialized regions, as a percentage of public budgets*

|      | BELGIUM | FRANCE | ITALY | NETHERLANDS | U.S.S.R. |
|------|---------|--------|-------|-------------|----------|
| 1955 | 10.8    | 9.6    | 11.91 | —           | 10.5     |
| 1956 | —       | —      | —     | 11.3        | —        |
| 1960 | 15.2    | 12.4   | 13.83 | 16.0        | 10.2     |
| 1961 | —       | —      | 13.85 | —           | —        |
| 1963 | —       | —      | —     | —           | 10.7     |
| 1964 | 17.1    | —      | —     | 20.7        | —        |
| 1965 | —       | 16.9   | —     | —           | —        |

*Sources:* For the tables in this appendix: (Austria): OECD, *Educational Planning and Economic Growth in Austria, 1965-1975, op. cit.;* (Belgium, France, Italy, United Kingdom, USSR): Poignant, *L'enseignement dans les pays du Marché commun, op. cit.;* (France): Poignant, *Education and Economic and Social Planning in France, op. cit.;* (Netherlands): OECD, *Educational Policy and Planning. Netherlands, op. cit.;* (Sweden): OECD, *Educational Policy and Planning. Sweden, op. cit.;* (United Kingdom): 1964, IIEP estimations; (U.S.A.): Past trends from *Digest of Educational Statistics, op. cit.,* 1965. (Prospects, IIEP estimation.)

APPENDIX 19

*Trend of government expenditures on education in the Netherlands*
1950-1975[a]

| CATEGORY | 1950 | 1955 | 1960 | 1965 | 1970 | 1975 |
|---|---|---|---|---|---|---|
| | | | (millions of guilders) | | | |
| Personnel | 350 | 645 | 1 160 | 2 280 | 3 200 | 4 550 |
| Material | 85 | 175 | 265 | 510 | 715 | 1 050 |
| Capital | 80 | 195 | 470 | 800 | 900 | 1 050 |
| Indivisable | 40 | 65 | 105 | 190 | 250 | 350 |
| *Total* | *555* | *1 080* | *2 000* | *3 780* | *5 065* | *7 000* |
| As percentage of GNP (at market prices) | 2.9 | 3.6 | 4.7 | 5.7 | 6.3 | 7.0 |

Source: *Educational Planning in the Netherlands, op. cit.*
a 1950-1965 current prices; 1970-1975 prices 1965, except for a real salary increase of 3.5 per cent per annum.
Note. 'The foregoing assessment of government expenditure on education must definitely be regarded as a *minimum* estimate. Measures likely to be taken, such as raising the school-leaving age, further lowering the ratio of pupils to teachers, increasing financial aids to students, the implementation of the new law on primary education, etc. . . . may, as calculations indicate, cause government expenditures on education to increase to 8 per cent/10 per cent of GNP in 1975.'

APPENDIX 20

*Projections of educational expenditures in the United States—a 'flattening' curve?*

1.   In *Projections of Educational Statistics to 1973-74* (1964), Kenneth Simon and Marie Fullam of the U.S. Department of Health, Education, and Welfare give the following trend of enrollment in educational institutions and of total expenditures on education:

| YEAR | TOTAL ENROLLMENT (in thousands) | TOTAL EXPENDITURES (in $ billions, 61-62 prices) |
|---|---|---|
| 1953-54 | 34 536 | 15.9 |
| 1956-57 | 39 547 | 21.0 |
| 1960-61 | 45 764 | 26.8 |
| 1964-65 | 52 575 | 33.8 |
| 1965-66 | 53 820 | 35.6 |
| 1968-69 | 57 397 | 40.9 |
| 1969-70 | 58 374 | 43.9 |
| 1971-72 | 60 176 | 45.8 |
| 1973-74 | 61 951 | 49.5 |

2.   The *Digest of Educational Statistics* (1965 edition) estimates the total expenditure devoted to education, in current value, in 1964-65 at $39 billion. These data make it feasible to estimate the importance of the financial effort devoted to education to 1973-74 in absolute values and as a percentage of GNP.

*Assumptions*

1.   Assume the same trend from 1964-65 to 1973-74 for the educational expendi-

tures as that given in *Projections of Educational Statistics to 1973-74* in constant prices. Thus the index is 146.5 (49.5/33.8) for the period 1964-1973/74.

2. Assume that the average annual rate of increase of GNP for this period is the same as that of the period 1950-65 at constant prices. From the United Nations statistical data, the indices of GNP at constant prices are:

$$1963/1950 = 155$$
$$1964/1963 = 105$$
$$1965/1964 = 106$$

Thus for the whole period (15 years) the index is 172.5 (155 × 105 × 106) or 3.6 per cent per annum, which gives an index of 138 for the period 1964-65 to 1973-74.

*Estimations*

1. The amount of expenditure on education in 1964-65 was $39 billion. Therefore the estimated expenditure on education in 1973-74 is:

$39 × 146.5 = $57.1 billion (at 1964-65 prices)

2. The percentage of GNP devoted to education was 6.3 per cent in 1964-65. In 1973 it will be 6.3 × 146.5/138 = 6.7 per cent at constant 1964-65 prices.

*Comment*

In fact, since the price index of the education sector can be expected to increase more quickly than the general price index, the percentage of GNP devoted to education will probably be higher than 6.7 per cent in 1973-74. However, if we compare the evolution with the trend of the last ten years, there is, in fact, some 'flattening' in the curve of expenditures in education as a percentage of GNP. The essential reason is that whereas the total enrollment increased at an annual rate of 3.6 per cent from 1949-50 to 1964-65, it is expected to increase only at a rate of 1.8 per cent per annum from 1964-65 to 1973-74.

APPENDIX 21

*Comparative economic growth rates for selected countries*

| | GROWTH | |
|---|---|---|
| | Over the period 1960-65 (1960 = 100) | Average annual rate 1960-65 (per cent) |
| *Developing countries* | | |
| Argentina[a] | 118 | 3.35 |
| Bolivia[a] | 127.5 | 5 |
| Ceylon[a] | 116.5 | 3.15 |
| Chile[a] | 123 | 4.25 |
| Cyprus[a] | 132.4 | 5.75 |
| Ghana[a] | 116 | 3 |
| India[b] | 114 | 2.7 |
| Iran[a] | 132.5 | 5.75 |
| Morocco[c] | 118.5 | 3.5 |
| Tanzania[d] | 116 | 3 |
| *Developed countries* | | |
| Austria[a] | 122.3 | 4.15 |
| Bulgaria[b] | 138 | 6.6 |
| Czechoslovakia[b] | 110.1 | 2 |
| Denmark[a] | 127 | 4.85 |
| France[a] | 128.2 | 5.10 |
| Germany (Fed. Rep.)[a] | 126.7 | 4.8 |
| Italy[a] | 128.4 | 5.15 |
| U.S.S.R.[b] | 137.5 | 6.5 |
| United Kingdom[a] | 117.3 | 3.25 |
| U.S.A.[a] | 125.8 | 4.7 |

*Source:* United Nations, *Monthly Bulletin of Statistics, op. cit.* (May 1967), table 63.
a Gross domestic product at constant market prices.
b Net material product at market prices.
c Gross domestic production.
d Gross domestic product at factor cost.

APPENDIX 22

*The population problem: the example of Uganda*
Consider the implications in terms of enrollments and recurring costs of two alternatives for development of primary education: (a) maintaining a constant enrollment ratio, and (b) maintaining a constant absolute nonschooling gap.

*Assumptions*
1.   Growth of population aged 6 to 12 assumed to be 3 per cent per annum, not 2.75 per cent as in the published statistics, because the second five-year plan (in its Table 3) assumes an increase of *total* population of 2.8 per cent.
2.   Primary teachers' salaries increase in real terms at the same rate as monetary GDP per capita; nonteacher costs remain constant; therefore, the total unit cost rises steadily.

3. Use monetary GDP rather than total GDP to measure education costs.

The results are shown in the table below. Points to be noted are: (a) it costs almost a constant 2.48 per cent of GDP simply to maintain an enrollment ratio of 43 per cent; and (b) to maintain the nonschooling gap with the figure pertaining to 1966 would mean a rise in the percentage of GDP devoted to primary education from 2.48 per cent to 3.49 per cent, and would also mean a quadrupling of the recurring costs in real terms.

*Uganda primary schools: enrollments and costs needed to (a) maintain a constant enrollment ratio; (b) maintain a constant nonschooling gap*

| | POPULA-TION 6 TO 12 (000's) | GDP (monetary) (£ m.) | UNIT COST £ (sal. + £1.5) | Enrollment (000's) | MAINTAIN ENROLLMENT RATIO 43% Recurring costs (£ m.) | Per cent of GDP | MAINTAIN NONSCHOOLING GAP OF 763,000 Enrollment (000's) | Recurring costs (£ m.) | Per cent of GDP |
|---|---|---|---|---|---|---|---|---|---|
| 1966 | 1 340 | 97.7 | 8.5 | 577 | 4.90 | 2.48 | 577 | 4.90 | 2.48 |
| 1967 | 1 381 | 211.9 | 8.8 | 594 | 5.23 | 2.47 | 618 | 5.44 | 2.57 |
| 1968 | 1 423 | 227.2 | 9.1 | 612 | 5.57 | 2.45 | 660 | 6.01 | 2.65 |
| 1969 | 1 465 | 243.6 | 9.4 | 630 | 5.92 | 2.43 | 702 | 6.60 | 2.71 |
| 1970 | 1 509 | 261.1 | 9.8 | 649 | 6.36 | 2.44 | 746 | 7.31 | 2.80 |
| 1971 | 1 554 | 279.7 | 10.1 | 668 | 6.75 | 2.41 | 791 | 7.99 | 2.86 |
| 1972 | 1 600 | 301.2 | 10.5 | 688 | 7.22 | 2.40 | 837 | 8.79 | 2.92 |
| 1973 | 1 648 | 325.6 | 11.0 | 709 | 7.80 | 2.40 | 885 | 9.73 | 2.99 |
| 1974 | 1 698 | 351.4 | 11.5 | 730 | 8.39 | 2.39 | 935 | 10.75 | 3.06 |
| 1975 | 1 749 | 379.1 | 12.0 | 752 | 9.02 | 2.38 | 986 | 11.83 | 3.12 |
| 1976 | 1 801 | 409.1 | 12.6 | 774 | 9.75 | 2.38 | 1 038 | 13.08 | 3.20 |
| 1977 | 1 855 | 441.4 | 13.2 | 798 | 10.53 | 2.39 | 1 092 | 14.41 | 3.26 |
| 1978 | 1 191 | 476.3 | 13.8 | 822 | 11.34 | 2.38 | 1 148 | 15.84 | 3.33 |
| 1979 | 1 968 | 513.9 | 14.4 | 846 | 12.18 | 2.37 | 1 205 | 17.35 | 3.36 |
| 1980 | 2 027 | 554. | 15.1 | 872 | 13.17 | 2.38 | 1 264 | 19.09 | 3.44 |
| 1981 | 2 088 | 600.0 | 15.8 | 898 | 14.19 | 2.36 | 1 325 | 20.93 | 3.49 |

Source: IIEP calculations based on: Uganda, *Education Statistics, 1965, op. cit.;* and *Work for Progress: The Second Five-year Plan 1966-1967, op. cit.*

APPENDIX 23

*Populations of developing countries are 'younger,' thus placing a heavier burden*
*of support on employable adults*

| | YEAR OF DATA | MEDIAN AGE OF TOTAL POPULATION | SCHOOL-AGE POPULATION AS PERCENTAGE OF TOTAL POPULATION |
|---|---|---|---|
| China, (Rep. of) | 1963 | 17.4 | 56. |
| France | 1962 | 32.9 | 28.2 |
| Germany (Fed. Rep. of) | 1961 | 34 | 21.4 |
| Ghana | 1960 | 18.3 | 48.3 |
| India | 1961 | 20.4 | 46.5 |
| Morocco | 1960 | 19.5 | 49.4 |
| Nicaragua | 1963 | 15.8 | 61.7 |
| Niger | 1962 | 18 | 54.4 |
| Sweden | 1960 | 36.5 | 23.1 |

*Source:* Prepared from data in United Nations, *Demographic Yearbook, op. cit.* (1964), table 5, 'Population by age and sex,' p. 130.

APPENDIX 24

*Trend of total public expenditures on education in developing countries*

| | YEAR | AMOUNT | INDEX | | YEAR | AMOUNT | INDEX |
|---|---|---|---|---|---|---|---|
| Bolivia (billion bolivianos) | 1960 1964 | 76.5 182.0 | 100 238 | Senegal (million CFA francs) | 1961 1964 | 7 143 10 658 | 100 149 |
| India (million rupees) | 1955 1965 | 1 897 6 000 | 100 316.2 | Tanzania ( £ million) | 1956 1963 | 4.71 8.13 | 100 173 |
| Libya ( £ 000's) | 1960 1963 | 3 322 7 797 | 100 234 | Tunisia (million dinars) | 1959 1964 | 9 112 25 012 | 100 275 |
| Mexico (million pesos) | 1960 1964 | 2 650 6 360 | 100 240 | Venezuela (bolivar 000's) | 1960 1964 | 795 000 1 730 000 | 100 218 |
| Pakistan (million rupees) | 1957 1963 | 268 910 | 100 339.6 | | | | |

*Trend of public educational expenditures in developing countries*
*as percentage of public budget*

|            | YEAR | PER CENT |          | YEAR | PER CENT |
|------------|------|----------|----------|------|----------|
| Argentina  | 1961 | 9.7      | Pakistan | 1961 | 6.5      |
|            | 1965 | 11.4     |          | 1964 | 10.6     |
| Honduras   | 1961 | 19.3     | Senegal  | 1961 | 13.0     |
|            | 1965 | 24.8     |          | 1964 | 13.7     |
| Mexico     | 1961 | 15.7     | Tanzania | 1956 | 14.7     |
|            | 1965 | 24.1     |          | 1965 | 15.6     |
| Morocco    | 1956 | 13.3     |          |      |          |
|            | 1965 | 17.3     |          |      |          |

*Trend of educational expenditures in developing countries as percentage*
*of national product*

|                        | YEAR | PER CENT |                         | YEAR | PER CENT |
|------------------------|------|----------|-------------------------|------|----------|
| Colombia[a]            | 1960 | 2.4      | Senegal[c]              | 1961 | 4.6      |
|                        | 1964 | 3.1      |                         | 1964 | 6.4      |
| India[b]               | 1955 | 1.7      | Tunisia[c]              | 1959 | 3.5      |
|                        | 1965 | 2.9      |                         | 1964 | 6.7      |
| Ivory Coast[c]         | 1960 | 3.9      | Venezuela[a]            | 1960 | 3.1      |
|                        | 1964 | 4.5      |                         | 1964 | 4.8      |
| Mexico[a]              | 1960 | 1.7      |                         |      |          |
|                        | 1964 | 2.8      |                         |      |          |

*Sources:* (All countries): Unesco, *Statistical Yearbook, 1965, op. cit.;* United Nations, *Monthly Bulletin of Statistics, op. cit.* (May 1967); (India): *Educational Expenditure in India* (New Delhi: National Council of Educational Research and Training, 1965); estimates given in *Report of the Education Commission (1964/66)* . . . , *op. cit.;* (Ivory Coast): Hallak, Poignant, *op. cit.,* annex A, page 39, table XVI; (Latin America): Unesco, 'The Financing of Education in Latin America,' Report of the Regional Technical Assistance Seminar on Investment in Education in Latin America, Santiago de Chile, 5-13 December 1966 (Paris, Unesco) (SS/Ed.INV.7); (Pakistan): International Bureau of Education/Unesco, *International Yearbook of Education,* Report on educational developments in 1963-64, presented at the 27th International Conference on Education, Geneva/Paris, 1964, Vol. XXVI; (Senegal): Guillaumont, Garbe, and Verdun, *op. cit.,* annex A, pp. 42, 43, tables XVIII and XXI; (Tanzania): J. B. Knight, *The Costing and Financing of Educational Development in Tanzania,* African research monographs, No. 4 (Paris: Unesco/IIEP, 1966), pp. 19, 21, tables 5, 7.

  a Percentage of gross national product.
  b Percentage of national income.
  c Percentage of gross domestic product.

APPENDIX 25

*Projected enrollments and financial requirements up to 1970 for Unesco
regional educational targets, by regions*

| | 1965 | PER CENT | 1970 | PER CENT | AVERAGE ANNUAL RATE OF INCREASE (*in per cent*) |
|---|---|---|---|---|---|
| **Africa** | | | | | |
| First level: enrollment (000) | 15 279 | | 20 378 | | 5.93 |
| participation rate | | 51 | | 71 | |
| Second level: enrollment (000) | 1 833.5 | | 3 390 | | 13.08 |
| participation rate | | 9 | | 15 | |
| Third level: enrollment (000) | 46 | | 80 | | 11.71 |
| participation rate | | 0.35 | | 0.55 | |
| Total expenditures (U.S. $mil) | 1 139 | | 1 701 | | 8.35 |
| GNP (U.S. $mil) | 19 694 | | 24 413 | | 4.39 |
| Percentage of GNP | | 5.78 | | 6.96 | |
| **Latin America** | | | | | |
| First level: enrollment (000) | 34 721 | | 43 438 | | 4.58 |
| participation rate | | 91 | | 100 | |
| Second level: enrollment (000) | 6 230 | | 11 457 | | 12.96 |
| participation rate | | 22 | | 34 | |
| Third level: enrollment (000) | 665 | | 905 | | 6.35 |
| participation rate | | 3.4 | | 4.0 | |
| Total expenditures (U.S. $mil) | 3 219 | | 4 937 | | 9.00 |
| GNP (U.S. $mil) | 71 130 | | 90 782 | | 5.00 |
| Percentage of GNP | | 4.52 | | 5.43 | |
| **Asia** | | | | | |
| First level: enrollment (000) | 110 368 | | 148 716 | | 6.15 |
| participation rate | | 63 | | 74 | |
| Second level: enrollment (000) | 14 545 | | 23 064 | | 9.66 |
| participation rate | | 15 | | 19 | |
| Third level: enrollment (000) | 2 206 | | 3 320 | | 7.86 |
| participation rate | | 3.4 | | 4.1 | |
| Total expenditures (U.S. $mil) | 3 261 | | 4 803 | | 8.05 |
| GNP (U.S. $mil) | 88 319 | | 112 719 | | 5.00 |
| Percentage of GNP | | 3.69 | | 4.26 | |

Source: Unesco, *Unesco's Contribution to the Promotion of the Aims and Objectives . . . ,
op. cit.,* pp. 35-37.

APPENDIX 26

*Trend of 'completed students'—primary level* (1960 = 100)

| | AFRICA | | | | ASIA | | | | LATIN AMERICA | | | |
| | Madagascar | Niger | Senegal | Uganda | Afghanistan | India | Korea (Rep. of) | Viet-Nam (Rep. of) | Guatemala | Paraguay | Peru | Venezuela |
|------|------|------|------|------|------|------|------|------|------|------|------|------|
| 1955 | — | — | — | — | 64 | 65 | 72 | — | — | — | 66 | — |
| 1956 | — | — | — | 59 | — | — | — | 51 | — | — | 72 | — |
| 1957 | — | 54 | 48 | 68 | — | — | — | 60 | — | — | 79 | 70 |
| 1958 | 95 | 67 | 73 | 83 | — | — | — | 71 | — | — | 86 | 75 |
| 1959 | 98 | 85 | 86 | 96 | — | — | — | 86 | 93 | — | 94 | 85 |
| 1960 | 100 | 100 | 100 | 100 | 100 | 100 | 100 | 100 | 100 | — | 100 | 100 |
| 1961 | 126 | 145 | 121 | 113 | 117 | — | 96 | 113 | 119 | 100 | 106 | 112 |
| 1962 | 137 | 96 | 113 | 119 | 124 | — | 106 | 127 | 133 | 107 | — | 127 |
| 1963 | 146 | 154 | 154 | 140 | — | — | — | 138 | 145 | 113 | — | 143 |
| 1964 | — | 216 | — | 151 | — | — | — | — | — | 123 | — | 165 |
| 1965 | — | — | — | — | — | 166 | — | — | — | 138 | — | — |

Sources: (Africa): *Madagascar, Niger, Senegal* (graduates): IEDES, *Les Rendements de l'enseignement* . . . , *op. cit.,* II, pp. 56, 78, 86; *Uganda* (enrollment in class VI): Ministry of Education, *Education Statistics, 1965, op. cit.,* table G6; (Asia): *Afghanistan and Korea* (graduates): Ministry of Education, Japan, *Education in Asia, op. cit.,* p. 77; *India* (enrollment in class VII): Ministry of Education, *Report of the Education Commission (1964-66)* . . . , *op. cit.,* p. 155; *Viet-nam* (enrollment in class VI): Unesco, *Projections à long terme de l'éducation en République du Viet-nam* (Bangkok: Unesco, 1965), p. 119; (Latin America): *Guatemala* (graduates): unpublished data; *Paraguay* (enrollment in class VI): unpublished data; *Peru* (enrollment in class VI): Ministerio de Educación Pública, *Estadística educativa, 1957-1961,* Lima, p. 14; *Venezuela* (enrollment in class VI): Oficina Central de Coordinación y Planificación, *La educación venezolana en cifras* (Caracas, 1965), I, p. 13.

APPENDIX 26 (*continued*)

*General secondary school graduates or final year enrollments in selected countries*
(1960 = 100)[a]

| REGION/COUNTRY | 1955 | 1965 | REGION/COUNTRY | 1955 | 1965 |
|---|---|---|---|---|---|
| *Africa* | | | *Asia* | | |
| E. Cameroon | 33 | 248 | China (Rep. of) | 66 | 122[b] |
| Ivory Coast | 38 | 217 | Korea (Rep. of) | 81 | 117[c] |
| Madagascar | 31 | 273 | Laos | 96[d] | 250[c] |
| Uganda | 42 | 203 | Nepal | 43 | 100[b] |
| *Latin America* | | | *Industrialized* | | |
| Colombia | 75[d] | 153[e] | *countries* | (1950/1) | (1965) |
| Paraguay[f] | — | 145 | Belgium[g] | 69 | 113 |
| Peru | 53 | 155[h] | France[g] | 54 | 141 |
| Venezuela | 35 | 144[h] | Germany | | |
| | | | (Fed. Rep.)[g] | 51 | 105 |
| | | | Netherlands[g] | 68 | 141 |

*Sources:* (Africa) *East Cameroon, Ivory Coast, Madagascar:* France, Ministère de la coopération, 'Statistiques scolaires des états africains francophones', Direction de la coopération économique et financière (unpublished paper); *Uganda:* Ministry of Education, *Education Statistics, 1965, op. cit.;* (Asia) *China, Korea, Laos, Nepal:* Japan, Ministry of Education, *Education in Asia, op. cit.,* table 42(2), p. 77; (Latin America) *Colombia:* Ministerio de Educación Nacional, Misión de Planeamiento de la Educación, Unesco/AID/BIRF, *Estadísticas* (Bogotá, 1965); *Paraguay:* unpublished data; *Peru:* Instituto Nacional de Planificación/OECD, *Desarrollo económico y social, recursos humanos y educación* (Lima, 1966); *Venezuela:* Oficina Central de Coordinación y Planificación, *La éducación venezolana en cifras, op. cit.;* (Industrialized countries) *Belgium, France, Federal Republic of Germany, Netherlands:* Poignant, *L'Enseignement dans les pays du Marché commun, op cit.*

a Where available, figures for graduates were used, but in some cases those for enrollments in final grades were all that were available.

b 1961.                                          e 1963.
c 1962.                                          f Index, 1961 = 100 (1963 = 126).
d 1957.                                          g Index, 1961 = 100.
                                                 h 1964.

*Graduates of higher education in selected countries* (1957 = 100)

| COUNTRY | 1960 | 1963 | COUNTRY | 1960 | 1963 |
|---|---|---|---|---|---|
| *Africa* | | | *Asia* | | |
| Ghana | 165 | 291 | China (Rep. of) | 178 | 255 |
| Sierra Leone | 171 | 302 | Iraq | 152 | 231 |
| Tunisia[a] | 128[b] | 132 | Pakistan | 191.5 | 270[c] |
| U.A.R. | 114 | 186 | Viet-Nam (Rep. of) | 191 | 304 |
| *Latin America* | | | *Industrialized nations* | | |
| Argentina | 120.5 | 169 | Denmark | 124.5 | 138 |
| Brazil | 117.5 | 123.5 | Romania | 85.5 | 118.5 |
| Chile | — | — | Japan | 103.5 | 125 |
| Guatemala | 113.5 | 242[d] | U.S.A. (+ Puerto | | |
| | | | Rico) | 111.4 | 140.5 |

*Source:* Unesco, *Statistical Yearbook, 1965, op. cit.,* pp. 326-38.
a Index, 1961 = 100.
b 1962.
c 1962.
d 1964.

APPENDIX 27

*United States: retention rates, 5th grade to college entrance*

| Year pupils entered 5th grade | RETENTION PER 1 000 PUPILS ENTERING 5TH GRADE Grade | | | | | HIGH SCHOOL GRADU- ATES | Year of high school gradu- ation | FIRST TIME COLLEGE STUDENT |
|---|---|---|---|---|---|---|---|---|
| | 5 | 6 | 8 | 10 | 12 | | | |
| 1924/25 | 1 000 | 911 | 741 | 470 | 344 | 302 | 1932 | 118 |
| 1934/35 | 1 000 | 953 | 842 | 711 | 512 | 467 | 1942 | 129 |
| 1944/45 | 1 000 | 952 | 858 | 748 | 549 | 522 | 1952 | 234 |
| 1954/55 | 1 000 | 980 | 948 | 855 | 684 | 642 | 1962 | 343 |
| 1956/57 | 1 000 | 985 | 948 | 871 | 724 | 667 | 1964 | 357 |
| 1957/58 | 1 000 | 994 | 954 | 878 | 758 | 710 | 1965 | 378 |

*Source:* United States, *Digest of Educational Statistics, op. cit.,* 1966, p. 7.

*United States: number of high school graduates as proportion of population of 17 years of age*

| YEAR | PERCENTAGE | YEAR | PERCENTAGE | YEAR | PERCENTAGE |
|---|---|---|---|---|---|
| 1870 | 2 | 1910 | 8.8 | 1950 | 59 |
| 1880 | 2.5 | 1920 | 16.8 | 1960 | 65.1 |
| 1890 | 3.5 | 1930 | 29 | 1965 | 72 |
| 1900 | 6.4 | 1940 | 50.8 | | |

*Source:* United States, *Digest of Educational Statistics, op. cit.,* 1966, p. 50.

APPENDIX 28

*Philippines: Employment status of high school graduates by age groups*

| AGE | TOTAL 000's | TOTAL per cent | WORKING (per cent) Full time | WORKING (per cent) Part time | OUT OF WORK (per cent) Looking for work | OUT OF WORK (per cent) Not looking for work |
|---|---|---|---|---|---|---|
| 15-19 | 224 | 100 | 5.7 | 9.1 | 29.5 | 55.7 |
| 20-24 | 235 | 100 | 22.0 | 12.3 | 36.5 | 29.2 |
| 25-29 | 131 | 100 | 33.0 | 22.7 | 28.5 | 15.9 |
| 30-34 | 77 | 100 | 50.6 | 15.0 | 18.3 | 16.1 |
| Over 35 | 14 | 100 | 48.5 | 24.2 | 18.2 | 9.1 |
| *All age groups* | 681 | 100 | 22.5 | 13.8 | 30.2 | 33.5 |

*Source:* Philippines, Office of Manpower Services, *Summary Report on Inquiry into Employment and Unemployment among Those with High School or Higher Education* (Manila: Dept. of Labor Office, May 1961), table 31, p. 37.

APPENDIX 29

*India: Distribution of applicants (matriculates and above) on live registers
of employment exchanges, by level of education, 1956-1962*

| | | | GRADUATES | | |
| YEAR | MATRICULATES | INTERMEDIATES | Engineering | Medical | Others |
|---|---|---|---|---|---|
| 1956 | 186 978 | 30 640 | 481 | 213 | 26 080 |
| 1957 | 236 509 | 38 762 | 511 | 171 | 31 605 |
| 1958 | 283 268 | 44 575 | 518 | 186 | 35 845 |
| 1959 | 344 329 | 49 141 | 598 | 143 | 38 900 |
| 1960 | 399 880 | 60 756 | 1 190 | 262 | 45 132 |
| 1961 | 463 633 | 70 811 | 1 255 | 265 | 54 266 |
| 1962 | 553 618 | 90 954 | 1 676 | 310 | 61 798 |

*Source:* Institute of Applied Manpower Research, *Fact Book on Manpower: Part 1* (New Delhi, 1963), table 3.23, p. 52.

APPENDIX 30

*Ivory Coast: Occupational aspirations and expectations of sampled students*

| | OCCUPATIONAL ASPIRATIONS | | | OCCUPATIONAL EXPECTATIONS | | |
| OCCUPATIONS | Males | Females | Total | Males | Females | Total |
|---|---|---|---|---|---|---|
| | (in percentages) | | | (in percentages) | | |
| Teaching[a] | 24.3 | 21.9 | 24.0 | 57.6 | 48.5 | 56.6 |
| Scientific technological[b] | 23.8 | 0.8 | 21.2 | 7.1 | 0.0 | 6.3 |
| Medicine, nursing[c] | 18.6 | 61.2 | 23.4 | 3.8 | 32.9 | 7.1 |
| Agriculture[d] | 14.1 | 1.3 | 12.6 | 3.1 | 0.0 | 2.7 |
| Administration[e] | 12.3 | 11.0 | 12.2 | 18.1 | 14.4 | 17.6 |
| Military, police[f] | 3.5 | 0.0 | 3.1 | 5.5 | 0.0 | 4.9 |
| Miscellaneous and no answer | 3.4 | 3.8 | 3.5 | 4.8 | 4.2 | 4.8 |

*Source:* R. Clignet and P. Foster, *The Fortunate Few: A Study of Secondary Schools and Students in the Ivory Coast* (Evanston, Ill.: Northwestern University Press, 1966), pp. 128, 140.

a Includes teachers from the primary to the university level, plus a small group concerned with the social sciences.

b Includes research scientists, engineers, technicians, and skilled workers at all levels.

c Includes doctors, pharmacists, veterinarians, nurses, and social welfare workers.

d Includes agricultural engineers, technicians, demonstrators, but *not* farmers.

e Includes all public and private cadres down to the clerical level, and law or politics.

f Includes both commissioned and noncommissioned categories.

*Ghana: Occupational aspirations and expectations of sampled students*

| OCCUPATION | OCCUPATIONAL ASPIRATIONS | | | OCCUPATIONAL EXPECTATIONS | | |
|---|---|---|---|---|---|---|
| | Males | Females | Total | Males | Females | Total |
| | (in percentages) | | | (in percentages) | | |
| Medicine | 17.3 | 11.2 | 16.1 | — | — | — |
| Law | 3.7 | 3.7 | 3.7 | — | — | — |
| Ministry | 0.1 | — | 0.1 | — | — | — |
| Other professional[a] | 1.0 | 0.5 | 0.8 | 0.1 | — | 0.1 |
| Higher administrative[b] | 6.8 | 4.3 | 6.3 | — | — | — |
| Higher commercial[c] | 7.2 | 3.7 | 6.6 | 0.1 | — | 0.1 |
| Politics | 1.5 | 0.5 | 1.4 | — | — | — |
| Clerical (government)[d] | 1.0 | 3.7 | 1.5 | 18.3 | 20.7 | 18.8 |
| Other clerical[e] | 3.6 | 16.5 | 6.0 | 31.3 | 40.5 | 33.1 |
| Scientific, technical[f] | 26.2 | 3.2 | 21.7 | 7.4 | 1.1 | 6.1 |
| Nursing and pharmacy | 2.4 | 18.1 | 5.5 | 0.8 | 10.1 | 2.6 |
| University teaching | 2.6 | 1.1 | 2.3 | — | — | — |
| Secondary school teaching | 14.8 | 22.9 | 16.4 | 1.4 | 0.5 | 1.3 |
| Primary school teaching | 4.3 | 6.4 | 4.7 | 34.1 | 23.9 | 32.1 |
| Other teaching[g] | 0.8 | — | 0.6 | 0.4 | — | 0.3 |
| Police, uniformed services | 4.6 | — | 3.7 | 4.5 | — | 3.6 |
| Minor commercial[h] | — | — | — | 0.1 | — | 0.1 |
| Farming and fishing | 1.0 | 2.1 | 1.3 | 1.0 | 1.1 | 1.0 |
| Miscellaneous[i] | 0.6 | 0.5 | 0.6 | — | 0.5 | 0.1 |
| No answer | 0.5 | 1.6 | 0.7 | 0.5 | 1.6 | 0.7 |

*Source:* Foster, *op. cit.*, pp. 276, 281.

a Economists, statisticians, sociologists.

b Senior civil servants, chief secretaries, directors of public corporations, district and regional commissioners, etc.

c Accountants and auditors, bank managers, business executives, etc.

d All choices specifying clerical work which indicated a specific preference for government employment.

e All choices specifying clerical work which indicated a specific preference for private employment.

f Including engineering of all types, surveying, agricultural research, veterinary activities, laboratory assistantships, and work in the field of the physical or biological sciences, etc.

g Primarily at technical institutes or commercial schools.

h Small shopkeepers and petty traders.

i Actor, dramatist, etc.

APPENDIX 31

'Adult call for further education

A sharp increase in the number of men and women of 30 and 40 wanting a university education was predicted yesterday at the opening of an international conference on the University Education of Mature Students at Birkbeck College, London.

'Dr. F. C. James, Principal Emeritus of McGill University, suggested that there were at least four significant reasons. One was a growing realization by employers in business, government, and teaching that a first degree was no longer adequate and that a higher degree was tending to become a minimum qualification.

'A second was the growing tendency for what was learnt as an undergraduate to become obsolete by the time a graduate was in the middle of his career. It was fundamentally true, he said, that someone not directly engaged in research needed to return to university at intervals of not more than 10 years for re-education; this was being recognized in medical practice, teaching, and scientific and engineering technology.

'A third reason was that as new areas of employment opened in the future—for instance in computers, communications, or nuclear energy—able and ambitious men and women would want university education in a new field to qualify themselves. One half of the working population today, Dr. James said, was working at jobs that did not exist at the start of the century.

'Lastly more than half the young people in Britain left school as soon as they could—at 15—and they were not necessarily the dullest students. Dr. James said it was important that in maturity, when these people realized their need for university education, it should be available for them.

*High dividends*
'He suggested that spending on the further education of members of their staffs by industry was an investment paying high dividends, a truth more widely realized in the United States and Canada than in Britain. He cited the example of the Bell Telephone Company, which for 15 years has been sending selected members of staff, on full salaries, to the University of Pennsylvania.

'Universities, also, had a duty to formulate educational programmes tailored to the special needs both of employers and of mature students, not solely watered-down versions of undergraduate courses.

'Dr. James said that there was a need for long courses, given at night; for the development of correspondence courses, using television and radio; for periods of residence within universities or colleges; and an equally urgent need for full-time short courses of from two weeks to three months. . . .'

*Source:* The *Times* (London), 21 July 1967.

APPENDIX 32

Following are some illustrative practical actions taken by members of village Rural Radio Forum participants in three districts of India as the result of their 'adult education':[1]

'Will grow fruit trees in back-yards; add fruit to daily diet.'
'Will use poison against rats; call on the agricultural officer for help.'
'Will keep a good breeding bull or otherwise will send cows for artificial insemination.'

'Will try to introduce better poultry; will vaccinate poultry.'
'Will start multi-purpose co-operative society and sell produce through that society.'
'Will see that there will not be any illiterates in the village in the next five years; they will read the newspaper aloud in one or two places in order to increase the knowledge of the people.'

'Will use cow dung for fruit trees, will not burn cow dung as fuel; even the refuse is more productive when used in the fields.'

'Will keep wells clean, prohibit the public from washing in the wells, fix sign boards, instruct the public not to make the water dirty.'

'Will introduce contour bunding to preserve wetness in land.'[1]

Source: Unesco/IIEP, 'Ten Years of the Radio Rural Forum in India,' in *New Educational Media in Action: Case Studies for Planners* (Paris: Unesco/IIEP, 1967), I, pp. 115-16.

APPENDIX 33

'*Summary of argument*

'A large part both of the natural and of the human resources of Tanzania is at present only partially developed. Less than one-tenth of the labour force is in paid employment. Most of the able-bodied men and women, 95 per cent of whom live in the rural economy, are still engaged in relatively low-yielding agriculture and herding.

'To increase the proportion in modernized production needs not only capital but much strengthened educative services. These include not merely formal education but all services which provide advice, technical assistance, and training in various forms to the producer. While the industrial sector will absorb an increasing but still small proportion, only a modernized rural economy is large enough to affect the great bulk of the labour force.

'At present it is impossible to provide modern productive employment for more than a small fraction even of those who have completed a full primary education, still less for those who have had only four years [of education] or less. It can thus be stated that investment in formal education has outrun investment in those other educative services directly aimed at increasing production and economic opportunity. To this extent, expenditure on formal education is partially wasted.

'It is therefore argued that, for the present, the highest priority is needed for services which actively foster an agrarian revolution, while the further expansion of formal primary education is temporarily restricted.'[1]

Source: Hunter, *Manpower, Employment and Education in the Rural Economy of Tanzania, op. cit.,* p. 39.

APPENDIX 34

*The over-all amount of external aid to education*

EVOLUTION OF OVER-ALL FOREIGN AID (DAC COUNTRIES, IN BILLIONS OF U.S. DOLLARS)

| YEAR | PUBLIC | PRIVATE | TOTAL |
|------|--------|---------|-------|
| 1956 | 3.3 | 2.9 | 6.2 |
| 1957 | 3.9 | 3.7 | 7.6 |
| 1958 | 4.4 | 2.8 | 7.2 |
| 1959 | 4.4 | 2.7 | 7.1 |
| 1960 | 5 | 2.9 | 7.9 |
| 1961 | 6.1 | 3.1 | 9.2 |
| 1962 | 6.1 | 2.5 | 8.6 |
| 1963 | 6.1 | 2.4 | 8.5 |
| 1964 | 5.9 | 3.2 | 9.1 |
| 1965 | 6.3 | 3.8 | 10.1 |

Note the steady increase up to 1961 and leveling off since that year with a new important increase between 1964 and 1965. The latter increase is mainly due, however, to *private* aid (long-term loans and investments) which probably does not affect education very much.

EVOLUTION OF TECHNICAL ASSISTANCE (DAC COUNTRIES)

| Disbursements (in billions of U. S. dollars) | | Number of teachers sent to developing countries | |
|------|------|------|------|
| 1962 | 0.725 | | |
| 1963 | 0.858 | 1963 | 34 592 |
| 1964 | 0.950 | 1964 | 33 839 |
| 1965 | 1.048 | 1965 | 35 316 |

| Number of volunteers | | | Number of experts in the educational field | |
|------|------|------|------|------|
| | Total | Teachers | | |
| 1963 | 6 927 | 3 619 | 1963 | 2 205 |
| 1964 | 9 903 | 4 571 | 1964 | 3 558 |
| 1965 | 15 995 | 8 033 | 1965 | 4 912 |

*Source:* Sources of all the above data are the latest OECD/DAC annual reviews, *Development Assistance Efforts and Policies.* The 1965 issue also contains data showing the geographic distribution of aid and its inequalities (French-speaking Africa south of the Sahara gets $11.00 per inhabitant, India $2.50, Algeria $23.00, Latin America $4.40).

# A Guide to Further Study

From the rapidly growing literature on the topics dealt with in this book, we have selected a limited number, available in English, as an initial guide to readers interested in digging deeper. Many of the documents listed below have good reference lists of their own which can provide further guidance.

*Education and Society* EDUCATION'S CAPACITY TO FOSTER SOCIAL OBJECTIVES · SOCIAL CONSTRAINTS ON EDUCATION · IMPACT OF EDUCATION ON SOCIAL CHANGE · INFLUENCE ON STUDENT ATTITUDES · EQUALITY OF EDUCATIONAL OPPORTUNITY · SOCIAL BIAS OF EDUCATIONAL SYSTEMS.

Anderson, C. A. *The Social Context of Educational Planning.* Fundamentals of educational planning, 5. Paris, Unesco/IIEP, 1967. 35p.
Discusses societal factors which educational planning should take into account but often ignores.
Ashby, Eric. *Patterns of Universities in Non-European Societies.* London, School of Oriental and African Studies, University of London, 1961.
Examines the impact of imported models of higher education in India and West Africa, and the contrasting British and French colonial educational policies in Africa.
Cremin, Lawrence A. *The Transformation of the School; Progressivism in American Education, 1876-1957.* New York, Alfred A. Knopf, 1961. xi, 387p. Index xxiv. Bibliography.
An historian's lively analysis of the effort made over fifty years to adapt education to the democratic aims of American Progressivism.
Durkheim, E. *Education and Sociology.* Translated from French by S. D. Fox. New York, London, Macmillan, 1956.
Halsey, A. H., Floud, J., and Anderson, C. A., eds. *Education, Economy and Society; A Reader in the Sociology of Education.* New York, Free Press of Glencoe, 1964. ix, 625p.
Hanson, John W., and Brembeck, Cole S., eds. *Education and the Development of Nations.* New York, Holt, Rinehart and Winston, 1966. xiv, 529p. Bibliography.
A wide assortment of articles written by outstanding authors, from various

vantage points, bearing on education's capacity to foster social, economic, and political development.

Hoselitz, B. F., and Moore, W. E., eds. *Industrialization and Society.* Report based on a North American Conference on the social implications of industrialization and technological change. Chicago, Illinois, 15-22 September 1960. Paris, Unesco, 1963. 448p.

Discusses major policy implications of the sociological view of education's role in promoting growth in developing countries.

Myers, Edward D. *Education in the Perspective of History.* With a concluding chapter by Arnold J. Toynbee. New York, Harper and Brothers, 1960. xii, 388p.

A sweeping review of the role which education played—or failed to play—in the rise and fall of thirteen civilizations and the historical lessons which Professor Toynbee sees in this vast body of human experience for helping mankind to cope with modern dilemmas.

Ottaway, A. K. C. *Education and Society: An Introduction to the Sociology of Education.* London, Routledge and Kegan Paul, 1964. 2nd edn. rev. xiv, 232p.

*Education and Economic Growth*    EDUCATION VIEWED AS AN
INVESTMENT IN HUMAN RESOURCE DEVELOPMENT AND ECONOMIC GROWTH ·
HISTORICAL EVIDENCE OF EDUCATION'S CONTRIBUTION · DIFFERING VIEWS
AMONG ECONOMISTS · THE PROBLEM OF HOW MUCH TO SPEND ON
EDUCATION.

OECD. *The Residual Factor and Economic Growth; Study Group in the Economics of Education.* Paris, OECD, 1964. 280p. Tables.

The record of a debate among able economists who broadly agreed that education is a good investment in economic growth, but who differed strongly about how to prove it; recommended mainly for economists.

OECD. *Policy Conference on Economic Growth and Investment in Education; IV. The Planning of Education in Relation to Economic Growth.* Washington, D.C., 16-20 October 1961. Paris, OECD, 1962.

The proceedings of a notable conference of economists and educators which gave encouragement to policy-makers to invest more heavily in education; includes main papers and addresses by leading participants.

Schultz, Theodore W. *The Economic Value of Education.* New York, Columbia University Press, 1963. xii, 92p. Bibliography.

A readable little book by a distinguished economist whose research and writings have given great impetus in recent years to the idea that education is a "good investment" in economic growth.

Unesco, *Readings in the Economics of Education,* selected by M. J. Bowman, M. Debeauvais, V. E. Komarov, and J. Vaizey, Paris, 1968. 945p. Tables.

A large and useful anthology of articles by leading economists and other social scientists on the role of education in economic growth and social development, and related matters.

Vaizey, John. *The Economics of Education*. London, Faber and Faber, 1962. 165p. Bibliography.

A standard work which reviews ideas on the economic returns of education, expenditures on education, productivity and efficiency of education and manpower aspects, with some reference to underdeveloped countries.

*Educational Planning and Management*   CONCEPTS AND TECHNIQUES · FORECASTING NEEDS AND RESOURCES · INTEGRATING EDUCATIONAL PLANNING WITH ECONOMIC AND SOCIAL PLANNING · MANPOWER ASPECTS · QUALITATIVE ASPECTS · CASE STUDIES · PROGRAMME BUDGETING · PLANNING AS A PART OF MANAGEMENT.

Beeby, C. E. *The Quality of Education in Developing Countries*. Cambridge, Mass., Harvard University Press, 1966. x, 139p. Index.

An internationally known educator responds to the economists and takes up the practical problems of achieving needed changes in education, pointing out that educational systems must develop by stages and what works at a later stage may not work at an earlier one.

Bereday, George Z. F., Lauwerys, Joseph A., and Blaug, Mark, eds. *The World Year Book of Education, 1967; Educational Planning*. London, Evans Brothers, Ltd., 1967. xiv, 442p. Tables.

A useful collection of new articles on various aspects of educational planning and development in many parts of the world, by an array of authorities.

Burkhead, J., Fox, T. G., and Holland, J. W. *Input and Output in Large City High Schools*. Syracuse, N.Y., Syracuse University Press, 1967. 105p. Index. Tables.

A total-factor-productivity model of American high schools, applied to a comparison of high schools in Chicago and Atlanta.

Gross, B. M. "The Administration of Economic Development Planning: Principles and Fallacies." In United Nations, *Economic Bulletin for Asia and the Far East*. XVII, No. 3, December 1966. Pp. 1-28.

Some practical guidelines drawn from experience regarding the implementation of plans, pertinent to educational as well as to economic planning.

Harbison, F. *Educational Planning and Human Resource Development*. Fundamentals of educational planning, 3. Paris, Unesco/IIEP, 1965, 24p.

A concise presentation of the views of a well-known scholar whose ideas have been very influential in the field of educational and manpower planning.

Harbison, F. H., and Myers, C. A. *Education, Manpower and Economic Growth. Strategies of Human Resources Development*. New York, McGraw-Hill, 1964. xiii, 229p.

A general discussion of problems and strategies of educational development

in relation to economic development, especially in developing regions; includes a composite index for ranking seventy-five countries into four levels
of human resource development; stresses the importance of nonformal as well
as formal education.

Hunter, G. *Manpower, Employment and Education in the Rural Economy of
Tanzania.* African research monographs, 9. Paris, Unesco/IIEP, 1966. 40p.

An illuminating case study of the practical needs and difficulties which educational planning must cope with in the vast rural areas of most developing
countries. One in a series of 13 IIEP African research monographs, focused
on planning problems common to many countries.

IIEP. *The Qualitative Aspects of Educational Planning.*

The papers and lively discussions of a symposium on the non-quantitative
dimensions of planning, with heavy emphasis on the need to raise the efficiency and productivity of educational systems by improving their "fitness"
to their changing environment. Participants include an international group
of leading educators and social scientists.

IIEP. *Manpower Aspects of Educational Planning. Problems for the Future.*
Paris, Unesco/IIEP, 1968. 265p.

An examination by an international group of leading experts of the "state of
the art" of manpower and educational planning, and of three major future
problems: manpower and educational needs for rural and agricultural development; unemployment of the educated; and the implementation of plans.

Lewis, W. Arthur. *Development Planning; the Essential of Economic Policy.*
London, George Allen and Unwin, 1966. 278p.

A small and useful book for educators who want to learn about economic
planning and its relation to educational planning, by an eminent authority
on the subject.

Lyons, R., ed. *Problems and Strategies of Educational Planning: Lessons from
Latin America.* Paris, Unesco/IIEP, 1965. viii. 117p.

Papers and summary of discussions of a five-week seminar series, including
statements by leading Latin American educators and economists, emphasizing the need for planning and the practical difficulties.

Nozhko, K., *et al. Educational Planning in the USSR.* Paris, Unesco/IIEP, 1968.
300p.

A comprehensive review and critical appraisal of educational planning in the
USSR, integrated with economic and manpower planning, including an historical picture of Soviet educational development over fifty years; prepared
by a group of experienced Soviet planners and scholars, with a commentary
by a visiting international team of experts, organized by the IIEP.

Oddie, G. *School Building Resources and Their Effective Use. Some Available
Techniques and Their Policy Implications.* Paris, OECD, 1966. 160p.

A practical discussion with useful guidance to those especially concerned
with the efficient construction and utilization of educational facilities, by an
architect-engineer who had a hand in improving educational construction in
the United Kingdom.

Parnes, H. S. *Forecasting Educational Needs for Social and Economic Development.* Paris, OECD, 1962. 113p.

A clear and systematic discussion of the various steps in educational planning employed in the OECD's Mediterranean Regional Project.

*Report of the Committee on Higher Education under the Chairmanship of Lord Robbins 1961-63.* London, HMSO, 1963. xi, 166p.

A landmark in the United Kingdom's approach to the planning of higher education, including an historical survey of growth thus far, some striking international comparisons, some bold projections for the future, and some controversial proposals.

Ruml, Beardsley, and Morrison, Donald H. *Memo to a College Trustee; A Report on Financial and Structural Problems of the Liberal College.* New York, McGraw-Hill, 1959. xiv, 94p.

A provocative little book which warns higher educational authorities and faculties that curriculum proliferation is the enemy of adequate teacher salaries and good quality learning. It proposes some planning principles and techniques for achieving the best use of available resources.

Skorov, G. *Integration of Educational and Economic Planning in Tanzania.* African research monographs, 6. Paris, Unesco/IIEP, 1966. 78p. Bibliography.

Though focused upon one sample country, this case study in the IIEP African monograph series portrays with clarity the problems faced by most developing countries in trying to integrate educational development with economic development, in line with their extremely scarce resources.

Unesco. *Economic and Social Aspects of Educational Planning.* Paris, Unesco, 1964. 264p. Bibliography.

An integrated set of papers on various aspects of educational planning and development by internationally known experts, including a paper by Professor Jan Tinbergen on "Educational Assessments."

Vaizey, J., and Chesswas, J. D. *The Costing of Educational Plans.* Fundamentals of educational planning, 6. Paris, Unesco/IIEP, 1967. 63p.

Presents some general principles and methods of costing, and shows their practical application in an illustrative African country.

Waterston, A. *Development Planning: Lessons of Experience.* Baltimore, Johns Hopkins, 1965. xix, 706p. Bibliography.

Reflections by a seasoned observer after conducting a number of country studies on planning, for the World Bank.

●

*Financing Education*  COMPARATIVE EDUCATIONAL EFFORTS OF DIFFERENT COUNTRIES · ALTERNATIVE FINANCING AND CRITERIA OF SELECTION · THE FINANCING OF HIGHER EDUCATION · METHODS FOR ANALYZING EDUCATIONAL EXPENDITURES.

Edding, F. *Methods of Analysing Educational Outlay.* Paris, Unesco, 1966. 70p.

A useful technical discussion by one of the most experienced international students of educational expenditures, whose work in the Federal Republic of Germany has aroused economists, educators, and politicians alike.

Harris, S. E., ed. *Economic Aspects of Higher Education.* Paris, OECD, 1964. 252p.

A collection of papers from a conference organized by the OECD's Study Group in the Economics of Education, led by Professor Seymour Harris, who has written prolifically on the financing of education.

Keezer, Dexter M. ed. *Financing Higher Education 1960-70.* New York, Mc-Graw-Hill, 1959. vii, 304p. Tables. Illustrations.

A useful collection of expert papers and observations, derived from a seminar at the Merrill Center for Economics, chaired by Dr. Willard N. Thorp.

Mushkin, S. J., ed. *Economics of Higher Education.* Washington, D.C., U.S. Government Printing Office, 1962.

A large collection of papers and data prepared by an eminent group of educators and economists under the auspices of the U.S. Office of Education, dealing with financial and other economic aspects of higher education.

OECD Study Group. *Financing of Education for Economic Growth.* Paris, OECD, 1966.

A series of papers dealing with educational finance in underdeveloped and developed countries, with discussion of criteria for external aid to education in developing countries.

Poignant, R. *Education and Development in Western Europe, the United States and the Soviet Union.* New York, Teachers College, Columbia University, 1968. 320p. Tables.

This recent study presents a provocative picture of the comparative postwar growth of educational enrollments and expenditures—relative to economic growth—in several industrialized countries. It has stimulated debate in some of the lagging countries.

*Educational Change and Innovation*   ACCELERATION OF EDUCATIONAL CHANGE IN THE PAST DECADE · TEAM TEACHING · INSTRUCTIONAL TV · CURRICULUM REFORMS · NEW SCHOOL DESIGNS · UNGRADED SCHOOLS · OTHER INNOVATIONS · THE NECESSITY AND PRESSURE FOR CHANGE · STRATEGIES FOR ACHIEVING IT · HOW RESEARCH CAN HELP.

Anderson, Robert H. *Teaching in a World of Change.* New York, Harcourt, Brace and World, Inc., 1966. 180p. Bibliography.

A readable, authoritative summary of recent innovations in school organization, team teaching, school design, and other matters; written for teachers but useful to a wider audience.

Bruner, J. S. *The Process of Education.* Cambridge, Mass., Harvard University Press, 1961.

A fresh look at the structure of knowledge in relation to the learning process, which prompts an imaginative search for more efficient methods of imparting and acquiring knowledge.

Goodlad, John I. *Planning and Organizing for Teaching.* Washington, D.C., National Educational Association, 1963.

A leading authority on the non-graded school discusses new ways of organizing the teaching-learning process in order to enable each individual to proceed at his own best pace.

Gore, H. B. "Schoolhouse in Transition," in *The Changing American School,* 65th Yearbook of the National Society for the Study of Education, Part II, Chicago, University of Chicago Press, 1966.

The President of the Educational Facilities Laboratories—a former school superintendent and noted educational innovator—sums up recent new developments and directions in school design aimed at creating school buildings that will foster rather than impede necessary educational changes. The EFL, New York, is the best source of publications on new trends in school design.

Harris, S. E., and Levansohn, A., eds. *Challenge and Change in American Education.* Berkeley, Calif., McCutchan Publishing Corporation, 1965. 347p.

A summary of papers and discussions of a series of Harvard seminars in 1961-62 involving numerous invited experts, to explore political, economic, qualitative, and organizational issues facing education in the future.

*Innovation and Experiment in Education.* A progress report of the Panel on Educational Research and Development. Washington, D.C., U.S. Government Printing Office, 1964. 79p.

Kidd, J. R. *The Implications of Continuous Learning.* Toronto, W. J. Gage, Ltd., 1966. 122p.

Lectures by a leading Canadian adult educator, in which he advocates lifelong integrated education for all and discusses the implications.

Miles, M. B., ed. *Innovation in Education.* New York, Bureau of Publications, Teachers College, Columbia University, 1964. xii, 689p. Fig. Index.

Miller, R. I., ed. *Perspectives on Educational Change.* New York, Appleton-Century-Crofts, 1967. 392p.

Ministry of Education. *Half Our Future.* A report of the Central Advisory Council for Education (England). Known as "the Newsom Report." London, HMSO, 1963. 299p.

A much discussed report on "the education of pupils aged 13 to 16 of average and less than average ability," with numerous recommendations for change, and emphasizing "above all a need for new modes of thought, and a change of heart, on the part of the community as a whole."

Morphet, E. L., and Ryan, C. O., eds. *Designing Education for the Future.* No. 1—*Prospective Changes in Society by 1980.* 268p. No. 2—*Implications for Education of Prospective Changes in Society.* 323p. No. 3—*Planning and Effecting Needed Changes in Education.* 317p. New York, Citation Press, 1967.

The results of an eight-state project designed to help educational systems to adapt themselves to new and larger tasks in a rapidly changing environment; the three volumes contain numerous informative and perceptive articles by leading scholars and educational officials; an antidote to complacency and a spur to the imagination.

Schramm, W., Coombs, P. H., Kahnert, F., and Lyle, J., *The New Media: Memo to Educational Planners*. Paris, Unesco/IIEP, 1967. 175p. Plus three volumes of case studies entitled *New Educational Media in Action*.

Summary and conclusions of a world-wide research project aimed at learning more about the over-all feasibility of using instructional TV, radio and other new media to solve educational problems; includes practical advice on how to diagnose any given situation and how to plan in order to maximize the chances of success.

Shaplin, J. T., and Olds, H. F., Jr., eds. *Team Teaching*. New York, Harper and Row, 1964. xv, 430p. Bibliography. Index.

A comprehensive review of the theory and practice of team teaching by a group of well-qualified observers and participants.

Skinner, B. F. *The Technology of Teaching*. Appleton-Century-Crofts, New York, 1968.

A new book of essays by the Harvard psychologist who has been called the father of "programmed learning"; here he couples his discussion of the learning process with severe criticism of the conventional educational practices which stand in its way, and he offers some remedies.

Stoddard, A. J. *Schools for Tomorrow: An Educator's Blueprint*. New York, Fund for the Advancement of Education, 1957. 82p. Bibliography.

This document, still available in most education libraries, is of special historical interest. After retiring from a distinguished career in educational administration, the author helped launch a major movement of educational reform and innovation in the United States. Shocking to many of his education colleagues in 1957, this booklet is widely accepted today as a prophetic view of things to come.

Trump, J. L., and Baynham, D. *Guide to Better Schools*. Chicago, Rand McNally, 1963. 147p. Fig.

The senior author, Lloyd Trump, an experienced educator, has been a leader of innovation in secondary education for many years.

*University Teaching Methods*. Report to University Grants Committee. (Hale Report.) London, HMSO, 1964.

Vaizey, John. *Education in the Modern World*. London, World University Library, 1967. 254p. Bibliography. Illustrations.

A leading authority on the economics of education, with a bent for sociology and politics, looks at education in a world of rapid change, and draws conclusions for policy, tactics, and strategy.

Young, Michael. *Innovation and Research in Education*. Institute of Community Studies. London, Routledge and Kegan Paul, 1965. 184p. Bibliography.

The author set out to "clear his mind" about priorities in educational research, in the process explored much literature about the nature of such research, and came out with the conclusion that the accent should be on innovation. A useful reading for those interested in using research to promote educational change and advancement.

*International Co-operation in Education*  VARIOUS FORMS OF
CO-OPERATION · RELATION TO FOREIGN POLICY OBJECTIVES · OPPORTUNITIES
AND DIFFICULTIES INVOLVED · SOME CASE HISTORIES · WAYS TO IMPROVE
EFFECTIVENESS OF FOREIGN AID · THE SPECIAL ROLE OF UNIVERSITIES.

Cerych, Ladislav. *The Integration of External Assistance with Educational Planning in Nigeria.* African research monographs, 9. Paris, Unesco/IIEP, 1967. 78p.

A case study in a particular country, designed to highlight practical problems—of rendering, receiving, and utilizing external educational assistance—which are common to many developing countries.

Cerych, Ladislav. *Problems of Aid to Education in Developing Countries.* New York, Praeger, 1965. xiii, 213p. Bibliography.

A comprehensive examination of the international flow of educational assistance in the 1950's and early 1960's; the needs for aid, the forms it took, and the practical problems involved.

Coombs, P. H. *The Fourth Dimension of Foreign Policy: Educational and Cultural Affairs.* New York, Harper and Row, 1964. xvi, 158p. Index.

An attempt to relate international educational and cultural interchange to the long-term objectives of foreign policy; based on comparative analysis of the educational and cultural exchange programs of the United States, France, Federal Republic of Germany, the United Kingdom, and the Soviet Union.

Coombs, P. H., and Bigelow, K. W. *Education and Foreign Aid.* Cambridge, Mass., Harvard University Press, 1965. 74p.

Burton and Inglis Lectures at Harvard on "Ways to Improve United States Educational Aid," and on "Problems and Prospects of Education in Africa."

Curle, A. *Planning for Education in Pakistan.* Cambridge, Mass., Harvard University Press, 1966. xxii, 208p.

An illuminating case history of the efforts of one developing country to strengthen its educational system, and the perplexing problems encountered, as seen through the eyes of a sensitive "foreign adviser" over a period of years. Required reading for any such "expert" before he starts giving advice.

*Education and World Affairs. The University Looks Abroad.* Approaches to world affairs at six American universities, Stanford, Michigan State, Tulane, Wisconsin, Cornell, Indiana. New York, Walker and Co., 1965. 300p. Bibliography.

Accounts of how six universities have progressively extended their international dimensions over 100 years, but at a greatly accelerated pace since 1960, resulting in an educational "extended family system" and a host of new opportunities and problems for the universities.

Gardner, John W. *A.I.D. and the Universities.* Report to the Administrator of the Agency for International Development. Washington, AID, 1964. xii, 51p.

A critical examination of the uneasy new partnership between universities and the government in the rendering of overseas assistance, with positive suggestions to both parties on how to improve the partnership.

Weidner, Edward W. *The World Role of Universities*. New York, McGraw-Hill, 1962. xii, 366p. Bibliography.

Synthesizes a series of regional studies of the international exchange programs of American universities (to the late 1950's), carried out by a team of social scientists, with conclusions drawn by the team's director.

Williams, P. R. C. *Educational Assistance*. London, Overseas Development Institute, 1963, 125p.

Though statistically out of date, this remains a useful description of the various types and channels of British international co-operation in education.

## Useful Reference Sources

Blaug, M. *Economics of Education: A Selected Annotated Bibliography*. Oxford, Pergamon Press, 1966. xiii, 190p. Index, plus Addenda I and II.

A useful bibliography which concentrates mainly on economic aspects and English language sources; kept up to date with frequent supplements; prepared at the Institute of Education, University of London.

IIEP. *Educational Planning: A Bibliography*. Paris, IIEP, 1964. 131p.

Annotated references to books, articles, etc. in several different languages, classified by (A) the purpose and value of educational planning, (B) the preparation of educational plans, (C) the organization and administration of educational planning, and (D) case materials. Includes listing of numerous other useful bibliographies.

OECD. *Methods and Statistical Needs for Educational Planning*. Paris, OECD, 1967. 363p. Tables.

Contains the results of a major effort to identify basic data needed for educational planning, to standardize definitions and statistical concepts, and to suggest methods of statistical analysis. Useful primarily for industrialized countries with relatively good statistics.

UNESCO. *Unesco Handbook of International Exchanges*. F/E/S/. II, Paris, Unesco, 1967. 1102p.

Gives information on the aims, programs, and activities of national and international organizations, and on agreements concluded between states, concerning international relations and exchanges in the fields of education, science, culture, and mass communication.

UNESCO. *World Survey of Education. Handbook of Educational Organization and Statistics*. I, *School Organization*. II, *Primary Education*. Paris, Unesco, 1958. 1387p. Fig. III, *Secondary Education*, Paris, Unesco, 1961. 1482p. IV, *Higher Education*, Paris, Unesco, 1966. 1435p.

Contains accounts of all educational systems in the world at three-year intervals. Developmental facts traced since about 1900 and present trends described. Because of different methods of reporting, however, the statistics are often not comparable and must be treated with caution.

# Index